Language and Political Understanding

Language and Political Understanding
The Politics of Discursive Practices

Michael J. Shapiro

New Haven and London
Yale University Press

Designed by Sally Harris
and set in Times Roman type.
Printed in the United States of America by
Halliday Lithograph, West Hanover, Mass.

Library of Congress Cataloging in Publication Data

Shapiro, Michael J.
    Language and political understanding.

    Includes index.
    1. Languages—Political aspects.   2. Languages—
Philosophy.   3. Sociolinguistics.   4. Social
sciences—Philosophy.   I. Title.
JF195.L3S45   306'.2   81-3069
ISBN 0-300-02590-4   AACR2

10 9 8 7 6 5 4 3 2 1

To my father,
Irving Shapiro,
whose generosity helped make this possible

Contents

Acknowledgments ix
1 Logical Positivism and Political Science 1
2 Language and Meaning 26
3 Normative Discourse and Political Understanding 65
4 The Problem of Human Action 95
5 Michel Foucault and the Analysis of Discursive Practices 127
6 Language, Theories, and Models 165
7 Political Relations 199
Notes 235
Index 249

Acknowledgments

I began working on this book in the spring of 1976 while a visitor in the Department of Government at the University of Essex, which provided an office, library, squash courts, assorted tea- and lunchrooms, and occasional interpersonal encounters in measures that were very felicitous for beginning my writing. I am therefore very grateful to my then colleagues Michael Taylor for arranging my visit; Ian Budge, who, as Department Chairman, saw to my eligibility for various, indispensable local services; and John Gray and Ernesto LaClau, with whom I had some valuable discussions.

At various stages in my writing, I thought that I had a finished manuscript, more or less ready for publication but became convinced otherwise. I am therefore especially indebted to my severest critics who were all encouraging enough to give me confidence in my basic project but firm and persuasive enough to make me reconsider some positions and/or consider additional literatures. These include Peter Manicus of the Department of Philosophy, Queens College; R. E. Goodin of the Department of Government, University of Essex; an anonymous reviewer for Yale University Press; and most especially my editor at the Press, Marian Neal Ash, whose persistence has made this a much better book.

Throughout the period of my writing my graduate and undergraduate students—too numerous to mention by name—provided the occasions and challenges that acquainted me with my ideas as I heard them both from my own lips and from theirs. I am very grateful to them and to my friends and colleagues who read various drafts, offering both criticism and encouragement: Bob Cahill, Henry Kariel, Manfred Henningsen, Deane Neubauer, and Bob Stauffer from my department, Jack Bilmes of the Department of Anthropology, University of Hawaii, Bill Connolly and Jean Elshtain of the Department of Political Science, University of Massachusetts, Daniel Heradstveit of the Norwegian Institute of International Affairs, Christer Jönsson of the Department of Political Science, University of Lund, Knut-Erik Tranöy of the Department of Philosophy, University of Oslo, and Fred Praeger of Westview Press.

Amplifying the considerable debt outlined above is that which I owe to Michel Foucault, not only for producing the corpus that stimulated me to rethink thoroughly my notion of what constitutes political understanding and to embark on this book, but also for his encouraging and helpful reactions to my manuscript and questions and for his warm and generous hospitality during a visit I made to Paris in the summer of 1980.

Finally, it is difficult to assess separately to what extent my wife Beppie, my son Kam, and my daughter Mandy helped to make this book possible. They help make *me* possible.

Honolulu, Hawaii
January 1981

1
Logical Positivism and Political Science

There is a variety of ways to characterize the major concerns that prompted me to write about issues in the philosophy of political science. One way is to frame those concerns in the context of decision-making problems related to conducting empirical political inquiry. Over the years, as I pursued various aspects of my research interests in political psychology and public policy decision making, I found increasingly that I had to make more decisions than could be comprehended and justified within the philosophical framework—contemporary empiricism—in which I had been instructed. Aside from the research step generally referred to as "choosing the problem," social science methodology texts tend to present the process of inquiry as a series of technical decisions oriented toward discovering the truth about one or another kind of social or political relationship. When an aspect of inquiry is discussed in a technically oriented discourse—for example, the problem of choosing an operational definition of a theoretical term— what is required seems to be nothing more than raising questions of reliability and validity: Do repeated measurements produce the same results when the measurement devices are the same (reliability) or different (validity)? If one pays attention to the society to which a given piece of research may be relevant rather than just to a body of social science literature that has sponsored particular measurement orientations, it becomes difficult to be satisfied with a technical understanding of concepts. To the extent that one sees as a political problem the possible understandings one can have of a citizen, a society, or any part of a social process, one must regard as complex and partisan the choices one must make to establish meanings for the concepts one uses. To neglect this complexity and potential partisanship by simply selecting the meanings one finds assigned by a given social science subculture is implicitly to affirm a normative orientation.

I found, therefore, that the prevailing self-understanding of the social sciences encourages a misleading account of political inquiry, one that obscures ideological commitments and problematic interpretations of ways of life by offering a language of inquiry that aims at an anachronistic philosophical ideal of objectivity. Having become convinced that assignments of meaning in the process of social science inquiry promote some interests and neglect others, I began to reassess the familiar notions of the relationships among those who use the language of inquiry and the persons and things constituted in that language. Because on the one hand I wanted to participate in a knowledge enterprise and on the other I found the familiar knowledge-justifying language to be an inadequate representation of my activities, I embarked on a search for alternative understandings of social and political inquiry, convinced, at a minimum, that the empiricist separation of normative (advocacy-oriented) and empirical (explanation-oriented) approaches was not viable. At the same time, my search for a viable understanding of the language of inquiry had to be guided by an applied political orientation, a guiding concern for the kinds of values and interests that must be elucidated by an alternative understanding of inquiry.

Many of the alternative models of social and political inquiry I encountered were just as troubling as the standard empiricist model—the object of my original discontent—but in concerning myself with problems in the philosophy of the social sciences, I found a felicitous focus for *my* problem and what I think is *the* problem for much of contemporary social science. It is not, as some antiempiricists have argued, that a systematic social science including quantitative approaches to social phenomena is entirely inappropriate. There is more to the understanding of human phenomena, however, than can be developed within the bounds of scientific, causally oriented explanations. To appreciate a more comprehensive rendering of what it means to understand, given the kinds of assumptions that have been popularized by empiricist accounts of explanation in the human sciences, it is necessary to raise *meta*-level questions, literally those lying behind the kinds of questions that direct social and political inquiry. Given my interest in *political* inquiry, the initial chapters in this book are accordingly addressed to metapolitical questions.

Politics and Metapolitics

The prefix *meta* affixed to a term implies an interest in analyzing commitments that are logically anterior to the usual referents of that term. If I were to say, "X and Y are engaged in a conversation," I would be assuming that the rules governing what constitutes a conversation are not at issue and that X and Y, untroubled by possible controversies as to what constitutes "conversation," are simply having one. If, however, I were to say, "X and Y are engaged in metaconversation," I would be saying that making an issue of what constitutes a conversation is precisely what they are doing. Because much of the emphasis in this book is on metapolitics, what I will be doing is making an issue out of what constitutes political phenomena, political analysis, and political inquiry. In this chapter I begin by exploring the metapolitics associated with the positivist philosophical tradition. My purpose is to raise doubts about that metapolitics by contrasting the rules for political inquiry which that metapolitics implies with other, incompatible rules for inquiry that derive from alternative philosophical commitments. In general, however, my analysis is not exclusively bound up with philosophical or meta-level issues, for my overriding purpose is to link metapolitics with politics.

In demonstrating relationships between positions at different levels of discourse—the more abstract, meta level with the more applied, substantive level—I hope to show how certain philosophical commitments, related to such issues as what it means to describe something, what it means to explain something, and what it means to understand something about social and political phenomena, both control the way that inquiry is conducted and determine the significance that the resulting knowledge can have. Although I will be demonstrating various links between meta and applied levels of analysis, my primary concern is not with the different kinds of connections between philosophical positions and modes of inquiry; it is with a particular perspective on the meaning of statements and discourses (systematically interrelated sets of statements) and with the implications that perspective can have for the conduct of political inquiry if they are pursued. So while the emphasis in the discussion at the outset is on the kinds of meta-level concerns one normally associates with an interest in the philosophy of social sciences—problems of meaning and truth, explanation and understanding, interpretation versus hypothesis testing, and so on—the treatment of issues at this level is selective rather than comprehensive, for it is intended to demonstrate the need for a reoriented perspective on the relationship between language and political inquiry.

From an emphasis on the relationship between language and political inquiry, it is a short step to talking about the practice of political inquiry or, more basically, about political relationships. When the discussion finds its way to this level, I will emphasize the controversial nature of the concept of what is political. Because one must unavoidably erect political standards to identify what is political, this aspect of the discussion should be viewed as tentative and necessarily elliptical. The verb *to be,* which seems serviceable in most conceivable rhetorical contexts, must inevitably appear to promise more than it can deliver when it disports itself in statements like "Politics is . . ." The rhetorical ground remains disturbingly shaky when criteria for bounding the domain of "the political" are offered, for it is just as misleading to state boldly for example, that, "Public relations *are* . . . , whereas private relations *are* . . . " When the level of discussion becomes grounded in "the political," the reader will accordingly find that there is still a lot of hovering going on.

Although it would be misleading to argue that there exists a single, identifiable political science culture, based on a relatively homogeneous set of norms that define the political science vocation, it is probably fair to say that there is at least an aggregation of subcultures and that, except among isolated subcultures, there are few well-developed expectations that one's meta-level commitments, for example, one's notions about the meaning of statements involved in political inquiry, significantly affect the direction and quality of one's applied political theory building or analysis.

Despite the relative absence of expectations linking philosophical positions with the craft of political inquiry, there is within what could best be termed the dominant political science subculture (that must prone to identifying its approach as scientific) a house epistemology, that is, an orientation toward the character of political knowledge that is most often purchased by scientific political researchers as a knowledge-justifying framework.

If we take, for the moment, an anthropological perspective, we can raise the question whether the culture makes sense in the context of its meta-level commitments. This kind of question was raised by Gregory Bateson in his inquiry into the problem of alcoholism. His analysis of the culture within which alcoholics struggle to achieve sobriety exemplifies the linking of meta-level and applied commitments.[1] Bateson identifies the major disabling ontological orientation of that culture as an acceptance of the "Cartesian dualism," the commitment to a radical separation between mind and body. By accepting such a dualism, he argues, alcoholics place themselves in a bind because their commitment to the Cartesian dualism produces a self-destructive personal ethic. Believing that their problem is one of needing to assert mind over matter, alcoholics engage in risk taking to try to overcome their craving for alcohol by force of will. They keep testing themselves by drinking to see if their mind is in control of their body, a control that would be evidenced by their ability to limit their consumption. Bateson asserts that the success of Alcoholics Anonymous is owed to its rejection of the mind–body dualism and the positing of an alternative model of the self. If, he points out, an alcoholic operates with a view of the mind as immanent (that is, not as a causal domain that is a separate part of the system, but as one residing in the system as a whole), he or she can reject the notion that achieving sobriety is a function of the mind successfully winning over the body and can instead view the total self as alcoholic. With such a view, the treatment consists in admitting defeat rather than constantly testing oneself in order to achieve a victory.

What Bateson has argued, then, is that because, as he put it, "the local epistemology is *wrong*," alcoholics tend to develop disabling beliefs about the nature of the self and its relation to the world. We can similarly view a major aggregation of social scientists in general, and political scientists in particular, as members of a culture that operates within a framework of epistemological premises which determine how they act in the conduct of inquiry. We can note, moreover, that the absence of elaborated expectations about the relevance of meta-level concerns supports the retention of what, I will argue, is an epistemological perspective that is politically insensitive. Specifically, *the retention of an inadequate and misleading theory of meaning (position on the relationship between persons and utterances and utterances and experience) has led to the neglect of the value commitments, institutional presuppositions, and models of individual and collective responsibility and interest implicit in the concepts employed in political inquiries.* These implicit presumptions, taken as a whole, comprise a significant aspect of existing or envisioned political arrangements. These political arrangements or institutions, which are implicit in the way we speak about politics, can be appreciated only in the context of an alternative model of the language/speech–reality relationship and language/speech–person relationship, a model that regards language as *constitutive* of political phenomena rather than as merely *about* political phenomena. To develop such a model, the initial focus of my analysis will be on metapolitical questions, beginning with an elaboration of the predomin&nt empiricist orientation of modern political science.

It should be noted, however, that while my critique emphasizes the shortcomings of the philosophy of the social sciences as influenced by the positivism of the Vienna Circle and subsequent developments under the general label of "empiricism," there have been a variety of other influences on modern political analysis. For example, the influence of the positivist tradition in Germany, particularly as represented in the writings of Max Weber, has had an undeniable impact on contemporary social science in the English-speaking world. Especially noteworthy is Weber's insistence on value-free inquiry and on a radical separation between the grounds for a proposition's validity and the process by which an interest in the proposition develops. These two commitments are part of the same frame of reference, for while Weber advocated a separation

of normative and factual judgments, he pointed out that normative commitments are essential for developing one's categories of analysis and
for establishing the experiential meaning of those categories. There is,
according to Weber, no presuppositionless knowledge. His argument
that social science must be value free resides in his commitment that
"it can never be the task of an empirical science to provide binding
norms and ideals from which directives for immediate practical activity
can be derived."[2] Like the Vienna positivists, Weber argued that there
can be a science of means but not of ends, that is, ultimately knowledge
and value must be separated. The separation of the grounds for presuppositions that provide an interest in a proposition from the truth of the
proposition is thus a part of his commitment to a value-free science.

Another aspect of Weber's influence on modern social science is his
indictment of the historical point of view that equates understanding
with exhaustive description. Explanatory schemes in the social sciences
are "inherently abstractive and selective,"[3] according to Weber. To this
extent he saw the natural and social sciences as sharing a methodological orientation. This argument of Weber's was, of course, echoed in
David Easton's influential call for a theoretical political science that
avoided what he called the "hyperfactualism" of descriptively oriented
disciplines.[4] Weber's influence on contemporary social science, moreover, extends to other than positivist orientations. His emphasis on the
subjective meaning that behavior has for the actors who are the focus of
sociological inquiry was, along with Husserl's philosophical writings,
the basis for Alfred Schutz's systematization of the phenomenological
approach to social inquiry.[5]

My emphasis in the following section of this chapter and in parts of
the next on the writings of both the positivists of the Vienna Circle and
the more contemporary empiricists such as Hempel should not be construed, therefore, as implying that contemporary social scientists are directly and exclusively influenced by these writings. I maintain rather
than an analysis of this school will underscore the difficulties and shortcomings in what I see as the central tendency in modern political inquiry
and will provide a basis for the development of an alternative perspective, because the approach to meaning and the analysis of discourse that
I subsequently develop begin with the significant critiques of logical positivism and empiricism.

The Positivist Mode of Theory Building in Political Science

Since roughly 1940, the "scientific study of politics" has operated
with procedural and justificatory principles resembling those of the philosophical school known as logical positivism (and its later development
known under the rubric of logical empiricism). Although in a discipline

as nonformal and informal as political science one can witness a vast diversity of activities that are not coordinated by any agreed-upon theoretical or metatheoretical commitments, many political scientists would place their theory building and analysis efforts within the framework of the following statement, produced fairly early in the development of "scientific political analysis":

> While theory building must begin with the establishment of existing fact, political facts may be significant only insofar as they are connected with other facts to form laws or generalizations. A major purpose of political research is to find such connections. When we have accumulated an adequate number of laws and significant concepts, it is generally useful to arrange this material into an axiomatic system or theory. This involves the construction of a set of axioms (laws temporarily taken for granted), definitions, and the theorems that follow from them. It is toward the development of a body of theory formally rationalizing experienced political phenomena that many political scientists are now working.[6]

That such a statement is undisputed by a large number of political scientists is surprising. Although it is generally in accord with the principles of inquiry set out by the early positivists of the Vienna Circle, it should now be very controversial, for there have been further developments in philosophy to which the positivists themselves have disproportionately contributed. The philosophy of modern empiricism, departing significantly from the commitments of early positivists, sees data as inseparable from theoretical formulations and therefore construes meaning as a function of theoretical coherence rather than of correspondence with or relation to facts.[7] It is very controversial, moreover, in the context of alternative philosophies of the social sciences with well-established traditions (e.g., hermeneutical and phenomenological). The statement is at least as controversial for what is left unsaid as for the commitments expressed. First, we can consider what is notably missing. What distinguishes this statement most strikingly from traditional ones about the craft of political theorizing is the absence of terms that refer to values and various related normative concerns. There is no mention of the ends toward which political inquiry ought to be directed of how individuals and collectivities ought to act and organize themselves to achieve the good life. In short, the statement is wholly method oriented. Not only does it fail to mention the traditional concern with the "good" to which political philosophers since Plato have addressed themselves, but it also contains no stipulations about the domain of the political, no directions as to the appropriate content of political theories.

The mention of "existing fact" would alert many that there is no mention of preexisting fact. The statement is rigorously phenomenalist, suggesting that the domain of meaning to which political theory is to be addressed is immediate. There is no intimation that the political theorist needs to attend to the historical context within which theoretical terms or categories function, or, for that matter, to any context—social, political, cultural, and so forth. There is no suggestion, moreover, that there is anything special about the subject matter of political theories (the "political relations" among persons and groups of persons), nor is there any attention to the relationship of the theorist to the subject matter. Thus, nothing distinguishes this statement about political theory from what one has come to expect of statements about theory building in the natural or physical sciences.

Finally, the statement fails to consider alternative modes of explanation. It would appear that only a deductivist model of explanation is countenanced, because the view is expressed that valid explanations consist exclusively in deducing descriptive and/or likelihood statements from general empirical laws that are, in turn, derived from statements about antecedent conditions. A concommitant of such an exclusive view of explanation is a narrow perspective on understanding, one which precludes any inquiry into human conduct oriented toward interpretation, empathic understanding, or any kind of knowledge other than that expressed in the form of empirical generalizations.

These omissions should not be ascribed to the absent-mindedness of the statement's author. Both what is included and what is excluded derive from a comprehensive, well-articulated, and still influential (in the social sciences if not in philosophical circles) metatheoretical position known as logical positivism. What are referred to as omissions are thus omissions only in the context of one or another of a wide variety of alternative metatheoretical viewpoints. In order to begin to gain a perspective on the major epistemological issues surrounding the statement, then, we need to consider, at least in their most general form, the enduring tenets of logical positivism and contrast them—though only sketchily at this stage—with alternative positions.

Curiously, despite significant departures from the classical Greek tradition in philosophy, particularly as it has been applied to the human sciences, much of the conceptual and motivational impetus of logical positivism can be traced to the classical period. Habermas has pointed out this continuity succinctly.

There is a real connection between the positivist self-understanding of the sciences and traditional ontology. The empirical-analytic sciences develop their theories in a self-understanding that automatically generates continuity with the beginnings of philosophical thought. For both are committed to a theoretical attitude that frees

those who take it from dogmatic association with the natural interests of life and their irritating influence; and both share the cosmo-
logical intention of describing the universe theoretically in its lawlike order, just as it is.[8]

But the logical positivists of the Vienna Circle also *departed* from
classical assumptions by identifying metaphysical or transcendental
commitments as both meaningless and as illegitimate supports for ideological claims. Because metaphysical statements are not, they claimed,
susceptible to public scrutiny, they are destructive of a disinterested,
scientific theoretical attitude. Arguing that statements about entities
which lie outside the grasp of experience are vacuous ("pseudo-state-
ments"), they sought to develop a theory of meaning that would attribute cognitive meaning only to statements that are analytic or logically
true (tautologies) or statements that are about experience and thus can
be verified by observation. As Ayer put it in his version of the logical
positivists' "verifiability theory of meaning," "A statement is held to be
literally meaningful if and only if it is analytic or empirically verifiable."[9]
Thus, for example, the positivists rejected as meaningless, statements
about the nature of reality, such as "reality is simple and undifferen-
tiated," or the converse, "reality is complex and many-faceted."

The positivists' position on meaning is closely related to their philosophy of mind, which, in the tradition of the British Empiricists, locates
the origin of ideas in the passive perception of "sense data." The influence of such a model of mind on social inquiry becomes evident when
the positivist position is contrasted with an alternative philosophy of the
social sciences like phenomenology. Interestingly, phenomenology was
also developed as a rejection of traditional metaphysical speculation. At
least this was a major aim of Edmund Husserl, the originator of phenomenology as a contemporary philosophical tradition. Husserl claimed to
be avoiding what he called "a historically degenerate metaphysics" by
establishing a presuppositionless view of consciousness. Whereas positivists sought an unobstructed base for dealing with the data of experience in a language of data or sensation, Husserl sought a similarly unobstructed view in a language of consciousness that would convey
"ultimate cognitions of being."[10]

Husserl used the notion of intentionality, after the psychologist Brentano, to refer to object-awareness. Used in this special way, the concept
of intentionality becomes the basis for a philosophy of mind, a position
on the nature of consciousness and the origin and nature of ideas. In
contrast with the positivist position that ideas are derived from sense
impressions, Husserl viewed mind as an active agent, engaging in ideational acts that confer meaning through the ex-pression of ideal entities.
While the more detailed aspects of Husserl's approach to meaning will

be developed below in chapter 2, here it is important to note that the desire to avoid traditional metaphysical speculation, which formed the underpinning of Husserl's philosophy, produced a philosophy of the social sciences wholly different from positivism, which began with a similar antimetaphysical posture but combined this posture with an empiricist philosophy of mind. If, in accord with Husserl's phenomenological philosophy, objects present themselves as a result of acts of consciousness, one would logically expect that a phenomenologically oriented social science would place significant emphasis on the standpoint of subjects, who, in a Husserlian view of mind, play a role in constituting the world of objects that give meaning to their conduct. This is precisely what has happened. Those who have developed the phenomenological approach to the social sciences, as a result of Husserl's influence, have in varying degrees emphasized the subjective standpoint of the actor. For example, Alfred Schutz insisted that the interpretation of a person's conduct by an outside observer must accord with the common-sense perspective of the actor if it is to provide a valid account of that conduct.[11]

It is understandable, therefore, that a positivistic social science based on a philosophy of mind that regards consciousness, not as an active constituting force that constructs a system of entities, but as a passive recorder of sensations, would develop a view that the scientific observer may disregard the standpoint of subjects involved in conduct. Whereas in the view of some philosophies of the social sciences, especially those influenced by phenomenological philosophy, the explanation of human conduct must be consistent with the meaning that acting subjects ascribe to their own conduct, the positivist position places an exclusive emphasis on the standpoint of the observer. This emphasis can be understood more clearly in connection with various supporting principles of inquiry which are exemplified in the above statement on political inquiry.

The absence of any reference to norms or value judgments in the statement is consistent with one of the positivist principles of inquiry, the radical separation between empirical inquiry and normative judgment, exemplified in the statement's reference to beginning with "existing fact." This commitment (which receives extended treatment in chapter 3), follows both from the denial of cognitive meaning to value statements and the empiricist construal of the role of consciousness. These commitments combine to justify a normative-empirical separation, because if sense data are conceived of as apprehended without the interpretive or constitutive activity of mind, the data of human experience must have a meaningful existence independent of the selecting-out activity of persons, whether the persons are the actors being investigated or the investigators. Given this posture, cognitive meaning must inhere in statements *about* an external reality. Since the positivists viewed value statements as subjective expressions of persons' attitudes or interests, they clearly cannot qualify as meaningful because they are neither analytic (logically true) nor "empirical," that is, about something external to the subject.

The positivist view that science ought to be value neutral makes sense, therefore, within the context of these positivist philosophical commitments. Because they viewed the world of experience as possessing a coherent structure unimposed by the perceiver, they approached the problem of developing a language of inquiry from a logical/structural perspective. If one is to make correct inferences about the world, one must develop conceptual systems or theories as sets of statements that are semantically and syntactically coherent. Hypotheses about experience must be logically derived from initial premises and statements that are more abstract, and observations must be linked to theoretical terms in an orderly, rule-governed way, for example, through the development of operational definitions that prescribe the method for identifying the data which are the referents of the theoretical terms.

Without a detailed analysis at this point, one may point out that alternative philosophical positions give rise to different perspectives on the role of normative judgment in inquiry. For traditionalists like Leo Strauss, for example, the realm of values cannot be separated from the realm of facts. Political inquiry for Strauss must be oriented toward "an attempt to discover and lay bare *the* true ends of man as man."[12] Strauss's perspective stems from a wholly different notion of what it means to speak truly or falsely. Whereas positivists have tended to promote a correspondence conception of truth, that is, a statement is empirically true if it corresponds or accords with observed experience, Strauss's conception preserves the meaning that truth had for the early Greek philosophers, for whom to speak truly meant to un-cover or discover something, not to speak *about* a thing.[13] This is not the place to analyze the Straussian position, which gives values the same kind of naturalistic "discoverability" as other aspects of experience. It is simply worth noting that various philosophical perspectives which evince principles contradicting the positivist separation between normative judgment and empirical inquiry are based on a rejection of the correspondence conception of truth.

Critical theorists of the Frankfurt school of philosophy also argue against the existence of an independent facticity that provides the basis for assertions that are true by virtue of correspondence. They, like others influenced by hermeneutical (interpretive) traditions of inquiry, argue that human experience is apprehended on the basis of categories that have meaning in the historical context of the persons analyzed *and* in the cultural context of the analyst/observer. Experience is thus always contingent on the normative standards that are presupposed in the selection and constitution of "facts." As Habermas has put it, "facts are first constituted in relation to the standards that establish them."[14] Modern analytic philosophers, whose position has been elaborated through the analysis of ordinary language, have developed a similar critique. Rejecting the notion that the meaning of statements inheres in their referral function and that truth is therefore a matter of speaking correctly about "things," philosophers like Wittgenstein and Austin—whose positions will be discussed in chapter 2—have suggested that norms or standards about the appropriate uses of utterances contribute to their meaning. What is to be taken as a fact within such a perspective is thus highly contextual, that is, it is rule dependent, and the content of those rules reveals, among other things, forms of life (as Wittgenstein put it). This approach to language clearly impeaches the normative-empirical distinction. As Austin wrote at the end of his analysis in *How to Do Things with Words,* "the familiar contrast of 'normative' or 'evaluative' as opposed to the factual is in need, like so many dichotomies, of elimination."[15]

Another principle or commitment that attaches to the logical-positivist metatheory is that methods, broadly conceived, for acquiring knowledge and justifying knowledge claims are the same for any domain of experience. This principle reflected the Vienna Circle's commitment to a unified science. Otto Neurath, who was concerned with the social sciences more than any other member of the Circle, argued, "All laws, whether chemical, climatological, or sociological, must . . . be conceived of as constituents of a system, *viz.* of unified science."[16] Neurath saw the pursuit of unified science as consisting in the attempt to establish correlations among entities with methods that are invariant across domains of experience. "No matter whether one is investigating the statistical behavior of atoms, plants, or animals, the method employed in establishing correlations is the same."[17] It is primarily because of this position that the same methods are appropriate for both the social and physical sciences, that the above statement about political theory makes no reference to contexts, whether historical, social, political, or cultural, and it is evident that the emphasis on a timeless or context-free approach to explaining the phenomena of human association is partly linked to the positivist approach to language. If speaking truly is construed as a matter of the structural properties of utterances, there is no incentive to attend to the particular context of the entities that are the focus of an investigation. The unified-science approach, moreover, is also a consequence of the positivist philosophy of mind. Because an emphasis on the standpoint of the observer follows from a rejection of the idea that actors themselves contribute, through their own perspectives, to the meaning of what they are doing, there is no need to treat persons differently from any other objects of investigation. There is, in short, no significance, for traditional logical positivists, that the objects under consideration in social science theories are persons who have minds and thus perspectives or conceptions of what they are doing. Accordingly a statement of a positivist approach to political science need not reflect any aspect of the subject matter. To study politics, as the above statement on theory building suggests, is to build theories, provide formal syntactic structures (to the extent that this is possible), and to test the propositions derived from the theories, after having invented "operational definitions" of at least some of the concepts in the theories.

There are several well-attended schools of thought that bear on this positivist position. The metatheoretical perspectives of traditionalists, phenomenologists, and analytic philosophers, for example, all challenge the positivist theory of meaning by suggesting that aspects of the context within which persons behave are relevant to the meanings ascribed to the observed behavior. Traditionalist Leo Strauss, in a statement worthy of many phenomenologists, states, "social science cannot reach clarity about its doings if it does not dispose of a coherent and comprehensive understanding of what one may call the common sense understanding of political things which precedes all scientific understanding; in other words, if we do not primarily understand political things as they are experienced by the citizen or statesman."[18] Strauss's statement here is reminiscent of Alfred Schutz's position that the social, as opposed to the natural, sciences require that theory building be in accord with "the postulate of subjective interpretation,"[19] which stipulates that human action must be understood in relation to the subjective meaning of that action for the actor.

Schutz's approach is clearly a departure from the positivist position because it emphasizes the common-sense world of subjects, but it remains an essentially objectivist approach to theory building inasmuch as Schutz prized scientific detachment as a basis for intersubjective knowledge. Rather than rejecting general laws and hypotheses, which are the major components of empiricist approach to explanation and understanding, Schutz *adds* a principle of adequacy, requiring that scientific understanding accord with common-sense understanding. The emphasis of Schutzian analysis is thus not wholly interpretive and is not a rejection of the scientific explanation of human phenomena on the basis of inductive generalization. A more radical departure from empiricist metatheory comes out of the critical theory and hermeneutical traditions. From the hermeneutical/interpretive approach to social phenomena comes the idea of *Verstehen* ("to understand"), which was juxtaposed to the idea of *Erklären* ("to explain") by thinkers like Dilthey, who argued that the understanding of human conduct, unlike the understanding of "natural" events, requires an empathic appreciation acquired through an imaginative reconstruction of the experience of the actors whose conduct is the focus of inquiry.[20]

The Verstehen approach to knowledge, as Dilthey conceived it, while not a wholly psychological approach to gaining knowledge through interpretive understanding—Dilthey saw interpretation as mediated through systems of signification—is still a more subjectivist approach to knowledge than is offered by some thinkers of the hermeneutical persuasion, who emphasize not empathic or subjective understanding but rather the placing of persons' actions in the context or way of life that gives those actions meaning. Here one sees an affinity between Wittgenstein, who maintained that a "form of life" is always presupposed in the meaning of actions and utterances, and interpretive theorists like Gadamer who advance the position of Heidegger that a form of "being-in-the-world" precedes any relationship between a subject and objects.[21] For Gadamer, to understand actions and utterances is to interpret them in such a way as to grasp the preunderstanding that gives them meaning, and that preunderstanding is manifest in language, not necessarily in the cognitions that are available to the actors' immediate consciousness.

The radical departure of this branch of hermeneutical thinking from the empiricist approach to understanding should be evident. Rather than understanding conduct by constructing concepts and establishing their meaning externally as observational or measurement rules in order to get on with the task of explaining by producing and testing hypotheses, hermeneuticists suggest that human conduct be understood by investigating the way of life or system of norms that underlies and gives meaning to what is said and done. Language, for hermeneuticists such as Gadamer, is thus treated as an expression of human existence rather than a symbolic structure that is external to existence and is to be used to represent or stand in place of things. This perspective is shared by Ricoeur, who has explicitly noted the compatibility of the interpretive approach to understanding, stimulated by the writings of Husserl and Heidegger, and the English linguistic tradition of Wittgenstein and others.[22] Both of these traditions view language as an aspect of conduct and as the primary medium through which conduct achieves meaning. From both perspectives, language becomes part of the data of analysis for inquiry rather than simply a tool for speaking about an extralinguistic reality, as it is for the naturalistic-empiricist tradition to which the positivist self-understanding contributes.

Critical theorists of the Frankfurt school of philosophy also emphasize interpretation rather than inductive generalization in explaining human conduct. Their most active current exponent, Habermas, develops his position from his rejection of the empiricist correspondence theory of truth. For Habermas, truth claims must be justified by resort to argumentation. Because experience supports the truth of a claim only through some consensus on the interpretation of that experience, one speaks truly to the extent that one's assertions can be warranted in unfettered argumentation.[23] Given that Habermas conceives of the grounds for justifying truth claims as pragmatic or interest related, the primary thrust of the kind of inquiry he promotes is toward clarifying the interests that are presupposed in statements rather than validating statements empirically (although this dimension is not totally neglected). Empirical explanation intended to produce generalizations in answer to "why" questions can serve no effective purpose, according to Habermas, unless it is incorporated into a dialogue that enhances "communicative competence." There is thus no meaningful empirical explanation outside of the context of some dialogue over interests into which the explanation can be placed. One way of characterizing this approach to understanding is to refer to it as dialectical. This means that, contrary to the empiricists, who presumes a gulf between theory and practice, that is, between the justification of knowledge and the justification of action, critical theorists see theory and practice as linked, because knowledge for them is contingent upon interests that justify action.

Finally, the linguistic philosophy tradition, whose influence on interpretive approaches has already been noted, suggests departures from the empiricist model of explanation that emphasizes inductive generalizations for both natural and social phenomena. But while the work of linguistic philosophers suggests that one cannot separate questions of meaning (requiring interpretation) from problems of explanation, the fact that meaning and explanation are inseparable does not necessarily imply that the human sciences require different methods and criteria for knowledge claims. Some philosophers of the social sciences, influenced by the analytic or linguistic philosophy tradition (e.g., Winch)[24] completely dismiss the understanding of social phenomena through inductive generalizations derived from theories, while others (e.g., Skinner)[25] see meaning accounts as complementary to such causal accounts. At a minimum, however, the linguistic philosophical tradition suggests that the account of explanation, developed in the statement on theory building in political science above, is inadequate because it neglects the problem of meaning. The implications of the various approaches to meaning of the different philosophical schools sketched briefly here are presented at some length in chapter 4. For present purposes, we can simply note some obvious contrasts.

Analytic philosophers generally agree that an adequate account of human conduct must refer to the rules which make that conduct one kind of action or another. For example, if someone forcibly prevents a bus involved in integrating public schools from delivering its passengers, the question of what kind of action is involved would depend on the rules that recruit conduct into various categories—political, criminal, economic, and so on. In a given case, what the relevant rules are may be controversial, but in general, analytic philosophers would hold that one must know the meaning of the behavior in question before the behavior can be interpreted, and it is some set of rules relating to the collectivity in which the conduct or behavior is undertaken that lends the meaning to the episode. One analyst, Charles Taylor, has referred to human action as "directed behavior," behavior that derives its meaning with reference to the intentions or purposes which guide it.[26] Intention is not, however, to be regarded as a motivating cause of an action. Intention, as Taylor and others tend to use the concept, is part of the description of an action.

Analytic philosophers therefore share the phenomenologists' preference for analyzing "action" rather than behavior, regarding the latter as a conception of human conduct that neglects the norms which guide and constitute what is done. The connotation of the concept of action, as it is used in social inquiry, then, is that it evokes "what" as well as "why" questions. To understand human *action* therefore is to know *what* is being done as well as *why* it came about. But there is an important distinction between the position on action developed by some phenomenologists (e.g., Schutz) and many analytic philosophers. While both argue that "intention" provides part of the context that gives meaning to conduct (and thus constitutes it as "action"), they employ different interpretations of the concept of intention. Schutz psychologizes the concept of intention, interpreting it as "a picture in our minds of what we are going to do." This orientation of Schutz's is not, strictly speaking, phenomenological, for Husserl and Heidegger both explicitly rejected the psychologizing of the concept of intention. What Schutz ends up doing with the concept of intention is treating all behavior as though it were purposive, that is, as behavior connected to what he calls "in order to" motives formulated by the actor.

In contrast, analytic philosophers tend to argue that intending, willing, and similar concepts should not be regarded as descriptions of mental events. Intention, they argue, is ascribed to persons in accordance with the rules governing the situation within which the conduct is deployed. Persons, as Melden has pointed out, follow rules habitually.[27] What is therefore required to understand human conduct is an interpretation of the conduct involved, in the context of the rules being followed, rules which reflect sociocultural norms used to interpret behavior. The analytic philosophical tradition thus stresses the need for a standpoint for the description of action based on an understanding of the context that can give meaning to a description. From the point of view of analytic philosophers, that standpoint may or may not include actors' own conceptions of what is to be accomplished, while for Schutz it is always involved. The implication of this contrast for the above example of forcibly detaining the bus is that a Schutzian analyst would tend to emphasize what the actors thought they were doing to decide what was done, while analytic philosophers would tend to emphasize the social/political context of the conduct. At a minimum, however, both phenomenologists (Schutzian or otherwise) and analytic philosophers agree that one cannot merely observe human conduct in order to develop explanations and understanding. One must rather interpret that conduct on the basis of the rules that give it meaning. The problem is, of course, whose rules?

Although some empiricist philosophers of science do argue that the meaning of persons' conduct provides an important kind of understanding, they separate out this kind of understanding from the kind derived from causal generalizations, arguing that meaning accounts are not involved in the explanation of human conduct. To "explain" according to the standard empiricist or positivist account is still simply to develop causal accounts as in the natural sciences.[28]

The phenomenological and analytic philosophical positions on human conduct (as well as the interpretive or hermeneutical) clearly have implications for another positivist principle reflected in the opening statement on theory building in political science, the principle of deductivism. If human conduct is to be regarded, at least partly, as consisting of behavior directed toward goals or purposes, or as behavior with meaning only in the context of the rules followed by the behavior, and if this kind of account is to be understood as noncausal, that is, as requiring interpretation, either as well as causal explanation or instead of causal explanation (depending on the orientation of the analysis), then the deductive-nomological paradigm of scientific explanation is an inadequate basis for understanding social phenomena. There have been additional problems associated with this model of scientific explanation, which have been pointed out by social scientists and philosophers within the empiricist tradition. One line of reasoning, popular among some social scientists, is that the deductive-nomological model of scientific explanation, as popularized in the writings of Carl Hempel[29] (and reflected in the political theory statement presented above), is inappropriate because it is not a good description of how social scientists actually conduct inquiry.[30] This kind of criticism can be dismissed by simply noting that this model of explanation is oriented toward justification and not discovery; it is a model or framework within which inferences are to be made and knowledge claims tendered. It does not purport to be a description of how one can discover or invent concepts, laws, and hypotheses.

There are, however, arguments that can be legitimately raised about the separation of discovery and justification. For example, a rejection of a correspondence notion of empirical truth leads one to consider the confirmation or acceptance of hypotheses as dependent on the interpretive rules that govern the meaning of the concepts involved. Such rules must also be involved in the "discovery" of concepts and hypotheses. One can thus show that just as the discovery of concepts and statements (laws, hypotheses, etc.) in theories is guided by the norms and conventions that comprise the standpoint of the theorist and orient the theorizing toward particular purposes, so too the criteria by which "empirical statements" (hypotheses) are to be regarded as true must be guided by the same norms and conventions.

If, contrary to the empiricist position, discovery and justification are logically connected, this raises questions about the function of explanations that tend to be neglected in the deductive account. For example, the deductivist model of explanation neglects the pragmatic dimension of explaining something.[31] It is not the case that there is no choice as to what to explain and how to explain something once the "what" questions have been decided. As Scriven has noted, "There is no such thing as *the* explanation of something unless a decision is made about *type*."[32] Decisions about the type of explanation to be employed in a particular circumstance have to do with the audience or constituency of an explanation, that is, with who is going to use it and for what purpose. Positivist philosophers of science have, since Mach, evaluated scientific explanations or theories on the basis of their structural properties. Aside from being concerned with a theory's truth value (its predictive or postdictive success), they have considered such dimensions as parsimony or economy of conceptual means and semantic and syntactic coherence, criteria that are reflected in the above statement about political theory. Hempel and other advocates of the deductive-nomological model of explanation have neglected what Scriven calls the "type-justifying grounds" of an explanation.[33] It is not clear, for example, when explaining why a person engages in a particular action, whether a psychological, biological, or even historical explanation is appropriate. The choice among these types of explanation depends upon the purposes for which the explanation is constructed, and, as will be elaborated below, those purposes are often best understood in the context of value frameworks or social and political ideologies.

Language, Political Analysis, and the Conduct of Inquiry

Although the succeeding analyses here and in subsequent chapters will be based on a rejection of the positivist side of most of the issues sketched above, the general tenor of the approach will be based on the premise that provided much of the coherence in the original writings of the Vienna Circle, the premise that the way to develop criteria both to acquire knowledge and to make knowledge claims is through a systematic analysis of language. What a science of any particular empirical domain requires, according to the positivists, is criteria for analyzing correct and incorrect ways of speaking, and the major principles of correct speech for the Vienna positivists emerged from their distinction between meaningful statements and pseudo statements. The domain of meaningful statements is divided, as was noted above, into those that are analytic and those that are synthetic. The former, of course, comprise statements whose sole function is syntactic, for example, a statement that is tautological or logically true, such as, "The sum of the interior angles of a triangle equals two right angles" (which follows logically from other statements in Euclidean geometry), while the latter, unlike the former, could be true or false, depending on the "facts" to which the statement refers. According to positivists, these two kinds of statements are involved in the discourse of any discipline that is to have scientific pretensions. Rudolph Carnap, who did more than any other Vienna Circle member to systematize the analysis of language as it relates to scientific inquiry, argued that "the questions dealt with in any theoretical field— and similarly the corresponding sentences and assertions—can be roughly divided into *object-questions* and *logical questions*."[34] The former kind of question, according to Carnap, involves inquiry into the properties and relations among "objects" in a particular domain, while the latter involves inquiry into terms, sentences, and various structures of sentences (e.g., theories) that "refer to objects."[35]

More will be said about the notion of referring to objects in the next chapter, which deals in part with the positivist theory of meaning. It will suffice now to note that the position to be presented here, on the relationship between language and the substantive domain to which it refers, contrasts sharply with the positivist position. An emphasis on correct speech in political theorizing and analysis, speech that is structurally sound (good syntax) and is appropriate (semantically sound) comes from the presumption that our political experience has a meaning of its own, an unreported coherence and integrity. It presumes that some entity called "political experience" exists fully formed, waiting for us to organize ourselves rhetorically and rewards correct speech patterns with enlightenment. It has been implied in the above statement on political theory that political scientists are working toward "the development of a body of theory formally rationalizing experienced political phenomena."

Throughout the analysis in subsequent chapters I will argue that the idea that we can speak *correctly* about objects and situations is predicated on a indefensible theory of meaning and is a misleading way to represent the relationship between speech and phenomena. Carnap and his Vienna Circle colleagues were bent on discrediting statements which, though presented in a descriptive mode, were not about anything. For some purposes it is sensible to distinguish between statements such as "The soul lacks material substance" and "Leopards have spots." But the matter turns out to be more complex than simply judging whether a nonanalytic statement is really about something. The position to be presented and elaborated throughout this analysis is that language is not *about* objects and experience, it is *constitutive* of objects and experience. This is not the subjectivist position that there is nothing (no thing) in the world until we cognize it or speak of it. Rather, it is the position that the world of "things' has no meaningful structure except in connection with the standards we employ to ascribe qualities to it. We therefore cannot speak about the world of experience without beginning with some presuppositions about the boundaries that distinguish one object or event from another. Even such seemingly trivial bits of materiality as "dirt" cannot be spoken of unproblematically, for, as Julius Kovesi has suggested, "Not only does the notion of dirt imply standards, but unless we understand why we list as examples of dirt custard on a waistcoat and sand on a lens but *not* custard on a plate or sand on a beach we would not know how to construct the list."[36]

Thus, statements are not appropriately thought of as being about objects or as representations of objects. They must be regarded as complex, rule-governed utterances that rely on implicit norms or standards which organize an otherwise shapeless material reality. Moreover those norms or standards are constitutive of human action, rendering episodes of performance as belonging to social, political, and other relations. For example, consider the concept "child." Conventionally, we would regard it as unproblematic to say that we speak about children; as competent users of the language we would expect to be reliably understood by others who possess the concept. We have this expectation because the degree of interpretation intervening between the concept of a child and the observations persons make in employing the concept, as givers and receivers of communications about children, is relatively small and, perhaps more importantly, is not currently contested by powerful, recognized interests.

Traditional positivists were relatively sensitive to the interpretive element involved in the relationship between words and statements and their referents. But rather than holding that interpretive element up to critical scrutiny, they endeavored to work out a metalanguage (a language to be used to speak about language) that would minimize the interpretive element, because they saw it as an impediment to communication and to the development of highly reliable scientific theories[37] rather than as a source of "date" for inquiry. The positivist approach thus places most of the emphasis in inquiry on the establishment of relationships among concepts and minimizes the process of establishing or constituting concepts, which depends on an emphasis on semantic rules linking concepts and experience. In the context of our present example, a positivist approach to theorizing about the children would begin with the assumption that identifying something as a child is relatively unproblematic. The inquiry would therefore focus on the development of hypotheses about relationships between children and other phenomena.

But to speak about children could be regarded as problematic. The emergence of the phenomenon of children is a relatively recent historical event, as Philippe Ariès has pointed out.[38] Before persons were recognized and treated as children, societies simply divided persons into the category of either infant or adult. Childhood, as a category, emerged from economic, political, and administrative changes as societies organized themselves differently in response to both immanent processes and changes in their external environments. Childhood has a meaning, therefore, not only by virtue of its current representation of part of the age spectrum but also because of the role that childhood as a conception has played in social and political processes for the past few centuries. Strictly speaking, then, we do not speak *about* children because there are no such "things" as children. *What makes something a child is the existence of rules that prescribe role entries and exits of persons into and out of the child category.* Moreover, those rules can be understood only in connection with the matrix of relationships comprising the social, political, and other processes within which the concept of childhood is used. Although it is not customary usage, it would be less misleading to say that "we speak children," that is, various persons are constituted as children in our use of language.

It should be noted that "use" here is being employed in a semantic rather than a pragmatic sense. The suggestion is not, in other words, that any given speaker arbitrarily employs rules to suit his or her purposes and thereby moves about in a world of personally constituted objects and events. Rather, the suggestion, is that the language used by a society or culture contains rules which provide boundaries around phenomena and thereby produce the objects and events that are the referents of our speech. The point is that we "speak children" not in an immediate cerebral sense. It is not a matter of our purposefully deciding that we will regard certain persons as children. We regard certain persons as children almost inadvertently because our language and thus our consciousness contains the rule-governed category :"child," which fits into a pattern of life reflected in our discursive practices.

The child example is especially important here for what it illustrates about the relationships between language and politics. In keeping with the traditional positivist influence on political theory, we are used to conceiving of theories as being *about* something. In the case of political theory, we think of political theories—when we are thinking about empirical theories—as being *about* political phenomena. But, as the example demonstrates, there is a political subject matter implicit in our language. A strictly causal explanatory approach to political phenomena that views language as a tool for orienting our conceptions about things and giving them coherence and articulation neglects the extent to which things, animate or inanimate, become political phenomena in our language. The moment we place the constituting activity of subjects into the theorizing process and reject the rigorous distinction between a theory and its subject matter, a distinction that is presupposed when we say such things as, "a theory about *X*," we can find a whole new domain of political relations that are worthy of inquiry, the political relations that precede and therefore contribute to the meaning of the rules linking word and object. If we tentatively designate political relations as those involving sanctioned individual and collective control over valued experience, it should be evident that the rules which constitute many concepts employed in political theories carry such control implications.

This can be illustrated by treating almost any concept that is an ingredient in political theories, the concept of "violence," for example. The traditional positivist approach to a concept like violence involves theorizing *about* it. Violence within such an understanding would be treated as either an independent or a dependent variable in a causal explanation, and the analysis would involve assessing the kind (linear-curvilinear, unidirectional, bidirectional, etc.) and degree of the relationship between violence and the other variable or variables, perhaps through the use of correlational and/or regression techniques. This type of inquiry might tell us something about the relationship between violence (whatever it is) and various political structures, demographic characteristics of populations, economic or exchange systems, and so forth. While such relationships may provide answers to some important and interesting questions and thus can be part of significant theory-building strategies, other kinds of questions are logically prior, whose answers locate violence as a phenomenon in the political culture of a society.

Traditional, empirically oriented research in political science has repressed such "what" questions as, "What is violence?" This repression is partly owed to the positivist perspective that effective political inquiry is a matter of discovering units of analysis that are clear and unambiguous, so that stable measurement criteria can be developed. If, as I have suggested, we regard the meaning of concepts as a worthy focus of inquiry in itself, the precausal or, in the case of some inquiries not oriented toward empirical generalization, the noncausal "what" questions become the orientating ones of the inquiry rather than problems that must be cleared away before the inquiry proper can commence. With such an orientation, predicated on the idea that the discourses within which violence is embedded reveal a political process, we can disclose the control implications that the idea of violence has for a given collectivity. Alternative meanings of violence derive from the different discourses in which it appears and have alternative control implications. These control implications come about because (1) discourses allocate control disproportionately to persons who are subjects in them, as in the case of professional discourses—legal, medical, penal, and so on—which allocate regulative control to those with professional credentials; and (2) violence as a concept implies illegitimate action, thereby positively sanctioning a regulative response. The identification of some activity as violent therefore legitimizes negative sanctions, whereas the identification of the activity in some other way would legitimize other responses. To identify violence in any way is to occupy a distinctively partisan standpoint that in effect legitimizes some kind of social control among a range of alternatives. To regard one event as violent, for example, a group of students occupying a university administrative office, and to regard another as nonviolent, for example, the decisions of university administrators to admit some students and reject others, thereby leaving the others to the vagaries of the post-high school job market, is to employ rules about the social and political relations that such a use of the concept of violence presupposes. Those rules in this case involve implicit decisions about who has the right to control entry into academic roles.[39]

The content of language is thus based on the social, political, and administrative relations (in short, the institutions) in the society that use that language. The objects and events about which language users speak emerge as a result of rules or principles of exclusion. These principles provide the content of a language by controlling what aspects of experience are to be regarded as identical or parts of the same wholes and what aspects are to be regarded as distinct. To discover how language reflects political processes, one can examine almost any concepts that have a content or a referral aspect, such as that of the child or of violence discussed above. Speaking about children presupposes a set of authority relations which, in the language of social or political theorists, would be called legitimized power, influence, and control relations, because the concept, child, implies not only particular objects but also a network of authority and responsibility relationships. Similarly, rules which recruit various events or actions into the category of violence are part of the aspect of language use that distinguishes right from wrong action. To speak of violence is thus to agree, at the same time, that certain models of responsibility obtain and thus that certain social control agencies should be involved.

The illustrations above demonstrate, therefore, that in addition to the political relations we can speak about are those involved in *what* we speak and, as will emerge in subsequent analysis, *how* we speak. This distinction can be understood only in the context of the rejection of the traditional positivist theory of meaning, which restricts the meaning of statements to the relationship between the utterance and that which the utterance is about, thereby ignoring the context that is involved in constituting what an utterance is about and the relationship between the speaker and the utterance. To say that context is important, however, is not to provide an adequate examination of the problem of meaning, much less a direction for political inquiry. Such an examination begins in chapter 2. The point to be noted at this stage is that an examination of the problem of meaning is oriented not toward refining a research tool but rather toward developing an approach to language that gives inquiry into questions of meaning the status of political inquiry—political inquiry that uncovers the political presuppositions inherent in language and in alternative speech practices.

The Conduct of Political Inquiry

Like the program that the positivists set out for themselves in attempting to devise a metalanguage of scientific inquiry, the analysis here and in subsequent chapters is aimed at suggesting how inquiry can be furthered by attending to the role of language. But the rejection of the traditional positivist position, which radically separates language and reality, broadens the subject matter of political inquiry while implicitly rejecting almost all of the epistemological norms that traditional positivism has lent to the social sciences in general and political science in particular. Rather than regarding language as a tool of political analysis, and the rules of language use as methods of organizing and dissecting a subject matter, one can regard language as the bearer of a subject matter in itself. Such a conception alters the relationship between language and inquiry, for, as it applies to political science, it suggest that *a substantial proportion of the political relations of a society must be scrutinized at what, given the nature of contemporary models of inquiry, would be a pretheoretical stage: deciding what, precisely, are to become the ob-*

jects and events whose relations a theory is to explain or comprehend. Despite an emphasis on language, however, the target of investigation remains human conduct, for, as will be clear in the development of the problem of meaning in chapter 2, speaking is a form of acting. Our utterances constitute our meaningful world. To inquire into our language is thus to inquire into the meaning of our conduct, and, to the extent that we focus on the controls allocated and legitimized in language and speech, that inquiry into meaning is manifestly political.

For some time the philosophical resources have existed for us to recognize and thus begin to systematize the aspects of political relations that are implicit in language and thus not apprehended by traditional theory-building techniques and modes of political analysis in general that are addressed exclusively to relationships among and between concepts, to the neglect of the relationships presupposed in concepts. English analytic philosophers such as Austin and Wittgenstein had developed understandings of the function of language and speech that should alter the language–inquiry relationship. Similar perspectives on language emerge from various elements of continental philosophy, notably Heidegger's version of phenomenology and the hermeneutical tradition exemplified in the writings of Gadamer and Ricoeur. Although the development of noncausal, meaning-oriented approaches to political inquiry has not been systematized and popularized in a manner approaching the empirical tradition of theory building, the direction that such an approach might take is exemplified in the historical investigations of French philosopher-historian Michel Foucault. Accordingly, after reviewing the positivist failure to establish an adequate theory of meaning in the beginning of chapter 2, I shall consider the contributions of those English and Continental philosophers whose analyses of language and discourse have important if unacknowledged implications for political inquiry.

2
Language and Meaning

Two dimensions of an approach to language can be seen to have significantly informed contemporary social science. One is the empiricist perspective that locates the meaning of terms or expressions in what they stand for. From this perspective, the primary function of language is to make assertions about the world of "things." The other is the view, represented in diverse strains of Western philosophy (e.g., both rationalism and empiricism), that a philosophy of language must be founded primarily on logic. This two-dimensional approach to language for social and political inquiry implies an emphasis on discovering the structure of social/political practices by preparing systems of statements whose logical structure (syntax) and empirical grounding (semantic rules linking concepts with observations) provides for correct inferences about those practices.

In this chapter I shall argue that both dimensions of this approach to language are problematic and that the approach to social and political inquiry which they influence would be restructured if language were differently understood. With respect to the first dimension, I shall emphasize the need for viewing speech as a form of activity and meaning as therefore inhering in the use to which utterances are put. This perspective was developed by Wittgenstein in his later writings and in the work of John Austin and other "ordinary-language philosophers." These contemporary conceptions of language and meaning have already influenced various philosophers of the social sciences, who have interpreted their implications for social and political inquiry in diverse ways.[1] Although my analysis will build on some of these interpretations, it will also make use of some perspectives on language developed by continental philosophers, particularly as those perspectives are represented in the inquiries of Michel Foucault, whose work is interpreted in chapter 5.

The perspectives of the contemporary English analytic philosophers, particularly those of Wittgenstein and Austin, have a bearing also on the second dimension of the old language paradigm that bases an understanding of language on logic, that is, the view that signs represent ideas and that the structure of statements can represent the structure of ideas without reference to the contexts of communication and ways of life that affect the use of signs. In developing the alternative perspective that language is better understood from a rhetorical rather than a logical frame of reference, Wittgenstein and Austin are supported by developments in continental philosophy. In the developing his phenomenological approach to ideas and meaning, Husserl opposed the first dimension of the old language paradigm, the location of meaning in the objects for which terms and expressions stand, but he continued to approach language from a logical perspective, viewing it as providing a structure to represent the constitution of ideal objects in consciousness.[2] His student Heidegger, however, while accepting Husserl's rejection of traditional empiricism, constructed a view of language as expressive of the way that persons dwell in the world. He argued that thinking and speaking are not forms of "objectifying."[3] More recently, in a critique of Husserl that was influenced by Heidegger's writings, Derrida has developed a perspective on language that, like Wittgenstein's and Austin's, emphasizes rhetorical rather than logical mechanisms.[4] He attacks the radical distinction, shared by Husserl and empiricists, between a sign and what is signified (i.e., between word and object). The meaning of a statement for Derrida is to be understood in the context in which it is expressed.

✗ Briefly, then, logic and rhetoric provide different perspectives on meaning. As Garver has noted, rhetoric is less a matter of the form of language (its logical structure) than it is the relationship of language to life. Rather than emphasizing the correctness or incorrectness of statements, those with a rhetorical perspective emphasize the "aptness and ineptness" of speech.[5] An elaboration of these alternative British and continental perspectives on language will be developed in a later section below. In order to provide a basis for turning to these alternatives, it is necessary to understand the breakdown of the logical positivist/empiricist positions on language and meaning.

The Development of the Positivist Position

The terms 'means' occurs in a variety of seemingly disparate types of utterances. The following list is suggestive if not exhaustive:[6]

1. This time I think she really means it (intends).
2. I suppose this means you won't be home for dinner (implies).
3. That choice is going to mean deprivation for a lot of people (cause).

4. When he says constituency he means the electorate (refers to).
5. The term carnivorous means 'feeding on animals' (symbolizes or translates as).

Traditionally, philosophical interest on the concept of meaning and epistemological positions designated as theories of meaning have been concerned with meaning in sense 5. But the distinctions among the uses of the term in the above list are not as easy to maintain as the parenthetical labels seem to suggest. For example, many would argue that part of what is involved in meaning in sense 5 is the intention of the person making the utterance (or other gesture), which would produce an obvious overlap with meaning in sense 1. Suspending ambiguities involved in the use of the term 'means' or 'meaning' for the moment, however (because the meaning or 'meaning' cannot be adequately understood until some consideration of theories of meaning has been undertaken), we can say, at a minimum, that the philosophical problem of meaning concerns the relationship between word (or any kind of sign— e.g., gesture) and object. It should be noted, however, that some philosophers of language hold that words have meaning only in the context of meaningful utterances like sentences. When I refer to meaning as involving word–object relationships, it should therefore be understood as a kind of shorthand at this stage in the discussion. Ultimately I shall argue that meaningful utterances involve a collection of words in a rule-governed relationship with one another.[7] That the word–object relationship has immense significance for inquiry in almost any field becomes obvious when we note that a large part of the concern with truth turns on whether a word or statement and some object(s) or event(s) have been appropriately conjoined. Although it sometimes appears that the idea of truthfulness is regarded as a characteristic of speakers rather than of what is uttered (e.g., "He speaks with a forked tongue"), the locus of evidence for the concept of truth, as it is commonly employed, is in three domains of relationships (corresponding to three kinds of meaning) in which signs (symbols that stand for objects or events) partake, only one of which involves the speaker.[8]

The first of these relationships is between or among signs and is usually designated by the notion of syntactic meaning. Syntactical relations are the formal property of language and are made up of the rules prescribing permissible relations among signs. So the syntax rules of a language constitute the orderly and standardized forms of utterance such as phrases, clauses, and sentences. Words like 'and,' 'or,' and 'but,' have only syntactic meaning or significance because they play no role in designating the phenomena to which an expression refers. Their role is strictly organizational, contributing to the *form* of the utterance. The use of such syntactic operators thus involves only rules for constructing statements, not for relating statements to users or to objects and events. Semantical relations are those that link signs and the objects or situations to which they are applicable. If one spoke about what distinguishes a table, for example, from other objects, one would do so with reference to semantical rules (which establish what one means by 'table'). The third relationship is that between a sign and its user. This relationship is called pragmatic meaning. In addition to the cognitive meaning (based on semantic rules) that the terms or concepts in a public language convey, individual speakers can make special use of signs (e.g., to arouse emotions, establish new meaning, mobilize collective action). So pragmatical relations involve the way that persons use signs to achieve their individual purposes, as compared with the purposes that are approached ipso facto by all users of the language because they are implied in semantic rules.

Because of their special concern with truthfulness and certitude as characteristics of linguistic performance, positivists focused on syntactical and semantical relationships and, for the most part, neglected pragmatical relations, which they felt involved noncognitive- and thus nontruth- related aspects of meaning. The most interesting and controversial aspect of the positivist theory of meaning as it developed from the writings of Vienna Circle members is the position on semantic meaning, identified as the 'verificationist theory,' which, because it locates the meaning of a term or expression in the methods one would use to determine its validity, closely identifies meaning with truth. But an appreciation of the positivists' position (or positions) on semantic meaning is better understood in the context of their firm commitment to a distinction between analytic (syntactic) and synthetic (semantic or empirical) truth. This distinction appears to be relatively straightforward and sensible if one examines only individual statements. For example, a statement from Euclidean geometry such as "The sum of the interior angles of a triangle equals two right angles" would be classified as analytic because it is tautological or true by definition, for it follows logically from other statements in Euclid's system (his theory of space). The statement is not "about the world," so assessing its validity is a matter of checking out the syntax or formal coherence of the Euclidean system to make sure that the statement is appropriate. By contrast, a statement such as "London is closer to Paris than to New York" would be classified as synthetic because its validity or truth would be determined empirically.

Despite the apparent simplicity of the distinction, however, the matter is quite complicated, owing to precisely what the positivists most vigorously committed themselves—the determination of something by empirical means. To analyze this commitment we can consider two questions. First, What does it mean to determine something by empirical means? and second, Does the answer to the first question support the distinction between analytic and synthetic statements? The answer to the first question is complex and not at all definitive, and the answer to the second question is no! To understand these answers, we can begin by focusing on the statement from Euclid's geometry offered above, "The sum of the interior angles of a triangle equals two right angles." As was noted, the statement is true analytically, that is, it is logically derivable from prior, more abstract commitments in the Euclidean system. There exist, however, two contradictory statements, which are also true in the same sense (analytically). One is logically derivable from the Lobachevskian system of geometry and can be stated, "The sum of the interior angles of a triangle is less than two right angles," and another can be logically derived from the Reimannian system of geometry and can be stated, "The sum of the interior angles of a triangle is greater than two right angles."

If one's attention is restricted to the concept of truth in the analytic sense, these three contradictory truths are not inconvenient. But because geometries are used to complement other conceptual systems in order to perform tasks in "the real world," some might find the situation perplexing. The philosopher-mathematician Karl Friedrich Gauss was sufficiently perplexed by the coexistence of incompatible geometries to attempt to settle the issue on "empirical grounds." He selected three adjacent hilltops and, from points on each of the hills, shone beams of light to one of the other hilltops. The three points on the hilltops were thus connected to form a triangle. He then measured his triangle as accurately as he could, given the instruments he had, and noted that the sum of the interior angles of that triangle equaled two right angles. He then claimed to have demonstrated that Euclid's is the true geometry, true in an empirical sense by virtue of its "correspondence with experience."

Because, once again, of the difficulty in sorting out what is involved in this second kind of truth, referred to in statements like "correspondence with experience" or "empirically true," Gauss's experiment was ill directed. As Poincaré was to point out, Gauss proved nothing in a definitive way about the relative merits of different geometries.[9] Euclid's geometry begins with some primitives (undefined terms), among which are points and lines. With these primitives and some axioms (underived statements) and some theorems (derived statements at a highly general level), one can derive the statement about the sum of the interior angles of a triangle. But Euclid's geometry says nothing about beams of light as representations of lines. That equivalence was supplied by Gauss and is an extratheoretical addition, in that its use cannot be justified in the context of the Euclidean system. All Gauss had shown is that, working within the earth's atmosphere and using light beams to represent lines, one can get accurate measurements for triangles by employing the Euclidean system to deal with the two-dimensional case. Later, Einstein was to demonstrate that a physics of motion in space, superior to that developed by Newton, can be achieved by employing, among other things, a Reimannian metric.

The importance of Poincaré's original point is that neither Gauss's nor Einstein's achievements with the different geometries constitute definitive empirical tests of the statements about the sum of the interior angles of a triangle, because those statements, by themselves, are not empirical statements or statements about experience in a direct, nonmediated sense (indeed *no* statement really is). It is, then, only a small additional step to see that the geometry anecdote seriously impeaches the analytic–synthetic distinction. To see why, we can turn to Quine's classic statement of why the distinction is invalid. Because no statement in a theory or conceptual system in general is, by itself, directly about reality, as was shown in the discussion of the Gauss experiment—extratheoretical conventions must be added to apply the statement to an experiential situation—it is not clear what part of a conceptual system, which purports to be empirically relevant, is "at fault" when an empirical test comes out with a negative result (or vice versa, we cannot be sure what is correct when the result is positive). The analytic–synthetic distinction can be reasonably maintained when one is dealing with the syntax of a theory, for statements in theories perform different functions within the theory, depending on the level of abstraction at which they reside, but the distinction breaks down when used to distinguish those statements that are or are not "about reality." As Quine puts it:

> For vividness I have been speaking in terms of varying distances from a sensory periphery. Let me now try to clarify this notion without metaphor. Certain statements, though about physical objects and not sense experience, seem particularly germane to sense experience and in a selective way: some statements to some experiences, others to others. Such statements, especially germane to particular experiences, I picture as near the periphery. But in this "germaneness" I envisage nothing more than a loose association reflecting the relative likelihood, in practice, of our choosing one statement rather than another for revision in the event of recalcitrant experiences to which we would surely be inclined to accommodate our system by reevaluating just the statement that there are brick homes on Elm Street, together with related statements on the same topic. We can imagine other recalcitrant experiences to which

we would be inclined to accommodate our system by reevaluating just the statement that there are no centaurs, along with kindred statements. A recalcitrant experience can, I have urged, be accommodated by any of various alternative reevaluations in various alternative quarters of the total system; but in the cases which we are now imagining, our natural tendency to disturb the total system as little as possible would lead us to focus our revisions upon these specific statements concerning brick houses or centaurs.[10]

What is "empirical," therefore, has meaning only in connection with some conceptual system constructed to interpret our experience. When that experience somehow evades the expectations involved in the conceptual system, it is possible to alter a variety of commitments in that system, some of which are relatively substantive and others of which are highly abstract. Because the more abstract commitments are more vital to the maintenance of the system, they are less likely to be adjusted to cope with what Quine calls "recalcitrant experience," but there is no adjustment that can be considered the *correct* one because no single commitment or single statement is directly *about* experience. The experience or empirical domain referenced by a conceptual system is constituted and shaped by the system as a whole.

Empirical truth, based upon semantic meaning or word–object relationships, is thus a fugitive and complicated phenomenon. It has nevertheless been vigorously pursued, especially by positivists, because of the value they felt that such a criterion of meaningfulness would have for scientific inquiry. In endeavoring to determine, as precisely as possible, just how a statement can be thought of as being about experience, the early positivists distinguished between the sense and the reference of a statement, thanks to the contribution of Gottlob Frege, a philosopher of mathematics and one of the first to subject the concept of meaning to rigorous analysis.[11] Frege showed that the sense of a statement or expression is not the same as its reference. For Frege the referent (*Bedeutung*) of an expression is that aspect of experience about which the expression says something or what the expression designates, whereas the sense of the expression (*Sinn*) is its meaning or what it expresses about that which it designates. Frege's now famous example involves the two expressions "the Morning Star" and "the Evening Star." Both refer to the planet Venus, but they clearly have different meanings in that they have different senses, or as Frege noted, they involve different thoughts about that to which they refer. One thought is about the star that is visible in the morning and the other is about the star that is visible in the evening. Frege thus showed that in explicating the relationship between words or expressions and objects, meaning depends on more than merely reference.

Reference remained an essential aspect of an expression, for in Frege's view, the truth value of a sentence depends on its referral function. The "proposition" contained in a declarative sentence is its sense. It is, according to Frege, what is said about what is designated. But unless there is a reference, the proposition cannot be true or false. This is evident in Frege's example "Odysseus was cast upon the shores of Ithaca in a deep sleep," which has a sense but not a reference. It is not meaningful to talk about the truth or falsity of the statement because Odysseus did not exist.

Frege's notions were influential in the development of an early version of the positivist position on meaning, known as the "referential theory," which was developed to a degree in Bertrand Russell's early position on meaning but found its elaborated expression, partly through Russell's influence, in Wittgenstein's early work, the *Tractatus*.[12] Wittgenstein's position on meaning in this work is usually designated the "picture theory," so called because there Wittgenstein argued that language provides images or models of reality and that if propositions are reduced to their "basic elements," those elements correspond to the basic elements in the reality or experience to which the proposition refers. Propositions thus provide a picture of reality because the elements in a proposition constitute a configuration of names that matches the configuation of the elements or objects in experience being designated.

That his picture theory, emphasizing the referent function of language, was inadequate as an account of all linguistic functions was obvious to Wittgenstein at the time he wrote the *Tractatus,* for he noted there that the words "and," "but," and similar connectives perform no referral function. A basic rejection of his picture theory of meaning was to come more than thirty years later, presented in his posthumously collected work, *Philosophical Investigations*.[13] Among objections to his original position was his argument that experience cannot be reduced to simple components (as was suggested in the *Tractatus*), for reality itself provides no standards for selecting particular features of objects or situations as the simplest or most basic. It also became clear to him that statements are more than lists of names which designate things. His emphasis in his later writing was to move from nouns to verbs, from speech as designation to speech as activity. Wittgenstein also rejected his earlier position on sense. In the *Tractatus* he had argued that the meaning of a proposition is supplied through the operation of the mind of the speaker who is, in effect, "thinking the sense of the proposition."[14] In *Philosophical Investigations* he noted that an expression's meaning cannot be arbitrarily altered through an act of willing (or, more appropriately, thinking). Rather, the meaning of a proposition is determined by the context or "language game" in which it occurs. In his later work, then, Wittgenstein was to reject a theory of meaning which simply indicates that language is *about* experience. His later work introduces complexities about how language relates to experience.

What is important here is the influence of the *Tractatus* on subsequent positions on the meaning of language developed by Vienna positivists. Interestingly, the Vienna positivists selected a minor theme from the *Tractatus* and never really adopted Wittgenstein's central notion that language conforms to reality by exhibiting the structure of relations among objects with its corresponding structure of the elements in prop- ositions. The verificationist theory of meaning, which is probably the best known and most influential commitment of the Vienna positivists, was partly encouraged by a remark of Wittgenstein. In the *Tractatus,* Wittgenstein says, "To understand a proposition means to know what is the case if it is true."[15] But this is not really a verificationist position that locates the meaning of a proposition in the method one would use to verify it. For Wittgenstein, in the *Tractatus,* propositions exhibit the structure of reality. So what he means by the above quotation is that if one understands what is meant by a proposition *and* if the proposition is true, then one knows what is the case. This interpretation is sup- ported by Wittgenstein's statement, "A proposition *shows* how things stand *if* it is true. And it says *that* they do stand."

The verificationist theory of meaning (a general label I shall use for a variety of positivist positions) does not assume that propositions show how things stand, only that they say that they stand. Within the verifi- cationist framework, meaning is thus not presumed to be contained solely in propositions or statements. To elucidate meaning, according to Schlick, Ayer, Carnap, and others in the Vienna Circle, one must go be- yond or outside of the statements themselves. If propositions do not re- semble reality in the way suggested by Wittgenstein the word–object gap must be filled with something to establish the linkage. After trying out a variety of candidates, described variously as the method of verification, method confirmation, testing procedures, reduction sentences, and so forth, the positivist attempt to establish the linkage, by its own reckon- ing, stands as a failure. The contemporary positivist position on mean- ing, as Hempel has stated it, is as follows: "It is a basic principle of contemporary empiricism that a sentence makes a cognitively meaning- ful assertion, and thus can be said to be either true or false, if and only if either (1) it is analytic or contradictory—in which case it is said to have purely logical meaning or significance—or else (2) it is capable, at least potentially, of test by experiential evidence—in which case it is said to have empirical meaning or significance."[16] But, as Ayer has noted, the principle of verifiability has never been adequately formu- lated, and Hempel has conceded that although the basic intent of what he calls "the empiricist criterion of meaning," as quoted above, is basically sound, he has little confidence that the idea can be stated precisely enough to provide criteria to distinguish, "(a) between statements of purely logical and statements of empirical significance, and (b) between those sentences which do have cognitive significance and those which do not."[17]

An appreciation of Hempel's pessimism can be gained by considering the various modifications the principle of verification has undergone in attempts to overcome the difficulties pointed out by its critics and/or discovered by its supporters. The original intent was, as has been mentioned above, to develop criteria that would distinguish cognitively meaningful, empirical statements from metaphysical or ethical statements, which the positivists regarded as either meaningless (in the hardliner's version) or possessing a noncognitive kind of meaning (the tolerant version maintained by Carnap, among others). But to claim that cognitively meaningful statements are either about objects or situations or are part of the conceptual system or rules for ordering statements (syntax) was inadequate because, in such a general format, it could not be used to cover the various metaphysical, or even mystical-religious statements, that purport to be about objects and situations of an ineffable variety, for example, the Bhagavad-Gita's statement about the self, "The self may not be wetted nor dried nor cut nor burned." Although this statement is clearly about something (the self), positivists wished to deny that such statements are cognitively meaningful, so they required a formulation that would address the distinction they wished to make between real and pseudo statements. The verificationist theory of meaning was invented to do just that. In its initial form, the principle simply identified the meaning of a statement with its method of verification. Since verification implied that the objects or situations referred to in the statement must be observable or recordable as sense impressions, the Ghita's statement about the self quoted above would not qualify as meaningful. So the principle of verification was introduced as a principle that, in effect, equated the questions "What does *P* mean?" and "What must be done to show that *P* is true?" As Schlick conceived it, for example, there is a requirement beyond that of a proposition indicating or referring to a state of affairs. If the terms in a proposition have meaning, one must be able to demonstrate that meaning. As Schlick put it, "the meaning of a word must in the end be *shown,* it must be given. This is done by an act of indication, of pointing; and what is pointed out must be given, otherwise I cannot be referred to it."[18] Although Schlick regarded this position as a commitment to a verificability principle, he had already softened his position to the point where he supported the claim that a statement, to have cognitive meaning, must be "verifiable in principle," recognizing that at the time one utters a statement or proposition, conditions might be such as to inhibit the actual 'pointing out' required to show that the proposition is either true or false.

A variety of objections were almost immediately raised to such early formulations of the verifiability principle. These have been extensively rehearsed in a number of places, so we can profitably restrict our attention to those that are most significant.[19] It has been demonstrated, to begin with, that there are important kinds of statements for which the verifiability principle is inadequate. The most troublesome, ironically, are scientific laws or generalizations, that is, general propositions to the effect that "all p's are q." Because the verification of such a statement would require one to observe all the p's that exist, there is no way to verify it. Since one can never know if all heretofore observed p's are q, there is no way of knowing if there exists at least one p that is not q and which would thereby invalidate the proposition. The same problem attaches, as Berlin and Hempel have pointed out, to propositions with 'any' and 'every' involved as elements, as in the proposition[20] "For any substance there exists some solvent," for here again, there could always be one or more invalidating instances that could not be examined prior to making a definitive test of the statement.

There have been some especially noteworthy attempts to save the verification principle. One is that of A. J. Ayer, who began by suggesting a weaker verifiability principle which requires simply that some observational evidence must at least be "relevant" to the truth or falsity of a proposition if it is to be cognitively meaningful.[21] But because of the vagueness of this formulation, no one hopeful of developing a plausible version of the principle, including ultimately Ayer himself, was satisfied. So Ayer tried a more elaborate modification, one to the effect that a sentence has empirical and thus cognitive significance if, from it, along with additional appropriate subsidiary hypotheses, one can derive observational sentences that one could not derive from the subsidiary hypotheses by themselves.[22] But a close inspection of this criterion and some subsequent, futile modifications reveals that almost any statement turns out to be cognitively significant, and this is certainly what the positivists had hoped to avoid.[23]

Another well-known innovation in the statement of the verifiability principle, constructed in part to address the principle's difficulty with general propositions, is Karl Popper's notion of falsifiability. Popper argued that empirically significant, scientific laws are those that can be 'falsified.' Falsification is equivalent to verifying the negation of the proposition that one is testing or validating.[24] One can verify the negation of a proposition simply by finding a single negative instance, such as, for the proposition "All p's are q," this would be accomplished by finding a p that does not have the quality q. Or, to say it another way, one could invalidate the statement "All *p*'s are *q*" by verifying the non-general statement "This *p* is not *q*." But this criterion, as Hempel has shown, denies empirical meaning to existential propositions of the type "There exists at least one unicorn," and to propositions of the 'any,' 'every', and 'some' variety (e.g., "There are some *p*'s that are *q*").[25] And, more importantly, it still does not address the main question, the sense in which general propositions may be thought of as being true. No failure to find a negative instance based upon a generalization can be regarded as exhaustive.

Perhaps the most thoughtful and rigorous attempts to work out an acceptable empirical criterion of meaning or cognitive significance are exhibited in the writings of Rudolph Carnap. Carnap, under the influence of his Vienna Circle colleague Neurath, took what he called a physicalist position on the appropriate method for reducing propositions to observations. Neurath had argued that propositions can be verified by resort to 'protocol sentences,' which are behavioristic statements about acts of perception. So, to use Neurath's example, the statement "The screeching saw cuts through the blue wooden cube" could be reduced to statements about received vibrations and/or statements about the attendant neural and cerebral changes a person undergoes in receiving the vibrations.[26] Although this position is what led to the developments in Carnap's method of employing protocol sentences to bridge the word–object gap, Neurath had a different epistemic position on the nature of the protocol statements than that which Carnap was to adopt. Neurath did not regard his protocol statements as direct reports of phenomena (whatever they might be). A protocol statement introduced into a system of statements in order to render that system testable must, according to Neurath, manifest coherence with the rest of the statements in the system. Protocol statements do not actually record experience, he argued, so the validity of a protocol statement, for Neurath, is not a matter of the extent to which it faithfully records experience but of its fit with the other empirical statements it is combined with in order to clarify the empirical meaning of the system of statements as a whole. What Carnap did share was Neurath's belief that all the sciences can be treated in the same linguistic mode—in the language of physics (hence the identification of the thesis as 'physicalist'). Neurath argued, for example, that a psychological statement such as "There is anger in this man" can, as in the case of the screeching-saw statement above, be analyzed on the basis of organic changes in the intestinal tract, internal secretions, blood pressure, muscle contractions, and so on. Thus the appropriateness of protocol statements to translate the psychological level statements into physical ones.

Carnap treated psychological statements very much as did Neurath.

He argued that a statement like "Mr. A is excited" should be analyzed by inferring the statement from one or more protocol sentences about the behavior of Mr. A. (e.g., facial expression, gestures, muscle tightening, etc.).[27] But for Carnap protocol sentences are "records of direct experience," whereas Neurath, as noted above, regarded protocol sentences as statements about experience (in physical language) and thus as corrigible statements like any other scientific statement. Because Carnap regarded the protocol sentences as direct references to the givens of experience, he felt that they are incorrigible and thus require no justification. Carnap's notion of protocol sentences reflected his commitment to bridging the word–object gap and thus avoiding any subjective, interpretive elements intervening between scientific systems (theories) and the data of experience to which they are addressed. The question that one might reasonably raise is "How does Carnap's notion of protocol statements relate to the verifiability principle? Carnap invented his own version of the verifiability principle, which was designed to achieve the objective, which he shared with Neurath, the unification of the sciences.

Carnap, recognizing the above-mentioned difficulties associated with the requirement of complete verifiability (in fact or in principle) suggested the idea of "confirmability." In his paper, "Testability and Meaning,"[28] he developed the view that a statement is cognitively meaningful if it is reducible to an empirical language. His empirical language, which he called a "thing-language" (his term for a language consisting of protocol statements) involves sentences which, "describe things by stating their observable properties or observable relations subsisting between them."[29] Carnap cautions, however, that the observation predicates in his thing language (terms like "warm," "blue," "longer than," etc.) are not perception terms—Neurath's protocol statements are constructed on the basis of references to perceptions—but are direct references to observable objects. The translation of scientific statements into the thing language cannot, according to Carnap, save the old positivist verifiability principle. In addition to the verifiability principle's failure to deal successfully with universal statements or lawlike generalizations (as was noted above), one cannot verify or, as Carnap put it, 'test' important scientific terms that are not definable or translatable into observation predicates. As examples of such "important scientific terms," Carnap speaks of "dispositional terms" like solubility, introspection, potential, and so forth.

As a result of these difficulties with the earlier positivist attempts to establish an empiricist criterion of meaning or cognitive significance, Carnap turned to the notion of confirmability, which he hoped would salvage an empiricist criterion of meaning. In searching for a valid way of speaking within the context of such a criterion, Carnap argued that

although laws or scientific generalizations cannot be conclusively verified, one can test instances or individual cases of general propositions,
and each such test can be regarded as an addition to the degree of confirmation of the general statement whose validity is being examined. So,
at this point, Carnap had withdrawn from the idea that a general scientific statement is verifiable. He asserted, instead, that although a scientific generalization cannot be verified in a complete sense, it is 'confirmable' if, according to Carnap, we know the conditions under which it
would be confirmed. This of course sounds very much like the earlier
hedge that Schlick invented when he suggested that cognitively meaningful statements must be verifiable "in principle." The idea involved
with "knowing the conditions" needed to confirm a statement is that if
the statement really has empirical significance, its primary function will
be one of referring to an experiential base, even if that base lies beyond
one's ability to record it in its entirety. So what Carnap is left with,
more specifically, is the idea that a statement is confirmable if it is capable of *being stated* in terms of observation predicates. Since some scientific terms, such as the above-mentioned disposition terms, are not in
themselves stated from the standpoint of observation predicates, Carnap
introduced the idea of "reduction sentences," which provide at least
partial specifications or operational definitions of concepts which are not
definable in observation predicates. As he put it, "Those predicates of
the thing-language which are not observable, e.g., disposition terms, are
reducible to observable predicates and hence confirmable."[30]

But Carnap's energetic and creative efforts to bridge the gap between
words or expressions and objects and events confronted the same difficulties as earlier attempts (e.g., Ayer's, discussed above), for as Carnap
himself and Hempel have both noted, any statement with empirical import cannot be exhaustively expressed by means of any class of observation sentences.[31] This difficulty has been extensively discussed by
Waismann in his well-known paper "Verifiability."[32] Waismann noted
there that one cannot translate statements about material objects into
an exhaustive set of observation predicates because of what he calls the
'open texture' of most empirical concepts. This open texture makes it
impossible, according to Waismann, to delimit empirical concepts in all
possible ways. The open texture of empirical concepts is complemented
by what Waismann calls the 'essential incompleteness' of empirical description. Explicating the idea of essential incompleteness, he notes that
while nonempirical concepts, such as a triangle, can be completely described by giving stipulations about three sides, empirical phenomena,
for example, his right hand, can be described in a variety of ways. One
could discuss size, shape, color, or any of several other qualities and
never exhaust the various possible descriptions.[33]

The Empiricist Criteria of Meaning and Their Prospects

The modern-day positivists have remained undaunted by their failure to produce an unimpeachable empiricist criterion of meaning. Waismann's answer to the 'open texture' and 'essential incompleteness' problems is essentially that although one cannot completely specify the empirical meaning of a concept, one must simply strive to do the best one can. Similarly, Carl Hempel has suggested that although he is pessimistic about the possibility of developing a valid verification principle, he believes that the general intent behind the empiricist criterion of meaning is basically sound. So Hempel also adheres to the "Do the best you can" thesis. Hempel's guidelines for doing so start with abandoning the attempt to develop an empiricist criterion of meaning for individual terms, or even individual sentences. Under the influence of Quine's attack on the analytic–synthetic distinction (discussed above), he suggests that cognitive significance, as an idea, should be applied to theoretical systems as a whole. Theoretical systems, then, can be regarded as empirical or as having empirical significance in a general sense to the extent that empirical specifications are provided for at least some of the terms and relationships in the system. Cognitive significance or empirical meaning for Hempel thereby becomes an attribute of theoretical systems, not terms or even statements, and it becomes a matter of degree, based on the theoretical system's clarity and precision, explanatory and predictive power, formal simplicity, and extent of confirmation by experiential evidence.[34]

The self-supplied critiques of the various positivist theories of meaning amount only to an ambiguous admission of failure. The various reformulations and ad hoc additions are reminiscent of pre-Copernican attempts to save the old Ptolemaic system of astronomy through such devices as the invention of epicycles. Waismann's open-texture argument, for example, is an initial recognition of a fundamental flaw in empiricist positions on meaning, but his analysis is hampered by his motivation to save traditional empiricism. Like Hempel, he fails to reflect adequately on why one cannot develop an exhaustive and noncontroversial empirical specification for either individual terms, statements, or conceptual systems as a whole. For either individual concepts or conceptual systems, the question can always be raised as to how one should select (or more directly, develop) empirical specifications by erecting or using standards, on the basis of which the experiential referents of statements and conceptual systems have meaning. This question can only be understood in connection with an adequate theory of meaning, one that explicitly addresses the rules or standards, linking word and object, because despite Carnap's suggestions to the contrary, objects do not impose those standards on us. More adequate approaches to language and meaning are available. They are developed in the later work of Wittgenstein, in John Austin's writings, and in Heidegger's reflections on language. But before discussing their approaches, all of which concern themselves with the rhetorical context of statements, I shall consider some consequences of contemporary empiricism for social science theory.

To address these consequences we may begin with an example of a relatively simple statement of "fact" that John Searle has used to illustrate a point about the relationship between factual and moral statements. Suppose someone says "Brown hit a home run," having been a spectator at a baseball game.[35] From a strictly positivist point of view, the sentence would seem to be susceptible to even the early, long-abandoned formulation of the verificationist principle. It appears, in other words, to be a simple description of a single event, one that could easily be observed by any person having normal human perceptual faculties. So a strict, empiricist approach to validating the statement would involve describing the behavior of Brown (e.g., his swinging the bat, the bat's connecting with the ball thrown by the pitcher, etc.) and describing the effects of his behavior (e.g., the flight of the ball over one of the stadium fences—in "fair territory," and in the increment to his team's score after he has run around the base paths, touching all four bases).

If we were to continue this exercise, however, we would discover that if we maintain an empiricist point of view, the validation problem begins to get out of hand, for it is ultimately a misguided effort. The validation procedure becomes rapidly unmanageable, because in the validation process one would run into Waismann's "essential incompleteness of descriptions" problem. Should we describe Brown's journey around the base paths? What aspects of his behavior are to be regarded as relevant to the performance, "hitting a home run," and which are not? Is it necessary for us to begin with an analysis of the situation obtaining before the ball is pitched? If so, what aspects of that "situation" are relevant to our ultimate characterization of what has happened? Do we have to describe such events as the submission of the batting order to the umpire (to indicate that Brown was not batting out of order—a situation that would avoid the invalidating circumstance of not being eligible for the kind of performance known as "hitting a home run")? If the question is posed in terms of the adequacy of a description—a question that empiricist positions on meaning inevitably raise—there can be no definitive answer. This is because even the contemporary empiricist positions on meaning would have us looking in the wrong place.

Proving that the statement "Brown hit a home run" is true is not simply a matter of accurate description or careful translation of abstract statements into "observation terms" (whatever those are). This becomes evident when we consider the problem from a different vantage point. We can ask, What are the various ways in which the statement that Brown hit a home run can be false, even when it has been observed that Brown hit a baseball over a wall in "fair territory"? It is clear that one could produce an extensive list of invalidating circumstances, including perhaps the possibility mentioned above about Brown's batting out of order. In any case, what is observed or recorded is not a home run but merely a sequence of behaviors and results of those behaviors. What is required to make the statement "Brown hit a home run" true is much more than the behaviors that one can observe. The suggested orientation toward looking for falsifying circumstances makes it clear that the list would be endless, implying that observations, no matter how acute or exhaustive, do not eventually yield up valid statements.

The statement about Brown and the home run, like all descriptively oriented statements, is rule governed. Neither its meaning nor its truth is simply a matter of the statement's correspondence with or precise reference to "sense data." A home run is not a thing that one can see, for to swing a bat at a ball and hit it to a given place is not, in itself, a home run. A complex set of additional circumstances must obtain before such events can be validly called "hitting a home run." The rules for those circumstances are the rules for the game of baseball.

A useful way, then, to characterize a statement like "Brown hit a home run" is to refer to it, as Searle has (following Anscombe's scheme), as an "institutional fact."[36] This suggests that the statement is constituted by a combination of "brute facts" and rules. The brute facts are the behavior of Brown and the other participants and the flight of the baseball, and so on, and the rules are the set of norms that, taken as a whole, define the institution (or game) of baseball. Now it is important to realize that facts, so called, are neither brute nor institutional intrinsically. If, as is the case at the moment, our concern is with "Brown hit a home run," we treat it as an institutional fact in order to analyze its meaning and validity, and we treat its smaller, constituent elements, which would be expressed in such statements as "He swung the bat," as brute facts which, for purposes of analysis, are regarded as unproblematic (i.e., we ignore the interpretive element in such statements). But what is an institutional fact in one context can be a brute fact in another. For example, if our analysis was concentrated on the statement "The Giants scored two runs in the third inning," then this statement would be the institutional fact, and among the relevant brute facts might be (1) "Brown hit a home run," and (2) "Evans was on base at the time that Brown hit the home run."

There is thus always an interpretive element involved in a descriptively oriented statement. Whether one wishes to expose and consider that element is a matter of the interest at hand. Even what Carnap called "observation predicates" (e.g., "taller than") can be treated as problematic. So, for example, a statement like "Charles is taller than William" is true only in the context of certain conventions and institutions, for example, that we take vertical measurements of a person's height when the person is standing as opposed to reclining. Because the terms found in social and political theories and analyses are more complex than the terms found in relatively simple descriptive utterances, the kind of analysis of interpretations and conventions sequestered in statements which has been just illustrated, applied to such conceptual systems designed to explain things, becomes even more significant. This has already been suggested in chapter 1. If, for example, one were to take a traditional positivist approach to the meaning of a statement in a theory of violence such as "Domestic violence is more likely to occur in nations with a high degree of social inequality than in nations in which there is a high degree of social equality," the analysis would be organized primarily around the problem of making valid inductive inferences. But the meaning of concepts like "violence," "social inequality," and the like depends not only on measurements and observations (based on "operational definitions") but also on the rules or norms which constitute the meanings of such concepts. So "violence" and "social inequality," like "hitting a home run," are not things that can be observed or recorded outside of a rule-governed context. Similarly, if a person is forcibly detained by a group of persons, the set of observable behaviors involved do not have an obvious or clear meaning by themselves. Depending on the norms employed, which govern the context of the behaviors and give them meaning, one might call the sequence of activities "law enforcement" (e.g., those doing the detaining are police officers "on duty"), "kidnapping," (the detainers have no authorized status), "playing" (the detainers are friends disguised as "hoods"), and so forth. The question as to whether any of these meanings that we attribute to the activities, given who the actors are and what the situation is in which they are acting, belongs to a conception of violence and is a matter of additional norms that govern such actions as law enforcement, kidnapping, and playing.

What are the implications of the rejection of a strictly empiricist approach to meaning? If we recognize that the relationship between speech and phenomena is mediated by rules or norms other than those which stipulate observation or measurement, and that those norms can be regarded as controversial or problematic, we can then see that much of the content of theorizing is involved at what is ordinarily regarded as a pretheoretical stage. For example, there are presuppositions about political relations involved in deciding how violence is constituted—pre-suppositions about the rules that govern its use.   ,

One kind of violent action, called "rape," is typically applied to situations in which a man has sexual intercourse with a woman "against her will." Given the way the concept is used, a woman who does not wish to give in to a demand for sexual intercourse must demonstrate her "will" by vigorous struggle. Therefore, if a woman's male employer asks her to engage in sexual relations, implying that she will lose her job unless she agrees, it would not be regarded as rape if she submits because that kind of relationship (structurally supported blackmail) is not regarded as coercive to the point where one can assert that the intercourse took place against the woman's will. Accordingly, to understand the kind of violence known as "rape" is to understand something about the kinds of human relationships that support the use of the concept. Any kind of interaction between persons involves some kind of influence. When the influence is regarded as in some way illegitimate, we characterize that with resort to broad conceptions about the role of a person's plans and intentions in the formulation of decisions to act in one way or another. Depending on where we draw the line, that is, on the situations we stipulate as relevant or irrelevant to issues of who is in control, we employ terms like "against a person's will."

Note that here the concept of intention is not to be understood as a matter of traditional empirical psychology. Both the language-analytic positions of Wittgenstein, Austin, and Ryle (among others) and the phenomenological philosophy of Husserl are based on a distinction between causal approaches to mental phenomena belonging to the discipline of psychology and philosophical/analytic approaches to mental phenomena. To ask, What does it mean to say that he remembered, he intended, he willed, and so on? is not to ask a causal-psychological question. Husserl, influenced by Brentano's distinction between experimental (causal) psychology and descriptive psychology, developed phenomenological analysis as inquiry into the nature of mental phenomena (his version of Brentano's "descriptive psychology"). One of his major concepts, intentionality, is treated not as a psychological cause of behavior but as what is intrinsic to consciousness. Intentionality is, for Husserl, "object-awareness." Similarly, language analysts like Ryle treat intentions, will, and other mentalistic concepts not as psychological causes but as concepts that make up what we mean by mind.[37]

The language philosophers' approach to concepts like willing and intending is particularly useful in understanding the meaning of "rape" in the present example. The determination of whether something is done "against a person's will" is not a matter of observation. We clearly do not observe mental processes in the sense of merely witnessing or recording a meaningful event. What we do is actively interpret the context of an activity or episode. Our use of an expression like "against her will" is based on a decision that it is legitimate in a given circumstance to ascribe the concept of willing to someone. When we say, therefore, that a person was raped, we evaluate the situation on the basis of our norms for legitimate versus illegitimate influence. In the final analysis, a justification of one versus another position on when we can apply the term "rape" to a situation would include arguments about the kinds of human relationships that ought to obtain in a society, particularly those that involve "control," and it is the norms about legitimate versus illegitimate control which constitute the political relations of a society.

Social scientists' contemporary empirical analyses of actions like rape are often flawed by a lack of attention to the problem of the meaning of complex and potentially contentious concepts like rape, violence, aggression, concepts whose meanings contain implicit prescriptions about legitimate versus illegitimate conduct. Much of the "empirical" literature on such concepts therefore constitutes partisan politics disguised as disinterested science. American researchers focusing on violence in international interactions, for example, usually predicate their descriptions of the behavior of national actors on a model of America's foreign-policy role that is invented in the U.S. State Department. In such studies, protest demonstrations are typically recorded as examples of "domestic violence," irrespective of what the content of the protest is, and reactions by foreign governments like the People's Republic of China to American attempts to influence them by placing missiles in Taiwan are recorded as belligerent. The theories guiding investigations linking foreign and domestic conflict have been most implicit, embedded in the identification and characterization of various "violent" and "nonviolent" behaviors. One must, as I shall argue below, ultimately take a normative stance in order to describe and explain something, but the bulk of the research on foreign and domestic violence has, because it has purported to be objective, rested on an uncritical acceptance of the norms of governmental agencies. The research has not been attentive to the standards for relationships presupposed in the concepts used.[38]

When we employ a positivist or empiricist notion of meaning and thus focus almost exclusively on causal relationships between entities that are the referents of statements, we therefore lose the opportunity to inquire into the political context that constitutes meaningful entities. By construing the problem of language as one of finding a logic of utterances that would illuminate a field of objects, empiricists have neglected the context or way of life that implicitly locomotes the movement from concepts or ideas to what is identified as a world of objects or data. The content of what is overlooked can be discerned if one examines almost any popular theoretically oriented treatment of political analysis. Robert Dahl's recently reissued *Modern Political Analysis* shows, in numerous instances, the limitations of implicity promoting an empiricist under-standing of concepts. For example, his definition of *the* government in a society is, after Max Weber, "any government that successfully up-holds a claim to the exclusive regulation of the legitimate use of physical force in enforcing its rules within a given territorial area."[39] Without ex-tended reflection, this definition appears quite serviceable. But Dahl's analysis is wanting in his understanding of the concepts in the definition. When, for example, he anticipates potential criticism of the application of his definition to the United States he notes that someone might ask, "What about criminals who go uncaught?" He wonders if this is a fail-ure to uphold the claim to the legitimate use of force, but he answers that the claim is upheld as long as there are few people who contest the state's *right* to punish criminals. He states, "Although criminal violence exists, it is not legitimate."[40] But isn't this statement both problematic and redundant? What is a "criminal"? Persons cannot be judged to be criminals by observation ("He's the one wearing the black mask"). Criminality is a social role, constituted by norms for legitimate and ille-gitimate conduct. So, among other things, one kind of criminal is one who makes illegitimate use of physical force. Given that many social in-teractions can be construed as involving some degree of "physical force," one interesting question about the political process in a society is precisely about which uses of force are legitimated and which are not. To base the idea of governance on the concept of legitimacy is promis-ing. But an empiricist approach to language leads to a neglect of the leg-itimizing norms inherent in the identification of such "things" as "crim-inals." Once violence is regarded as "criminal" it is merely redundant to say that it is illegitimate. The adoption of an empiricist understanding of concepts implicit in Dahl's discussion of government thus makes elu-sive a welter of political prescriptions which constitute social roles such as that of the criminal. To the extent that we regard political analysis as applicable only to relationships between agencies like governments and "entities" like criminals, we lose the ability to investigate the relation-ships presupposed in the use of such expressions as "criminal vio-lence." In order to include the content of relationships which give meaning to concepts, then, we need an alternative epistemological pos-ture to that developed by logical positivists and logical empiricists. The following philosophical interludes are included to help answer that need.

Wittgenstein, Austin, and the "Ordinary Language" Approach

Linguistic philosophers have provided a radical departure from the positivist view of the relationship between speech and phenomena.

Viewing speaking as a form of acting, Wittgenstein and Austin, among others, pointed out that there are many functions that statements perform beside describing or designating, and that even descriptive utterances cannot be understood without paying attention to more than their referral dimension. Wittgenstein's position, developed in his later writings, remains one of the most influential, if variously construed, philosophies of language. It is evident that in his later philosophy, Wittgenstein had rejected the early view, which he had shared with Carnap, that philosophy as an activity should be modeled on science (Carnap has gone so far as to argue that philosophy should deal exclusively with the logic of science).[41] Rather than attempting to create an ideal language whose form would provide a calculus for relating facts to each other (Carnap's view) or as a structure that has the effect of revealing, through its resemblance, the structure of the relationship between 'facts' or 'basic elements' (Wittgenstein's view in the *Tractatus*), Wittgenstein now urged that language be analyzed on the basis of the roles that words play in 'ordinary language' (hence the designation, ordinary-language philosophy). To understand the meaning of terms and expressions, according to Wittgenstein in his later view, one must avoid the temptation to regard words as names, as was the view sponsored in Russell's denotative theory of meaning, which influenced the view expressed in the *Tractatus*. Meaning becomes clear if we consider the various ways that words are used. In several places, Wittgenstein compares language to a tool chest, "containing a hammer, chisel, matches, nails, screws, glue. It is not chance that all these things have been put together—but there are important differences between the different tools—they are used in a family of ways—though nothing could be more different than glue and a chisel."[42]

Wittgenstein explains how this functional approach to the meaning of terms and expressions differs from the denotative approach by inviting us to imagine someone pointing something out to someone else, as in the case of "those games by means of which children learn their native language,"[43] for example, where the learner names objects as they are pointed out by a teacher. Wittgenstein calls such games "language games," but the language-game concept, according to Wittgenstein, attaches not only to the verbal interaction involved in the process of learning to name things or in other such communication processes but also to the linguistic and action context in which the communication is embedded. If we consider the great variety of language games, he notes, we will see that learning a language and subsequently using it are more than the process of learning the names of objects. As examples of different kinds of language games, Wittgenstein offers:

Giving orders, and obeying them—

> Describing the appearance of an object, or
> giving its measurements—
> Constructing an object from a description (a drawing)—
> Reporting an event—
> Speculating about an event—
> Forming and testing a hypothesis—
> Presenting the results of an experiment in tables or diagrams—
> Making up a story and reading it—
> Play-acting—
> Singing catches—
> Guessing riddles—
> Making a joke; telling it—
> Solving a problem in practical arithmetic—
> Translating from one language into another—
> Asking, thanking, cursing, greeting, praying—[44]

This multiplicity of language games indicates that knowing a language is, in effect, knowing a vast and intricate system of rules of how words are appropriately used. Therefore, when someone points something out to us, the occasion involves more than a correlation of word and object. We do not, as Wittgenstein observes, simply follow someone's finger with our eyes when something is pointed out. On such occasions, to the extent that we know the language, we know from the nature of the language game involved what aspect of a thing is being singled out for our attention, for example, its shape, color, and so on, just as understanding a move in the game of chess is more than knowing what piece is moved to what place. We understand the move because we know the game of chess.[45]

In order to interpret correctly the way the words are used, or in Wittgenstein's vocabulary, the particular language game involved in a given circumstance, a person, according to Wittgenstein, must know the 'depth grammar' of an utterance, not just the 'surface grammar.'[46] The surface grammar of an utterance has to do with the uses to which the words are put in the construction of a meaningful utterance such as a sentence. So, for example, the surface grammars of the sentence "All the world's a stage," the sentence "All the third floor is a laboratory," and the sentence "All the Eastern District is an army camp" are the same in that all three have the structure of a description.[47] But the latter two sentences have a different depth grammar from that of the first because, as Wittgenstein would argue, the first belongs in a different language game. "All the world's a stage" is not meant to be taken literally as a description. Thus a hearer in touch with the depth grammar of the sentence realizes that it is to be understood as a metaphor. The linguistic rules that constitute a metaphor are the rules of the particular language game that governs the meaning of the sentence. Inferring the correct meaning of the sentence therefore requires an understanding of the language game, constituted by the depth grammar of the sentence and not just its surface grammar, on the basis of which one could not distinguish it from an ordinary description.

Wittgenstein felt that much of the confusion in attempting to understand the language game or depth grammar of sentences results from the similarity that sentences like those illustrated above exhibit on the basis of their shared surface grammar. Although descriptively oriented statements of the form "The sky is blue" represent one kind of use among the many to which language is put, many other statements, which perform different functions, share their syntactic structure (or 'surface grammar') with descriptive statements. This is the case, for example, with statements meant to attribute features to something as in "Killing is wrong," a statement that clearly performs a different kind of function from description, although appearing, on the surface, to be descriptive.

By introducing, then, the distinction between surface and depth grammar in the explication of his notion of the language game, Wittgenstein sought to develop a theory of meaning that, by focusing on the use of terms and expressions rather than on what they designate, would clear up confusions stemming from the surface similarities of simple descriptions and other kinds of statements. Wittgenstein's abandonment of his earlier 'picture theory' of meaning was complete in that he came to regard it as an inappropriate account of even simple descriptions. In *Philosophical Investigations* he argues that ordinary descriptions, like other kinds of statements, are to be understood in the context of the language game in which they are employed. In a particular language game, for example, we may treat certain objects as though they are 'simple' so that they can function as unanalyzed elements in a sentence. But they, like Anscombe's 'brute facts' (above) are not simple in any ultimate sense. They are not to be taken as basic constituent elements of the experience to which terms and statements refer, as was suggested by the position taken in the *Tractatus*.

Wittgenstein illustrates the implications of his new approach to descriptive statements with an imaginary interaction between a doctor and a nurse who are discussing a patient. The doctor asks, "How is he feeling?" and the nurse replies, "He is groaning." Wittgenstein notes that one might justifiably wonder if groaning really expresses anything like what the nurse seems to interpret. One could question what is in fact being described by such a report of the patient's behavior. But such questions are beside the point, given what is going on here between the doctor and the nurse. Their interaction is about keeping the patient comfortable. So rather than wondering what is really being described by the descriptively oriented statement "He is groaning," one should pay attention to the kind of use being made of that description. As Wittgenstein says, "Isn't the point the service to which they put the description?" In this case, as in all cases of descriptions, according to Wittgenstein, the doctor and nurse share a tacit presupposition upon which the language game rests. "Simple descriptions" are thus only simple on the surface. Their interpretation demands acknowledgement of the presuppositions that orient them. Since it is the case that they rest on presuppositions, a circumstance which adds complexity to their meaning, why don't we therefore, asks Wittgenstein, preface them with expressions like "Naturally I am presupposing that . . ." We don't, he states, because presuppositions imply doubt and we may not wish to suggest a doubt in most cases in which we are describing things or situations.[48]

We can therefore understand one of the most important contributions of Wittgenstein's later theory of meaning, developed in his *Philosophical Investigations,* as not only inhering in its capacity to illuminate and account for the various functions for which language is employed in statements other than descriptions but also its account of simple descriptions, in which we are shown that the word–object relationship is based upon tacit presuppositions rather than on simple correspondence. John Austin's analysis of language, particularly that developed in his posthumously assembled Harvard lectures, *How to Do Things with Words,* makes a similar contribution.[49] Austin, like Wittgenstein, regarded the use of language as an activity to be understood as part of other activities. Wittgenstein had said that language is "woven" into other activities,[50] and Austin, making this view even more explicit, invented the expression "speech-act," which is an utterance in which saying something is doing something, as when someone says, "I hereby christen you the *Molly B*." (spoken by a person at a christening ceremony).

Austin, like Wittgenstein in his later work, began his analysis by noting that ordinary descriptions represent only one kind of statement among a variety of possibilities. But rather than concentrating on the diversity of functions involved in speaking, he focused his analysis on the particular kind of sentences that, unlike descriptions, do not seem to describe or report anything. These utterances, for instance, "I promise to buy you a balloon," "I bet you that the stock market will fall tomorrow," and so on, do not appear to be the kind of statement that one can regard as either true or false in the sense that ordinary descriptions are so regarded. Austin calls such sentences 'performatives,' because the process of uttering the sentence constitutes the doing of an action (making a promise and making a bet in the two examples above). He contrasts performatives with 'statements,' his label for utterances whose primary function is to describe or report something.

A major emphasis in Austin's analysis is based on what he asks of performatives—if performances or speech-acts do not appear susceptible to analysis in terms of their truth or falsity, as in the case with statements, is there *any* sense in which performatives can be regarded as valid or invalid or, as he put it, is there any sense in which performative can 'go wrong'? To distinguish his analysis of the ways that performatives can go wrong from the familiar true-false criterion that one ordinarily applies to descriptive statements, Austin invented the concept of 'infelicities,' which are the kinds of situations or contexts within which performatives go wrong or are invalid. For example, one type of infelicity is a situation in which the act that a verbal formula is supposed to achieve is not achieved. In such a case, the performative 'misfires,' as, for example, in the case where the purser of a ship, rather than the captain, says, "I now pronounce you man and wife," with the intention of effecting a marriage. The act is not performed in such a case, because the purser is not in a position (lacks the appropriate credentials) to perform the act.[51] In another broad category of infelicities are what Austin calls 'abuses,' as in promises that are made with the intention of not keeping them. This kind of infelicity covers acts that are 'professed' or 'hollow,' as contrasted with those that misfire and are thus 'purported' or 'empty.'

Austin's extensive analysis of infelicities produces the conclusion that saying something cannot make it so. This conclusion is obvious for familiar kinds of utterances like descriptions, because we tend to think of the criteria for "something being so" as existing independently of the statement. When we come, as Austin suggests, to consider the case of performatives, however, the conclusion is less obvious, because a speech-act of the form "I promise you," "I christen you," or "I dub thee" appears to be consummatory by virtue of the verbalization itself. But, as Austin's analysis of speech-acts demonstrates, saying something does not make it so, even in the case of performative utterances that are designed to be actions. This is the case because an utterance like "I now pronounce you man and wife" must, if it is to bring about the intended result, be said by the correct person, under the correct circumstances, to persons with the correct eligibility qualities, and so on. Therefore, Austin concludes, performatives, like descriptions (statements), are governed by criteria of application, that is, rather than being self-constituting, they stand or fall in the context of rules linking them to given circumstances.

After analyzing the various kinds of infelicities to which performative utterances fall victim, Austin pursued a parallel analysis of descriptive or factual statements, and like Wittgenstein, who spoke of the 'tacit presuppositions' underlying such statements, he argued that there is an implicit, nonverbalized context upon which the truth or falsity of a description depends. Because the context must be considered in the evaluation of descriptions or factual statements, they can be thought of as going wrong in precisely the same way as performatives. As Austin states this conclusion: "we see that in order to explain what can go wrong with statements we cannot just concentrate on the proposition involved (whatever that is) as has been done traditionally. We must consider the total situation in which the utterance is issued—the total speech-act—if we are to see the parallel between and how each can go wrong. Perhaps indeed there is no great distinction between statements and performative utterances."[52]

But, Austin notes, one would expect that at the very least performatives and descriptions can be distinguished on the basis of their relation to the facts. It would appear, after all, that a simple report like "I saw the bull charge" would have a different relation to facts than a statement like "I bet you that the bull will charge." Austin found, however, that as he continued to compare the two kinds of utterance, the distinction could not be sustained, even on this kind of basis. He found not only that the unhappiness characteristic of performatives is relevant to descriptions (i.e., they go wrong unless the situation is appropriate) but also that "the requirement of conforming or bearing some relation to the facts, different in different cases, seems to characterize performatives, in addition to the requirement that they should be happy, similarly to the way which is characteristic of supposed constatives." The conclusion is thus that descriptions (statements) can be infelicitous like performatives, and performatives or speech-acts—utterances in which saying something is doing something—can be treated as true or false, for, Austin states, "there is no necessary conflict between (a) our issuing the utterance being the doing of something, (b) our utterance being true or false."[53]

These conclusions are most clearly illustrated with Austin's example of the sentence "I warn you that it is going to charge" (speaking of a bull). This utterance seems to be a speech-act, because something is being done (a warning is being issued), and there are grounds for the statement's being true or false (the bull may or may not be about to charge). How such a statement is to be analyzed depends, obviously, on various factors not apparent in the form of the statement itself. If, for example, the statement is not said with the appropriate inflection, and the intended hearers are not positioned in a certain way, it would be inappropriate to regard the utterance as a warning. And whether or not the statement can be evaluated on the basis of the bull's behavior subsequent to the statement (leaving aside, for the moment, the problem of interpreting that behavior) is also a matter of inflection and/or other aspects of the context of the statement. The utterance may have been issued in such a way and in such a situation that it may be inappropriate to evaluate it as a prediction of the bull's behavior. The 'level' of meaning, in short, that is emphasized in a statement is a matter of more than what appears in the statement's form and content.[54]

After having exhaustively explored whether performatives and descriptions can be distinguished on the basis of the ways that they can go wrong and that they relate to 'the facts,' Austin raises the question as to whether the performative utterances lack anything that applies to statements. He concludes that they do not. Our temptation to distinguish rigorously statements and performatives is based, he argues, on an oversimplified account of what it means for a statement to correspond with or relate to facts. Here his analysis is similar to that which was offered above in connection with the statement "Brown hit a home run," and to Wittgenstein's discussion of the language games within which 'simple' descriptions function. Austin notes that, for example, the truth or falsity of the statement "France is a hexagonal" depends not on the accuracy of measurement but on the context within which the statement is made, for example, on such factors as the purposes for which such a statement is made. The identification of France as a hexagonal would be appropriate, he notes, for an army general planning a campaign but not for a geographer, whose criteria would demand more than a simple geometric model. As he sums up this part of the analysis, "in the case of stating truly or falsely, just as in the case of advising well or badly, what is judged true in a school book may not be so judged in a work of historical research."[55]

We are left, perhaps, with the question of why, if seemingly different kinds of utterances are actually to be judged in the same way rather than on the basis of different kinds of criteria, we use such different rhetorical styles, given that they have relatively little impact on the *kind* of meaning one can attribute to them. We can infer that Austin's response would be very much the same as Wittgenstein's. For Wittgenstein, the rhetorical style we select (descriptive, imperative, interrogative, etc.) is a matter of what we wish to emphasize, that is, of what language game we wish to establish as our context. So, for example, we rarely verbalize the tacit presuppositions implicit in our statements because we do not wish, as Wittgenstein suggested, to raise doubts (see above), even though what we are saying is either tentative or context dependent and thus more controversial than the rhetorical style would indicate. Austin provides a similar answer by suggesting that, depending on the force we intend our utterance to have, we emphasize one or another aspect or level of its meaning. Utterances, according to Austin, are not, on their face, one kind or another. There exist different levels of meaning in every utterance, and we emphasize the level that is compatible with the particular task we are performing when we issue the utterance. To understand what Austin means by "levels of meaning," we must adopt his special vocabulary for speaking about aspects of utterances.

There are, Austin states, three distinguishable aspects or levels of meaning in utterances. The first is the locutionary meaning that sentences or other meaningful linguistic entities contain. The locutionary meaning of an utterance is based on its content, or what it is about. For example, the statement discussed above, "I warn you it is about to charge," concerns a bull and its imminent behavior. The second and third levels of meaning in an utterance are what Austin calls its performative force. He refers to the second level as the utterance's illocutionary force or meaning. This has to do with what a person is doing *in* making the utterance. In the case of "I warn you it is about to charge," the illocutionary force of the utterance is that a warning is being given; in issuing the utterance, the speaker is warning the listener(s). Finally, the third level of meaning in an utterance is its perlocutionary force or meaning. This level consists in what a person is doing *by* making the utterance. The perlocutionary force of the "I warn you . . ." statement is based on the effect of the utterance on those who hear it, for example, it may cause them to take flight or, more generally, shift their attention away from wherever it might be and toward the bull. One cannot tell from the form of the utterance what level of meaning is governing the interpretation. The *primary* force, whether constative or performative, of an utterance is thus a matter of emphasis, as Austin puts it:

> (a) with the constative utterance, we abstract from the illocutionary (let alone the perlocutionary) aspects of the speech-act, and we concentrate on the locutionary; moreover we use an oversimplified notion of the correspondence with facts—oversimplified because essentially it brings in the illocutionary aspect. We aim at the idea of what would be right to say in all circumstances for any purpose, to any audience. . . . (b) With the performative utterance, we attend as much as possible to the illocutionary force of the utterance, and abstract from the dimension of correspondence with facts.[56]

This passage represents what is, for Austin, all that remains of the distinction between constative and performative utterances. He, like Wittgenstein, offers in *How to Do Things with Words* a functional theory of meaning, a commitment to the effect that the meaning of an utterance depends on the use to which it is put. Thus whether a particular utterance is to be regarded as a speech-act (performative) or as a constative (description) is not evident from the statement or sentence itself, because within the framework of his theory of meaning, whether an utterance is governed primarily by sense and reference (criteria for descriptions) or performative force (applying to speech-acts) is a matter of what is emphasized. As one interpreter of Austin has noted, "neither sense and reference nor performative force constitute a kind of meaning: rather . . . they constitute different levels of meaning.[57]

Husserl and Heidegger

In some social science subcultures, phenomenology, a philosophical perspective primarily associated with the writings of Husserl and Heidegger, provides an alternative philosophy of the social sciences and thus an alternative mode of inquiry. As was suggested briefly in chapter 1, part of the impact of the phenomenological perspective is owed to the philosophy of mind it offers, one which conceives of consciousness as an active, meaning constituting process. Clearly, if the data of persons' experience are constituted by "ideational acts" that inhere in consciousness, as Husserl suggested, rather than out of sense impressions which originate independently of the minds that record them (an empiricist view), the locus of evidence concerning social phenomena of interest to the social scientist exists somewhere in the interface between consciousness and the objects of consciousness, that is, between consciousness and that which persons are conscious of. But how do we construe the impact of consciousness on experience when individual or groups of persons are the subject matter? We could, for example, emphasize the ideational acts of the subjects and therefore locate the meaning of persons' conduct by emphasizing the standpoint of the subject. This emphasis in social science analysis, which has been influenced by phenomenological philosophy, has placed particular importance on the perceptions of the actors who are the focus of inquiries, because of the principle that their perspectives of what they are doing provide the basis for the meaning of their conduct. This emphasis on the subjects' perceptions, evidenced in the phenomenologically oriented psychology of Merleau-Ponty and the phenomenologically oriented sociology of Schutz and, to a more limited extent, Garfinkel will be explored in chapter 4. Here, the focus is on another emphasis influenced by Husserl's phenomenology, a linguistic rather than a perceptual emphasis.[58]

The linguistic aspect of phenomenology was addressed more by Heidegger than Husserl, but it has never had the same impact on the social sciences as the perceptual emphasis. An emphasis on signs or on language (a system of signs) transcends an exclusive or primary concern with the perspective of the subject, because persons as users of language acquire systems of meaning, a world of entitities and episodes,

that predates and preorganizes and affects their personal constructions
and perceptions. Moreover, the social science investigator or "observer" must ultimately describe or characterize social phenomena with
resort to one or another kind of discourse, and this contribution to the
meaning of conduct is both inescapable and problematic in relation to
the perspectives of the subjects themselves.

To understand the problem of language and meaning as it emerges
from the phenomenological philosophy of Husserl and Heidegger, it is
necessary to begin with a brief sketch of Husserl's view of meaning,
which is closely tied to his view of consciousness (his philosophy of
mind). Husserl approached the problem of meaning with a twofold distinction that is reminiscent of Frege's distinction between sense and reference. Signification, the relating of signs (meaningful words and expressions or gestures) to experience involves, according to Husserl, both
expression and indication (*Ausdruck* and *Anzeichen*), the former being
the conscious representation of things and the latter being the process
of identifying a "physical" referent of an expression.[59] Meaning for
Husserl inheres in expression rather than indication, that is, it inheres in
the presentation of ideal objects to one's imagination, a consciousness
of objects that Husserl generally referred to as intentionality. Meaning
does not therefore consist in the process of relating word and object or
sign and what is signified. As Husserl put it, "To mean is *not* a particular way of being a sign in the sense of indicating something." He suggested, however, that meaning as persons experience it is always bound
up with indicative relations, for indication, or the physical side of
speech, makes communication possible. Husserl excluded indication,
the grounding of signs in experience, from meaning because he saw the
process of selecting actual referents of expressed ideas as a subjective,
psychological process that should be "bracketed" (held separate) lest it
interfere with the objectivity that meaning finds in pure expression. To
understand this separation, it is necessary to be acquainted with Husserl's notion of the "solitary mental life." He argued that expression,
the presentation of ideal objects to oneself, can function meaningfully in
solitary mental life, that is, in pure imagining in which no indication
takes place.[60]

It is important to note that Husserl's position on meaning, constructed
with his idea of expression as a basis, is not subjectivist. He is not asserting that person's ideational acts of consciousness produce the subjective, perceptual universe of the ego. He is arguing, rather, that
"expression" is not just a process of expressing oneself but of expressing oneself *about* something.[61] Meaningful speech, for Husserl, can
therefore be described in terms of its ideality. There is a possibility of
univocity (sameness of speech between persons) so that signs can

achieve an objective permanence, but this permanence is not to be found "out there" in the world but in acts of repetition by the consciousnesses of the persons who express or represent objects to themselves. There are thus objective expressions, according to Husserl. Like some contemporary language philosophers (e.g., Grice[62]), Husserl distinguished timeless, permanent meaning of signs from occasional meanings that individual speakers appropriate in specific situations. It is the permanent expressions that are objective, and Husserl regarded as ideal a situation in which all occasional expressions would be replaced by objective, permanent ones.[63]

This brief exposition of Husserl's approach to language should indicate why social analysts, influenced by phenomenological philosophy, have emphasized the role of consciousness in giving meaning to human conduct and have seen the problem of truth as one of reflexivity rather than verification—validating with resort to subjects' reports of their conceptions rather than with data external to persons' conscious awareness. According to Husserl, speaking, writing, or any form of signification deposits ideal objectivity, it produces truth rather than simply recording it. So if we are to understand what "is," we must not simply look outward at the world but inward at the consciousness that constitutes the world as it is. This again raises the question of what kind of reflexivity is involved. As was suggested above, many contemporary social scientists, influenced by phenomenological philosophy, have emphasized the perceptual mirror. They have investigated the perceptions of the actors as they constitute their worlds. It is possible, however, to emphasize the linguistic mirror and thereby avoid the subjectivism that some have fallen into (e.g., Schutz) in their attempts to apply Husserlian philosophy to social inquiry. In applying such a linguistic mirror one examines social and political life by focusing on the way that it is reflected in language. This kind of application of the phenomenological orientation is much more encouraged in the writings of Heidegger, whose approach to language departed significantly from that of Husserl.

For Husserl, as for logical positivists and empiricists, the analysis of language is based on logic. "Expression" for Husserl is a pure logical grammar, for speech as he understood it is systematically aimed at objects, even though the objects are ideal rather than real in the sense of being wholly external to consciousness as they are for empiricists.[64] Heidegger departed from Husserl's logical approach to language. Like Wittgenstein and Austin, he developed a view of language that emphasizes the context and therefore the rhetorical rather than the logical structure of statements or expressions, arguing that it is the context or "way of being-in-the-world" that one must grasp to understand meaning. One cannot understand meaning, according to Heidegger, by simply following a logical relationship between utterances and their intended objects. Heidegger argued that it is misleading to focus on objects, whether external in the empiricist sense or immanent in consciousness and thus accessible as ideals to a transcendental ego in Husserl's sense. Ways of "Being" or the structure of human existence precede subject–object relationships and provide a framework for interpreting them, according to Heidegger. Therefore, when we seek to understand thinking or speaking, we must avoid construing them as primarily or exclusively "objectifying" processes. With respect to thinking, Heidegger says, "Thinking is not necessarily a representing of something as an object," and on language he says, similarly, "the saying of language is not necessarily an expressing of propositions *about* objects."[65] If language is not to be construed as strictly representational, as Heidegger argues, how are we to understand it? Heidegger, like Wittgenstein and Austin, bids us to focus not on individual words or signs but on the total meaning context in which signs are deployed. He says, "A sign is not a thing which stands to another thing in the relationship of indicating; it is rather an item of equipment which explicitly raises a totality of equipment into our circumspection so that together with it the worldy character of the ready-to-hand announces itself." Language for Heidegger thus has a referential function which he understands as an uncovering of what is there. The function of signs is not, however, to be understood as simply corresponding to something but as raising "the total meaning context, the referential totality, into our circumspection."[66] His emphasis on uncovering rather than correspondence is owed to his etymological investigations. Greek philosophers, as was noted above, regarded speaking truly as uncovering rather than corresponding.

Much of Heidegger's investigation of language involved him in the interpretation and exegesis of Greek thinking, particularly as it related to the original meanings of words with philosophical currency. He described his efforts as an attempt to preserve the force of words. To do so, he thought, was to discover the way of life that gives words and utterances meaning. It is in this sense that Heidegger's treatment of phenomenology, a philosophy that seeks to go directly to "the phenomena," emphasized the linguistic mirror. By reflecting on language and its meanings, we are viewing human conduct. The analysis of language for Heidegger is thus a hermeneutical or interpretive task, one oriented toward the recovery of what has been covered over by faulty interpretations. If we regard language as merely a tool that we can use to point out phenomena that exist "out there" in extralinguistic purity, we can neither understand what language is nor appreciate the meaning of human conduct, according to Heidegger. By recovering what is meant through correct interpretation, we recover, at the same time, the way of life that the language reflects.

The significance of Heidegger's position on language as reflecting a way of life is much the same as what one can derive from the positions of Wittgenstein and Austin. Many of the conceptions that represent the norms of human association are implicit in language. Heidegger called them "foreconceptions." As he put it, "The foreconception which is always implied in an assertion remains for the most part inconspicuous because language already conceals in itself a developed way of conceiving."[67]

The Wittgenstein, Austin, and Heidegger conceptions of language share, then, the view that the use of language is an activity and that language is, in itself, a representation of norms for activity rather than a static, denotational tool. Heidegger's position, however, would appear to differ in at least one important respect from the orientation of Oxford and Cambridge language philosophers, Heidegger does not view persons as users of language in an immediate active sense of doing things with words. Rather than viewing persons as having a language which they use, Heidegger suggests that perhaps the reverse is the case. It may be, he says, that language is something that "has human beings."[68] The activity of language is therefore a congealed activity residing *in* language. To speak is therefore to be caught in the flow of that activity rather than to create or initiate a wholly new activity. Two of Heidegger's statements on language convey their orientation clearly. He says, "language is not a work of human beings," and "Humans may be able to invent artificial speech constructions and signs, but they are able to do so only in reference to and in terms of an already spoken language."[69] This view of Heidegger's, that persons as users of a language are caught in a way of conceiving that may be inconspicuous to them, is a change in emphasis from what has been stressed by English linguistic philosophers and is a way of thinking that shares much with contemporary French structuralists and philosophers whose ideas will be treated in chapter 5.

But careful attention to what is meant by the idea of "use" in the functional or use-oriented theories of language of the ordinary-language philosophers shows that Heidegger's emphasis on how speakers are controlled by the foreconceptions in language is not an entirely radical departure from their view that the meaning of an utterance depends on its use. Before summarizing some of the implications of modern philosophy of language for social and political inquiry, it is therefore pertinent to clarify the meaning of the concept of use in the functional theories of meaning.

Recently, William Alston has noted that there exists a widely shared conviction (owing to the work of Wittgenstein and Austin) "that the meaning of a linguistic expression is to be elucidated in terms of the use of that expression in terms of the way it is employed by the users of the language."[70] After offering several versions of the use theory, however, he points out that despite the wide acceptance of "use" theories in modern philosophical circles, no one has gone very far toward illuminating what "use" actually means in the context of "use" theories of meaning, nor have they clarified what actually constitutes the illumination of the use of a term. Following Austin's idea of illocutionary meaning, Alston equates the use of a sentence with the set of illocutionary acts it can be employed to perform. He then relates the concept of use to meaning, arguing (with some additional complications) that two expressions have the same meaning if they have the same "illocutionary act potential." Although one would encounter problems accounting for the meaning of all words and expressions with Alston's concept of illocutionary act potential, this approach to elucidating the concept of "use" is well conceived because it indicates that the understanding of the use of an expression is not simply a matter of understanding what a particular person making an utterance might "have in mind" (although there are certainly cases in which knowledge of something like formulated intentions or plans—as the "have-in-mind" expression connotes—does contribute to the meaning of an expression). To speak about the meaning of an expression, according to Alston, is to inquire into "what people do in their employment of the expression in question." So meaning is not just up to the individual user of an expression, because in order to produce a meaningful linguistic expression and, in some cases, thereby to act appropriately, one must use language *correctly,* and using language correctly involves following syntactic and semantic rules.

It is especially important, therefore, when speaking about the "use" of expressions, that we distinguish between the semantic and pragmatic sense of the use of language. As was noted above, semantic rules are those governing the relationship between signs and the objects and situations to which they refer, whereas pragmatic rules are those governing relationships between signs and users of them. Persons can do a variety of things with language. They can 'use' it to achieve various purposes—influencing someone, mobilizing a collective behavior incident, and so forth. These uses are pragmatic, that is, people use individual words and groups of words with an eye toward the effects of using one set of signs versus another. The emphasis in "use" theories of meaning such as those developed by Wittgenstein and Austin, however, is on the semantic dimension of "use." "Use" theory in this sense is based on the idea that an utterance's meaning depends on the use to which it is put in a given context, but "use" here is not meant to imply that the person employs language in a deliberative way to achieve personal goals. The implications of the use concept as it is employed in Austin's position, for example, is simply that when a person wishes to warn someone, as compared with describing a situation, that person selects the correct emphasis for the purpose when saying such things as "I warn you it is about to charge." The employment of the appropriate emphasis is learned by the person who is a competent user of the language and thus need not be contrived for a particular occasion. Similarly, when a person employs what would ordinary be regarded as a simple description, as in the above example "Charles is taller than William," the semantic rules followed by the speaker are learned rather than planned or contrived in an immediate conscious sense. To employ the rule that "height" measurements are to be taken vertically with persons standing is to know what the expression "taller than" ordinarily means and therefore to use it correctly.

This distinction between the pragmatic and semantic connotations of the concept of use should help to clarify not only what is meant when someone refers to "use" theories of meaning but also what is meant by the expression "ordinary-language philosophy" and by the kinds of statements one hears ordinary-language philosophers making, for example, such generalizations as, one means *p* when one says *q,* or such questions as, "What does one mean when one says *X?* When one speaks of ordinary language in reference to the philosophical movement of that name, one is not referring to the kind of language used by "the man in the street." Rather, the expression "ordinary language" refers to the standard (as opposed to special or narrow) use of terms or expressions. As Ryle has pointed out, one can refer to the ordinary use of the term "infinitesimal" without implying that it is "on the lips of every man."[71] There is, as he suggests, an ordinary or standard use of the term and a specialized one that would be employed in mathematics.

So when one says such things as, "When we say *p,* we mean *q,*" we are making, as Stanley Cavell has shown, either an analytic or a synthetic kind of statement, that is, it is not an inference which follows formally from prior, more abstract claims, and it is not, as many have inferred, a generalization about what people do. Statements about ordinary language are references to semantic rules governing the use of terms and expressions. Austin, in his essay "Other Minds," provides a convenient example.[72] There he argues that when we speak of "knowledge," we are referring to procedures, not to states of mind. To support this claim, he contrasts the way one would ordinarily phrase a question about knowledge, noting that whereas we might say "*Why* do you believe thus and so" (belief *is* regarded as a state of mind), we would say "*How* do you know thus and so." If we simply reflect on Austin's suggestion, we see that these two expressions do seem to be the standard ones for phrasing the two different questions. Knowledge, therefore, seems to be a matter of procedures (as implied in the "how" question), and belief seems to be a state of mind (as implied in the "why" question). It is thus not necessary, as Cavell has argued, to take a poll of all users of the English language (or even of a random sample) to determine whether Austin's claim is valid, for his claim about ordinary usage is not an empirical generalization.[73] Functional or 'use' theories of meaning are thus based on the rules in use when persons make utterances or employ other kinds of signs.

Some Implications

There are some important consequences of these alternative conceptions of the functions of language that relate to contemporary positions on social science inquiry. If we accept the view that the language–phenomena relationship is mediated by sets of norms which, taken as a whole, constitute social/political prescriptions, a rethinking of the distinction between normative and empirical theory, a guiding principle of much theory building in the social sciences is suggested. This reassessment is presented in chapter 3. In addition, closely related to the question of the norms that provide the meaning context of utterances is the problem of "agency," that is, the question of whose norms are involved in ascribing meaning to the conduct of those under investigation— those of the observer, those of the actor(s), those implicit in the discourse, and so on. This problem is taken up in chapter 4. For present purposes it is useful to treat, briefly, one important concept in political inquires and analyses from the standpoint of the views on language just elucidated, the concept of legitimacy.

In the discussion of violence above it was pointed out that the concept of legitimacy functions implicitly to distinguish the kinds of conduct that are recruited into the category of violence. And in the above discussion of Dahl's identification of *the* government of a society, the concept of legitimacy was shown to be an important part of that identification. In those discussions, I noted that an empiricist position on language, one that treated the concept of violence as if its meaning were a matter of simply pointing to cases of violence, failed to monitor political commitments implicit in the use of the concept. Certainly many of the norms that produce legitimacy are explicitly recognized and can therefore be spoken about with relatively little problem. When we ask, for example, who may legitimately decide who can become the secretary of state of the United States, we can find the answer in rules that attach to the office of the American presidency. The president has the authority (legitimate power or control) over the incumbency of that position. But much of the authoritative structure of a society (rules for who has legitimate control over what) is implicit. As was noted above, for example, it is redundant to speak about the legitimacy of criminal violence because the meanings of both "criminal" and "violence" derive from, among other things, rules about what kinds of conduct are regarded as legitimate. To some extent, then, an exploration of legitimacy, as it relates to political power or control in a society, requires a look into the linguistic mirror. Therefore, although it is sometimes reasonable to say that we can speak *about* legitimacy, it is also the case that we affirm structures of legitimacy in our speech. When we use familiar forms of discourse to identify "things," we express in our speaking a form of life that contains within it rules about who has legitimate control over what. It is obvious, for example, that when someone asks, "What is the value of the table over there," and we say something like, "About \$50," we are probably affirming a particular model of person–object and person–person interaction and a model of political economy, one based on exchange in a market controlled primarily by producers and those who enable producers (e.g., political leaders who execute, legislate and adjudicate in their behalf). This is because, first of all, to identify a thing as a table is not just to point something out but to identify a relationship between persons and things, because what constitutes something as a table is the set of rule-governed activities in which it has a role. Then, to speak of its value is to ascend to a more complex level of social, political, and economic practice and employ norms about how persons can interact in acquiring things. Thus, embedded in our everyday discourse about the value and significance of various objects and episodes that emerge as we actualize our language in speech are affirmations of a system of authority, that is, acceptances of various allocations of control as legitimate. The familiar language of economic value is one that allocates legitimate control over commodities primarily to producers and their allies. This is why when Marx attacked the theory of value implicit in the capitalist exchange discourse, he had to invent a new discursive practice, one that would give more legitimacy to the persons who worked to produce things. One can, of course, develop a radical departure from the Marxian discourse, for Marx's political economy shares with capitalist political economy the elevation of productive capacity as the legitimate basis for developing a theory of value.[74] If we were to speak of a table in a different way, therefore, as we would if we adopted the Marxian model of political economy and thus a Marxian discursive mode, we would accord legitimate control over commodities to workers rather than to owners of the means of production. Subsequent discussions in the chapters that follow are therefore oriented toward building a mode of political inquiry that emphasizes the analysis of language as a bearer of political content rather than as just a tool to speak about extradiscursive political phenomena that reside independent of what we say and therefore conceive and affirm.

3

Normative Discourse and Political Understanding

The reorientation toward the problems of language and meaning presented in chapter 2 has important implications for understanding normative discourse as well as for understanding human conduct, for if that reorientation is accepted, one finds a much more intimate relationship between normative concerns and political understanding than is supposed within the standard, empiricist frame of reference. Normative discourse, whose primary focus is on the value of various practices and goals, has had a marginal role in contemporary social and political inquiry. Its relegation to the nonrespectable fringes of social science cultures has primarily resulted from the influence of philosophical traditions like logical positivism and empiricism that have radically distinguished between the meanings of normative and empirical statements. Positivists/empiricists have argued, as was noted above, that any science, whether physical or social, must be predicated on a view of language that rigorously distinguishes cognitively meaningful from cognitively meaningless statements, the former including analytic statements that are "formally true" (e.g., "Equals subtracted from equals gives equals") and statements that are "empirically true" or about something (e.g., "Giraffes are taller than camels") and the latter including every kind of statement that is neither analytic nor empirical.

For the early positivists, moral statements like "Lying is wrong" fell into the category of cognitively meaningless statements. To the extent to which such statements were to be accorded meaning at all, positivists like Carnap and Ayer suggested that they can be regarded as having "emotive meaning" only, that is, their meaning is of a noncognitive variety, stemming from the effect that such ethical statements have on persons (effects like arousing emotions, motivating action, etc.). "Evaluative statements," by which they meant statements containing explicit evaluative terms, were accorded cognitive significance by the positivists only if they could be regarded as instrumental commitments. So, for example, the statement "Lying is wrong" could be regarded as having cognitive significance only if it is tendered as a contingent commitment, based on prior commitment such as the belief that lying prevents the achievement of some more basic moral purpose. If the commitment about lying is tendered as a fundamental judgment, one that is not supported with reference to any other commitments, it would be regarded, within the positivist frame of reference, as lacking cognitive significance.

The obvious implication of this position on moral statements in particular and evaluative statements in general is that normative and descriptive (or empirical) discourse should not be conjoined in conceptual systems like theories, for there is clearly no compatibility between statements with different kinds of meaning. This implication has been realized in contemporary political science through the familiar distinction between normative and empirical political theory, which is used to distinguish separate vocational commitments within the discipline. But if we reject the idea that one can radically separate the empirical and normative functions of language, a rejection that follows from the reoriented view of language and meaning I introduced above, we must rethink and perhaps legitimize the role of normative discourse in social and political inquiry. In this chapter, therefore, I shall, with special attention to contemporary, functional, or 'use' perspectives on meaning such as Wittgenstein's and Austin's, reexamine the distinction between descriptive and evaluation discourses and suggest an alternative way of distinguishing normatively and empirically oriented approaches to social and political phenomena.

To understand the complementary relationship between the functions of describing and evaluating—stating what is the case and prescribing conduct—it is useful to *begin* by radically distinguishing "factual" and evaluative assertions. In the history of political theorizing, those who have emphasized the distinction were often responding to evaluative arguments by other theorists that were presented as though they followed from noncontroversial, factual statements. Critiques of such theorizing have emphasized the "gap" between facts and values and pointed out that what often appears to be a logically consistent combination of descriptive premises and subsequent evaluative assertions is actually based on one or another kind of linguistic sleight of hand. Hume's still influential remarks are:

> In every system of morality which I have hitherto met with, I always remarked, that the author proceeds for some time in the or-

dinary way of reasoning, and establishes the being of a God, or makes an observation concerning human affairs; when all of a sudden I am surprised to find, that instead of the usual copulations of propositions, *is* and *is not,* I meet with no preposition that is not connected with an *ought,* or *ought not.* This change is imperceptible; But is, however, of the last consequence. For as this *ought* or *ought not* expresses some new relation or affirmation, 'tis necessary that it should be observed and explained; and at the same time that a reason should be given, for what seems altogether inconceivable, how this new relation can be a deduction from others which are entirely differently from it. But as authors do not commonly use this precaution, I shall presume to recommend it to the readers; and am persuaded that this small attention would subvert all the vulgar systems of morality and let us see that the distinction of vice and virtue is not founded merely on the relations of objects, nor is perceived by reason.[1]

Since Hume, others have produced similar critiques of arguments that combine descriptively and evaluatively oriented claims. More recently Margaret MacDonald has shown how contract theories of the origin of the state are based on what she calls "pseudo-empirical" statements to the effect that the state is predicated on an implicit contract. Because such statements are used to justify evaluative assertions about citizens' obligations, she objects that "to be told that you are party to a contract of which you were unaware, and which is nothing like what anyone would ever call a contract, seems to have little to do with giving your vote at a general election, sending your child to a state school, or paying a fine for exceeding the speed limit."[2]

There do appear to be, as MacDonald suggests, disguised aspects of the argument or justification in contract theories of the state, but it is misleading to speak of "pseudo-empirical" statements as though some statements are genuinely empirical. The Hume–MacDonald kind of critique is misleading because (1) it focuses on individual statements rather than on the rhetorical force of utterances, connected to the context in which they are produced, and (2) it assumes an oversimplified notion of the meaning of "is"-type or empirical statements. It is a valuable service to highlight the illegitimate derivation of evaluative positions from disguised value premises, sequestered in descriptively oriented statements, because such derivations are usually incomplete and rely on principles which are not explicitly stated. But if we recognize that understanding the meaning of expressions requires more than focusing on individual statements and terms, we can take a different perspective on the normative–empirical distinction as it relates to political theory and analysis. At present, it is still the case that many political scientists, often influenced by their interpretations of the writings of the early positivists, ordinarily distinguish normative and empirical political theories with reference to the *terms* that appear in the statements of a theory. This practice stems from attention to only the surface appearance of various statements. As Wittgenstein has noted, however, the meaning of a statement derives from its depth grammar as well. For example, a statement like "Killing a man for his ideas is wrong" seems to be clearly evaluative or "normative," while a statement like "The greater the religious heterogeneity in a society, the more likely it is that persons will be killed because of their ideas" seems to be clearly empirical (in the ordinary sense of the term). Such an inference would be defended no doubt by pointing to the ethical term, "wrong," in the first statement and to the absence of such terms in the second. But, as has been pointed out in previous discussion, the surface appearance of a statement can be misleading, as in the above-mentioned example "All the world's a stage," which has the surface structure of a simple description. We do not treat it as a description because we use rules about the context of utterances that guide us as to when we should take descriptively oriented utterances literally and when we should not. Similarly the statement "Killing a man for his ideas is wrong" could be descriptively oriented (i.e., not meant as ethical injunction) in some contexts, for example, in a situation where the statement is among a list of rules someone is providing as a guide to the understanding of the practices of a particular collectivity.

Terms and statements alone are thus insufficient guides to meaning. This applies to the problem of distinguishing descriptions and evaluations. As Hare has stated, the descriptive–evaluative distinction "is not that between the descriptive and evaluative *terms,* but that between the descriptive and evaluative meaning which a single term may have in a certain context."[3] If terms are inadequate, then, is there any way to distinguish descriptive-oriented from normative-oriented theories? There is, but we can only approach it by repairing some of the damage done by the overzealous acceptance of Hume's caution about the is–ought gap. Rather than focusing on the gap between description and evaluation, a gap that cannot be inferred by such artifacts as what kinds of terms are involved in statements, we must be concerned with, if we are to understand the way that language functions for either descriptive or normative purposes, the gap between word and object or, better, speech and phenomena. Ironically, Hume also had something to say about *this* gap. Noting this, C. I. Lewis pointed out that attention to Hume's caution about this gap might clarify the confusion stemming from a preoccupation with the is–ought derivation problem. Lewis states:

In the modern period, it is Hume who raises this issue as to whether any ought can be derived from an is. But Hume also denied any valid knowledge of what is. . . . In Hume's terms, it hardly appears in what way we are the worse off for the non-derivability of an ought from an is, since in any case we do not have valid knowledge of what is, to serve as a premise of our normative conclusions. . . . The question is not how we can validate an ought on the basis of an is, but how, or whether, we can validate any conviction as to objective matters of fact without antecedent presumptions of the validity of normative principles.[4]

The redirection of emphasis for understanding the status of the normative–empirical distinction was also suggested in a recent treatment by Kovesi. Employing Waisman's open-texture concept (discussed above in chapter 2), he argues that actions and things can never be exhaustively defined in terms of their material properties, for example, one could provide an almost endless list of properties which are often included when someone is speaking about a 'chair,' but these properties do not, by themselves, give us license to call a thing a chair. There must also be some rules or principles that provide guidance in collecting various of these properties in combination so that we can validly use the word 'chair.' There is thus a gap, according to Kovesi, between what we perceive and what we can validly say. There is no such gap in relationships in formal systems. For example, the word 'rectilinearity' can be used if we assemble a fixed number of angle measurements, and there is no gap in the sensing of colors and the use of the appropriate word for the color, for example, between something being yellow and the judgment that it is. But, considering actions and things and moral notions (e.g., lying), Kovesi states, "the 'gap' between what is given to our senses and what we claim an act or thing to be exists in the case of both descriptive and evaluative terms."[5]

In summary, then, because the old descriptive–normative distinction has been predicated on a faulty model of the relationship between language and reality in general, and on a faulty conception of what a description is in particular, a useful reinterpretation of normative discourse can only be ventured by comparing the descriptive and normative *functions* for which language is employed. In the explication of John Austin's notion of performative utterances in the previous chapter, an introduction to this comparison was provided. It became clear to Austin, in the process of comparing statements and performatives, that what makes a performative or speech-act valid or invalid (or felicitous or infelicitous, in his language) is the rule-governed context in which it functions. But this is what also makes a 'statement' or descriptive utterance valid or invalid (true or false). This discovery has obvious implications for the normative–empirical distinction. Neither single statements nor conceptual systems like theories embodying many statements are empirical or normative on their face. The grounds for distinguishing whether an expression is normative or empirical have to do with emphases and purposes. Normatively and empirically oriented utterances do not possess different *kinds* of meaning. Rather, they may each be treated as containing different *levels* of meaning. In some cases the emphasis of an utterance is such that it becomes comprehensible when we see that it is meant to be treated as empirical, that is, to be governed almost exclusively by criteria of application. In other cases, the emphasis is on other levels of meaning, for example, on a statement's performative force. If a judge says, "The Brown Case is a precedent," the utterance is best regarded as performative or normative in emphasis and thus in meaning because the judge is acting to establish norms. When, subsequently, a commentator states, "The Brown Case is a precedent," the same utterance is now best interpreted as descriptive or empirical in emphasis and meaning because the commentator is 'using' the already established norm to report, not to judge.

Rather than distinguishing normative from empirical theory on the basis of such semantic artifacts as whether or not 'should's or 'ought's appear in the statements of the theory, we should therefore consider what is behind a theorist's choice of emphasis—either normative or empirical. Take, for example, the statement used above, "The greater the religious heterogeneity of a society, the more likely it is that persons will be killed because of their ideas." If a theory about 'domestic violence' contained such a statement the theory could be regarded as normative despite the lack of explicit normative emphasis in the statement or in any of the other statements in the theory. There are many different implicit norms in the statement, but for purposes of illustration, we can restrict our attention to those associated with the notion of "killing persons because of their ideas." If one were to do actual empirical research to 'test' the statement and thereby attempt to validate the theory in which it is embedded, it would be necessary to consider some rules of application that would clarify its meaning. It is likely that if a person is executed after due process of law because he or she killed another person in a dispute over property this would not be classified, by the ordinary empirical political theorist, as a case of someone's being killed because of his or her ideas. Why not? One *could* construe such an action as being based on some 'ideas.' The classificatory decision would probably be defended on the basis of a distinction between ideas that are related to personal, material self-interest and those that are construed as either other-regarding or community oriented, or at least matters of personal conscience which transcend attitudes toward worldly gratification. Certainly the rules or norms one could use to defend such classificatory decisions which constitute the meaning of "killing persons because of their ideas" could be regarded as controversial. All empirical theories (that is, those emphasizing the relationships between concepts for which observational equivalents have been selected, rather than emphasizing the norms underlying the concepts and guiding the selection of equivalents) are *potentially* normative in that they embody such classifactory decisions. Thus, the same characteristics that make a theory empirical—the rules of application linking speech and phenomena (concepts and data in empiricist language)—also make it normative, for the *norms* are the links that constitute the meanings of the terms which are the empirical nodes of a theory. So one could just as well reconstruct the supposedly empirical expression "killing persons for their ideas," treating as problematic or controversial the implicit norms which distinguish killing for (or because of) ideas from other kinds of killing. If this were done, such statements as "Persons who disagree with authorities on the basis of conscience should not be executed as criminals" would emerge as an explicit part of the theory or conceptual system.

This raises an important question. If we are to regard the normative–empirical distinction as a matter of emphasis, how are we to explain why a particular theory emphasizes either the empirical or the normative mode of discourse? The answer is that the choice of one versus the other emphasis is based on the theorist's level of concern with the concepts in the theory. Any concept could be treated as controversial or problematic. When a concept is so treated, this is symptomatized by the use of normatively oriented discourse. A theorist tends, on the other hand, to employ only empirically oriented statements when the assumption is that the concepts and links between concepts and observations are unproblematic or noncontroversial. In the absence of explicitly normative language, we can assume that the theorist's argument focuses on the links between concepts (syntactic or formal links—what are called by social scientists "the relationships between variables") rather than on the rules or norms that constitute or give meaning to the concepts. Thus, if we wish to study suicide from a wholly empirical standpoint, that is, to emphasize the relationship between suicides (whatever they are) and other phenomena, we would tend to deemphasize all the normative commitments underlying our concept of suicide and would construct a conceptual system emphasizing relationship between those "things" or events that we call suicides and other phenomena, such as the degree of community solidarity in high versus low suicide areas, the victims' social status, current trends in the economy, and so on. When we wonder, however, what suicide ought to be (if anything), we examine the rules that constitute the phenomenon of suicide and perhaps investigate the reasons the various phenomena fall within or outside of the conception as it is generally or perhaps variously used. Moreover, if we decide to assume a standpoint on the value of one versus another conception of suicide, our discourse in our argument would become explicitly normative.

Of course we could engage in social and political theorizing from both a normative and empirical perspective at the same time (even though this is relatively unfashionable). To do so would be to begin with the normatively oriented task of either investigating or creating rules which constitute the basis for various concepts and perhaps to argue about what rules should be involved in setting the boundaries of various concepts. The empirical analysis would then be to analyze some aspect of the relationships among the concepts developed and either antecedent or consequent conditions hypothesized to relate to them.

Theories are thus intrinsically neither normative nor empirical. The emphasis selected by the theorist, which is reflected in the mode of discourse used to express the theory, is a matter of what aspect of the concepts in the theory are assumed to be problematic. Although we cannot therefore distinguish clearly between normative and empirical theories, we can distinguish between normative and empirical emphases in theoretical discourse. With this in view, we can examine normative discourse more closely in order to understand the problem of meaning with which it is associated and to consider how it fits into political inquiry. The more relevant level of inquiry required to understand normative discourse involves questions at the meta level, which, in the case of normative discourse, are termed metaethical questions. Substantive ethical questions are those about the human goals or purposes that are thought to be valuable and about the various courses of action directed toward these goals that are thought to be right or appropriate. But contrary to the arguments found in standard ethics texts, one cannot identify ethical discourse by the presence of terms such as "good," "right," "should," "ought," and so on. Any of these terms can be employed descriptively. What makes a discourse ethical or nonethical is the performative force of its statements, a force that derives from the rhetorical context in which the statement is produced, and the purposes for which the statement is made. If someone says, "I ought to pay her something," the ought is not, by itself, sufficient to make the statement normative in emphasis or force, because the "ought" could be regarded as a descriptive commentary on the existence of a particular obligation. The statement is normative only if the context and emphasis of the statement highlights the action implied in the statement, that is, the acknowledgment of obligation.

Metaethical questions function at a higher level of abstraction than substantive ethical questions. Metaethics involves what is ordinarily called ethical theories, theories about the meaning of substantive ethical statements. So in order to understand how we can usefully apply the functional theories of meaning introduced thus far to normative discourse, we must raise questions about metaethical positions. In order to do this systematically, it is worthwhile considering various well-known metaethical commitments, which are still taken seriously as frames of reference for interpreting normative discourse.

Naturalism

It is difficult to put together a coherent discussion of naturalism or any of the well-known metaethical commitments, because many of the familiar presentations of such positions as naturalism, intuitionism, and emotivism are carried out in the context of outmoded conceptions of language. One view that is often identified as a naturalistic metaethic, for example, is the position that evaluative expressions, principles of conduct, and ideas of obligation can be derived from descriptive expressions. How can one evaluate such a claim? Traditional attacks on naturalism, like the position itself, have been based on the old language paradigm that sharply differentiates descriptive statements from evaluative ones. For example, one may encounter the following kind of "naturalistic argument" in traditional political theorizing that I have suggested elsewhere:[6]

1. Society functions to protect the property of each of its members.
2. A major threat to the institution of private property in a society is a set of rules that allows public ownership of land.
3. Public ownership of land ought to be disallowed in order that society might function properly.

Clearly this is precisely the kind of argument that provoked Hume to complain about arguments which begin with seemingly descriptive assertions, as in statements 1 and 2, and then proceed to produce valuational ones, as in statement 3. The argument in this particular example is quite deceptive because the evaluation in statement 3 appears to follow logically from the prior statements. This is because the "surface grammar" of statement 1 makes it appear to be descriptively oriented, but it would be less misleading to regard the statement as a normatively oriented argument to the effect that a society ought to be oriented toward the property maintenance for individuals who claim to hold it. If the contention were stated in such normative language, as I have just suggested, we would be prepared for a controversy and would be able to predicate our acceptance of statement 3 on our attitude toward the claim evinced in statement 1. When traditional naturalists smuggle such recommendations into seemingly descriptive premises, it appears that the world is being simply presented as it *is* rather than being fitted into a moral-ideological system that would, if revealed, in the appropriate normative language, invite critical evaluation.

The kind of naturalistic argument just presented has been evidenced frequently in the history of political theory by theorists who begin with a premise about the nature of man, which contains implicit premises about the appropriate kind of social organization. It is then a short and difficult-to-refute step to statements that justify a model of political order which provides a felicitous environment for the kind of political man "described" in the initial premise. Generally, the acceptance of such naturalistic arguments about the kind of political arrangements we ought to have rests on our agreement with a particular model of political man as self-evident. By deriving their rules for conduct and human organization from a norm-laden description of political man, naturalists put together moral arguments that appear to possess the same inference structure as ordinary empirical theories. This is, of course, a vulgar kind of naturalism, and it was practiced by theorists who never thought of themselves as engaged in an enterprise that falls within a particular metaethical school. There is a more sophisticated version of naturalism, however. Some ethical theorists are called naturalistic because they argue that terms like "good" refer to natural qualities. They do not, like "vulgar naturalists," imply that evaluative expressions refer to qualities that exist out in the world, independent of persons' perspectives, but rather to qualities which create pro or anti attitudes in persons. For this kind of naturalist, the justification for a descriptive premise at the beginning of what turns out to be a moral argument is that the description refers to naturally engendered attitudes or feelings, and these attitudes and feelings are the referents of normatively oriented statements appearing subsequently in the argument.

Underlying this more sophisticated kind of naturalism is the intention to relate normative discourse to something that persons actually experience. There is, however, a difficult gap to be bridged in moving from references to experienced attitudes and feelings to speaking about the intrinsic value of purposes. One such attempt, Paul Henle's, demonstrates the shortcomings of this kind of naturalism.[7] Henle compares the structure of ethical systems to the structure of epistemological systems, claiming that pleasure relates to values in an ethical system as sense data relates to objects in an epistemological system. A hypothesis about the existence of an object in an epistemological framework is then equated with aims or intentions which serve as hypotheses about pleasure in an ethical framework. The comparison is thus oriented toward showing how an ethical system can be thought of as no less cognitive than an empirical basis for knowledge about the world. But this kind of naturalism faces two serious difficulties. First, it provides no structure for moving from conceptions of individuals' feelings and motives for satisfying desires to concepts about what generally (or universally, if one is trying to produce an objectivist naturalism) ought to be desired. Second, the position is predicated on a faulty, empiricist philosophy of mind, one that regards meaningful ideas as the result of the recording of sense data. What we regard as "values," just as what we regard as "objects," are not impressed upon us. Rather, they are constituted by values by active interpretations that persons provide in mediating relationships between what they experience and what significance they ascribe to that experience, given the categories they possess from the collective meaning system within which they function.

If we adopt this alternative view of mind and the view of language and meaning that it supports, we reject the very distinction between descriptive and evaluative assertions. This rejection in turn impeaches any attempt to reduce evaluative assertions to descriptions. Because such attempts have, according to predominant ethical theory, been the defining characteristic of naturalism as a metaethical position, we are left wondering if their remains a viable kind of naturalism that could be constructed on the basis of a different philosophy of mind and a related alternative philosophy of language.

There *are* modern versions of naturalism that are constructed on alternatives to the traditional empiricist philosophies of mind and language. Although ethical theory is ordinarily associated exclusively with British and American views, phenomenological philosophy, primarily a continental phenomenon, has influenced the development of an ethical naturalism that is worth exploring. Rather than attempting to distinguish value judgments as one kind of discursive practice to be contrasted with judgments about facts, some continental philosophers have treated evaluation as an activity that is immanent in persons' active perceptual processes. For example, Georges Gusdorf has stated, "the most general definition of value would characterize it as a reality structure that is immanent to our action, as a manner of meeting the world and of qualifying it as a function of our constant or momentary exigencies."[8] He argues, in a manner reminiscent of Heidegger, that "intellectual philosophy" has misunderstood values because it projects the concepts of values within the framework of discourse rather than seeing values as part of a way of life that prestructures our discourse and our perceptions and interpretations. To be conscious and to have knowledge, according to Gusdorf, is in effect to affirm values.

Gusdorf's position clearly derives from a phenomenological conception of consciousness as an active, reality-constituting agency; but in what sense can one say that his ethical theory is naturalistic? His position can be called naturalistic, not in the British-American sense of reducing the idea of value to statements about perceptions or sensations, because he rejects the construction of values as such a discursive phenomenon to be understood by contrasting value judgments and judgments about "reality." Rather, he argues that values originate in the "sphere of our instincts" but that they then become reconstituted as concepts in language. He calls this reconstitution the "second intellectual birth of values." His naturalism thus resembles the kind developed by Dewey and Lewis. Gusdorf argues, basically, that given various human instincts and needs (and therefore derivative purposes), we construct our meaningful world. Our knowledge of what "is" for Gusdorf, as it is for Lewis, is therefore predicated on commitments about values. As he puts it, "we never face a universe that is indifferent and given as flatly lying before us, in its personal determination. Our knowledge of the universe always remains partial and biased, demanded by the exigency of this or that need."[9]

What emerges from some contemporary versions of naturalism, then, is not the familiar metaethic that seeks logically to interrelate valuational and factual statements or judgments, because one cannot clearly distinguish statements as descriptive or valuational. Naturalists such as Gusdorf and Dewey and Lewis argue that any apprehension of experience expressed through a set of utterances with meaning is a complex combination of judgments, inseparable from projected needs, purposes, and standards, about what is the case. If we accept this view, we cannot build an understanding of normative discourse with a traditional ethical analysis based on comparing the logic of factual versus valuational assertions. We must, rather, consider the rhetorical force or orientation of utterances, recognizing that evaluative components are always involved, whether or not they constitute the major claims involved in a particular utterance or set of utterances. Utterances, as has been noted above, derive their meaning in the context of what is being done with them. This functional approach to normative discourse will be taken up more fully below in a discussion of Austin's influence on ethical theory. First, I shall consider two more traditional metaethical positions, intuitionism and emotivism.

Intuitionism

Like traditional naturalists, intuitionists have argued that ethical terms and expressions refer to qualities and can thus be objectively vindicated, but intuitionists maintain a different position on how these qualities are apprehended. Whereas traditional naturalists argue that terms such as "good" and "right" refer to qualities discernible through "sense experience," intuitionists argue that such terms refer to qualities that are apprehended with a special moral faculty or sense. This provides an interesting contrast with the naturalist position on the relationship between ethical terms and data or "evidence" in moral arguments. Some naturalists, claiming that "*X* is good," would respond, when asked "Why is *X* good?" by describing qualities of *X*. But an intuitionist separates the concept of good from the idea of evidence in this sense. G. E. Moore's position on the meaning of "good" clarifies this separation. Two of his arguments should suffice to explain the intuitionist model of the evidence/moral-claim relationship. The first is his "open question" argument. He argued that the concept "good" functions much like the concept of a point or a line in a geometric system; it is a simple and undefinable term. This idea of "good" as undefinable can be contrasted, he asserted, with terms like "horse," which are definable. "When we say . . . the definition of horse is 'a hoofed quadraped of the genus Equus' . . . we may mean that a certain object, which all of us know, is composed in a certain manner: that it has four legs, a head, a heart, a liver, etc., all of them arranged in definite relation to one another. It is in this sense that I deny good to be definable." This indefinability leads to the open question that arises when someone tries to define "good." If, as in Moore's example, someone tries to define "good" as "that which we desire to desire," we could then substitute for the expression "*A* is good," *A* is one of the things that we desire to desire.[10] But, as Moore pointed out, we could still intelligibly raise the question, Is it good to desire to desire *A*? Thus whenever we attempt to define "good," an open question, such as the one just supplied, remains. This is what led Moore to his notion that "good" is indefinable.

If we now ask about what kind of status "good" has, we come to Moore's second argument. Moore suggested that we should regard "good" as supervenient, that is, as a term which cannot be derived from other terms. Therefore we cannot expect statements with the term "good" in them to be derivable from other statements. The statement "*X* is good" can thus never be a matter of either deductive or inductive inference. It can be known only through direct perception (through the operation of Moore's special moral sense). "Good," for Moore and for intuitionists in general, is thus taken outside the bounds of ordinary knowledge criteria. Inferential arguments are impossible because "good" is simple (it is not definable on the basis of a combination of properties) and deductive arguments are barred because "good" is supervenient.

The contribution of intuitionism to the understanding of moral arguments and to the comprehension of the role of moral discourse is dubious. There is no way within the intuitionist frame of reference to account for moral disagreement, for example, for persons to hold different views about whether something is good or not. If moral terms refer to simple qualities perceived by a special moral sense, one can only fall back on the notion of false perception to account for moral disagreement. To retreat to the false-perception argument, however, when the perceptual mechanism is a special faculty such as a "moral sense," leaves no way of maintaining the objectivist stance, which is part of the foundation of the intuitionist metaethical posture. One cannot, as in the case of disagreements over perceptions of colors, employ objective criteria (e.g., wave-length measurements in this case) to resolve disputes over moral perceptions. Given this difficulty, intuitionists have tended to argue that there are actually no real moral disagreements. They argue that there exists basic agreement on "fundamental values" and what appears to be a moral disagreement is usually a disagreement in belief(s) of a nonmoral variety. If ethical judgments are to be regarded as faulty, argue the intuitionists, it is only because in the process of reasoning about ways to achieve moral values, bad inferences from evidence become involved. P. F. Strawson has dealt with this claim effectively. He has argued, "We say, warningly, that ethical judgments are corrigible, because ethical disagreement sometimes survives the resolution of factual disagreement. We say, encouragingly, that ethical judgments are corrigible because the resolution of factual disagreement sometimes leads to the resolution of ethical disagreement. But the one kind of agreement leads (when it does lead) to the other, not in the way in which agreed evidence leads to an agreed conclusion but in the way in which common experience leads to sympathy."[11] Strawson's point is that there *do* exist disagreements at the level of moral values or judgments, and that these disagreements produce ethical disputes which are not resolvable with resort to evidence in the sense in which arguments with empirically oriented contingencies are. The resolution of such disputes results not from evidence or from a more careful set of inferences but from a heightened awareness or appreciation by one of the parties to the dispute of the moral level value(s) maintained by the other party.

Apart from these traditional critiques of intuitionism, it is evident that Moore's type of position rests on the same disabling view of language and meaning that plagues traditional naturalistic positions. Moore asked, in effect, what it is (i.e., what is the property or "thing") for which good stands. If we view the concept of good from a speech-act perspective and ask instead what is being done in expressions that employ the concept of goodness, we must reject intuitionism for the same reason we reject early versions of naturalism: because it seeks to understand expressions in which ethical *terms* exist by comparing them with other *kinds* of expressions, as though the meaning of discourses can be under-

stood by attending to the vocabulary involved and its referents. As Warnock has noted in reinforcing the general argument in this chapter, "any
expression which occurs in the context of the evaluation of something
could also occur in the context of the description of something and vice
versa."[12]

Subjectivist Approaches to Normative Discourse

Subjectivist metaethical positions, as the name implies, do not seek to
establish an objectivist basis for moral discourse. This is a good beginning because it is not clear what establishing such a basis might mean.
The very idea of objectivity, as it has been traditionally conceived and
used, is based on the problematic philosophical commitment that we apprehend objects (entities with meanings expressed in utterances) through
our reception of sense impressions. There is a variety of subjectivist approaches, all of which, in one way or another, base their position on the
meaning of ethical terms and expressions on a psychological theory of
meaning. Such theories locate the meaning of a statement in the psychological processes of either the speaker, the listener, or both. Here I shall
concentrate on one of the most influential varieties of ethical subjectivism, the emotivist position, best known through the writing of Charles
I. Stevenson. Articulating a position which remains influential in social
science circles, Stevenson argued that moral judgments are best understood if we distinguish their belief and attitudinal components. These
components perform different functions in the discourses surrounding
ethical disagreement, according to Stevenson. "When ethical issues become controversial, they involve disagreement in belief . . . but there is
also disagreement in attitude . . . the central problem in ethical analysis—one might also say 'the' problem—is one of showing in detail how
beliefs and attitudes are related."[13]

This distinction between disagreements in belief and disagreements in
attitude provides the basis for Stevenson's position on the meaning of
ethical statements. Ethical statements, he argued, differ from scientific
ones in that arguments involving the latter take into account only disagreements in belief. Ethical statements possess extra scientific meaning.
They encourage or alter aims and conduct, whereas scientific statements
describe or report something. Ethical statements, for Stevenson, thus
have two *kinds* of meaning, a descriptive meaning and an "emotive"
meaning. The descriptive meaning in an ethical statement relates to the
aspect of the statement that directs one's attention to particular objects
and/or situations, and the emotive meaning in the statement relates to
the aspect that is directed toward the attitudes of persons auditing the
statement.

We can see that the theory of meaning underlying Stevenson's analysis of normative discourse conforms neither to the verificationist position belonging to traditional positivism nor to the functional approach of analytic philosophers. Stevenson is basically promoting a causal theory of meaning, or, as it is sometimes known, a psychological theory of meaning. Such a theory locates the meaning of an utterance in the mental processes that it provokes. So when Stevenson speaks of the descriptive meaning of a moral utterance, he is not emphasizing its referral function, for its meaning is not a function of the procedural rules required to link the statement with that to which it refers. Rather, a moral statement's descriptive meaning inheres in its tendency "to produce *cognitive* mental processes."[14] Similarly, when Stevenson refers to a statement's emotive meaning he is emphasizing the tendency to produce or arouse feelings or attitudes.

The first question to raise about Stevenson's position, as in the case of any position on meaning, concerns its validity. What is the status of a position that equates the meaning of a statement with what it produces in its hearers? It is clearly a more narrow theory of meaning than that advanced by Austin in his analysis of the different functions performed by an utterance. Stevenson's theory emphasizes only the part of an utterance that Austin called perlocutionary (what one does *by* saying something). For Stevenson, the meaning of a statement like "You ought to defend your country" would depend solely on the beliefs and attitudes produced or aroused in those who heard it. This clearly neglects such aspects of an utterance as the emphasis that attends its expression, an emphasis that cannot be inferred from simply looking at the statement but can be gathered through such aspects as the way it is stated, the status or role of the speaker, the context in which it is uttered. We are certainly dealing here with an inordinately anemic theory of meaning. Within the frame of reference of such a theory, one cannot even tell to whom a statement such as the one in this example, which appears to be ethical or normative, is addressed. It may, for example, engender many cognitive and emotional/attitudinal processes in persons for whom it is not intended. We would want to be able to say in such a case that such unintended productions are gratuitous to the meaning of the statement, but if we cling to Stevenson's model of meaning we cannot.

Can we say anything encouraging about Stevenson's ever-popular theory of meaning? Yes; some subjectivist approaches are worse. Stevenson avoids the radical psychologizing that can be found in some subjectivist approaches to moral discourse. For example, he explicitly dissociates himself from "naive subjectivism," the position that moral judgments merely describe the speaker's attitude, for he argues that ethical sentences express rather than describe a speaker's attitude(s). As he puts it, "a man who says, for instance, that democracy is a good form of government, is expressing his attitude toward democracy, and is not describing his attitude toward it. If he was merely describing it, he . . . would be engaged in introspective psychology; and whatever else ethics may be, it is clearly not introspective psychology."[15]

On the positive side, it can also be said that within the bounds of Stevenson's subjectivist account of the meaning of moral statements, there is considerable room for reasoning and argumentation in ethical disputes. Stevenson saw the role of attitudes in moral discourse as similar to the role of beliefs in scientific discourse. He noted that, whereas in science we concern ourselves with reasons for believing and disbelieving, in ethics we concern ourselves with reasons for approving or disapproving.[16] "We disagree when someone approves of something and someone else disapproves, but in such cases, reasons can be adduced which may bring about a change in attitude."[17] But Stevenson's position on the place of reasons in moral discourse is not very productive for the understanding of moral positions, primarily because of the difficulties associated with his narrow, psychological theory of meaning. He fails to establish a logical relationship between beliefs and attitudes, viewing the connection as a causal-psychological one. This leads him to the view that one gives reason in the course of a moral argument in order to evoke or produce beliefs in the hearer that will result in changed attitudes. The attitudes are thus regarded as being changed not because they are inconsistent or otherwise logically inappropriate but rather because they happen to have a psychological relationship with the belief(s) evoked. An astute ethical debater will therefore select reasons on the basis of their psychological impact rather than their logical relationship with what is at issue. In effect Stevenson's position produces a model of ethical discourse for the debater rather than for one who seeks clarity. As a result, his metaethical position is seriously restrictive in its implications for understanding the various dimensions of normative discourse and moral arguments, however relevant it may be for making them successfully (i.e., persuasively). This shortcoming of Stevenson's metaethical position is owed to his inadequate theory of meaning. Clearly, whatever the psychological correlates of an ethical statement (i.e., whatever the speaker's affect toward what is being said and whatever the statement's psychological impact), its meaning is a function of semantic and syntactic rules that govern its use. So, an utterance of the type "You ought to get off that land immediately" would have the same meaning whether, for example, it was said in anger or not and whether it produced fear or not in the hearer. There are, of course, a variety of meanings that the utterance could have, depending on its context (the circumstances in which it is uttered) and depending on its emphasis (e.g., it could be meant primarily as a warning or as a descriptively oriented conclusion, given the speaker's knowledge of the hearer's already formed intentions). In no case, however, would the meaning be wholly controlled or determined by the psychological processes involved.

Some contemporary ethical theorists, having noted the failure of Stevenson's emotivism to provide an adequate account of the "cognitive" aspects of moral or ethical utterances, have invented modified versions of emotivism. Paul Edwards, for example, has suggested that only a limited number of moral statements lend themselves to an emotivist type of analysis. Most moral judgments, he argues, can be regarded as objective in that they refer to objects and/or situations and therefore most moral disputes can be resolved using only empirical statements. Edwards, in explicating his metaethical approach, employs the belief–attitude distinction that we find in Stevenson's position, but his notion of the interrelationship of these two cognitive components is different. Analyzing the statement "The steak at Barney's is nice," he points out that although taste or attitudes determine what features of the steak are being designated as part of "niceness," "the statement itself refers to those features and not to my taste."[18] For Edwards, statements with ethical predicates, which include both value statements (with "good" or "worth" in them) and statements of obligation (with "ought" or "should" in them), are "polygynous," that is, they possess multiple dimensions of meaning. For example, a statement like "Abortions are wrong" can have an affective significance in that it may express the speaker's approval, but it also refers to qualities that would be produced if the speaker were asked to supply reasons supporting the position. For example, he or she might say, "Killing is never justified, performing an abortion involves the taking of a life, therefore, abortions are wrong."

Edwards goes beyond Stevenson toward providing a logical basis for moral arguments, in that he allows a greater scope for the cognitive dimension of moral statements. Because, he argues, moral judgments refer to objects and situations as well as expressing approval, there are possibilities for supplying empirical statements that might be *logically* relevant to the judgment. Indeed, moral disputes can often be reduced to disagreements of "fact" when the parties are forced to give first- and second-order reasons behind each moral judgment. For example, the judgment "Schoolchildren should not be publicly ranked on the basis of abilities in cognitive domains such as reading and quantitative skills" might be defended by a belief like "Such ranking procedures produces negative attitudes toward cooperation among children." This first-order reason might then be supported by the second-order reason, "Children with negative attitudes toward cooperation are not adaptive to social organizations that require cooperation." Ultimately, the argument might be pushed to a point where differing models of collective relations and differing aspirations for human development are at issue and serve to provide the standards of last resort for the justificatory systems in contention, but it is conceivable that these models and/or aspirations are sufficiently shared by the parties involved so that the argument could be resolved by obtaining evidence for some of the belief commitments involved, for example, by assessing attitudes toward cooperation in groups of children who have been publicly ranked on reading and quantitative skills and in groups of children who have not been so ranked.

Edwards's position is useful therefore if we are concerned with providing a way to relate "empirical matters" to normative discourse. But there are serious deficiencies in his argument. As should be clear from the discussion above, Edwards employs an oversimplified model of what it means for something to refer to facts or qualities. For example, in the hypothetical dispute about publicly ranking schoolchildren, the reduction of the moral judgment to factual assertions that would lead to an empirical inquiry requires that we treat each empirically oriented concept (i.e., each term with a referral dimension to its meaning) as unproblematic. Were we to regard major constituents in the argument as problematic, however, we might find that a dispute is located in a place that involves norms which are *implicit* in the seemingly belief oriented statements. For example, the meaning of the concept of cooperation could be at issue, and such an issue can become evident only if we realize that statements do not refer to facts or qualities without, at the same time, embodying prescriptions which bound the phenomena they are referencing.

There is also a serious inconsistency in Edwards's position. He fails to maintain his notion of the polyguity of meaning for all moral judgments. When, for example, a participant in a moral argument gives first-, second-, and third-order reasons in support of a moral statement and the other participant agrees to all the "factual claims" and still rejects the moral statement at issue, the disagreement must be over what Edwards calls a "fundamental moral judgment" (in this example the judgment would be about the desirability of the conditions mentioned in the third-order reasons). Edwards abandons his basic theory about the polyguity of moral judgments with respect to this type of judgment. He states, "I have so far omitted any discussion of one peculiar kind of moral judgment, which must be exempted from the objectivism advocated in this work. I am referring to what are sometimes called 'fundamental' or 'basic' moral judgments. When a man is unwilling or unable to support a moral judgment with anything that would be considered a reason, we shall say that he has made a 'fundamental moral judgment'.

These judgments, unlike nonfundamental moral judgments, have 'emotive meaning' only, they express a stand or an attitude on the part of their author.''[19]

Edwards's retreat to emotivism opens him up to the same kind of criticism I directed toward Stevenson. Whether one emphasizes the emotions expressed in a moral judgment (as does Edwards) or those caused or aroused by the statement (as does Stevenson), the meaning of a statement like "I order you to leave the premises" is not determined by the attitudes or emotions evinced in the speaker and hearer. Moreover, Edwards's bifurcated account of the meaning of moral judgments rests on a dubious distinction. His distinction between fundamental and nonfundamental moral judgments creates a difficulty similar to that which afflicts his notion of moral judgments referring to qualities. Just as Edwards oversimplifies the way any single statement can be thought of as referring to an empirical domain, he also oversimplifies the way that *systems* of statements apply to an empirical domain. It is not clear that just because a person cannot directly supply reasons for a moral judgment, the judgment should be regarded as fundamental or basic and therefore unrelated to reasons which involve empirically oriented statements or commitments, while other moral judgments (nonfundamental ones) for which the "basic" one is a superordinate principle, *are* related to empirically based reasons. To understand why the distinction is problematic we can compare a moral justificatory system to a scientific theory. If we do so, we can observe that the function of "basic" moral judgments in moral arguments is similar to the function of axioms in scientific theories. Ordinarily, primitives (undefined terms) and axioms (underived statements) are considered part of the analytic portion of a theory, whereas hypotheses derived from them and other statements are regarded as "synthetic" or part of the empirical portion of the theory (when the concepts in the hypotheses have been supplied with measurement rules linking them with sense data). But recall the above quoted position of Quine on the analytic–synthetic distinction (supra, chapter 2). His point can be applied equally to moral justificatory systems. The relationship between any statement in either type of system, moral or scientific, and an object or situation referenced by the system as part of the relevant empirical domain is a matter of degree. Moral systems need not be thought of as hierarchical as regards relations between statements and phenomena. This point has been made by Scriven, who notes that the distinction between more and less basic values is a matter of degree. Radical distinctions between basic and nonbasic values (which are parallel to Edwards's fundamental-nonfundamental moral judgments) are predicated on a hierarchical model of the relationship between values and experience. Scriven states:

It is widely supposed that a man's system of values can be thought of as pyramidical hierarchy, and, conversely, as a tree structure. These have, at one end, a large number of specific practical values (liking today's issues of *The Times,* preferring one's nephew James to the neighbor's Johnny, and so forth) which are justifiable by, or derivable from, a smaller number of more general values (liking the most compendious paper in the country and not caring that it also has the most typographical errors, liking little boys that are intelligent but rather quiet), which are themselves instances of still fewer and more general values (liking the quality of being well informed, intelligent, secure). Now if this were a realistic account, all one's values would derive from a relatively small number of "highest" (or "more basic") values, which by definition are not derived from any other values. Where do *they* come from? It seems very plausible— if one is thinking in terms of this model—to suppose that they must be simply a free choice by the individual. The model cuts them off from any visible means of support, and in doing so it misrepresents the extensive interaction between values and experience that actually exists.[20]

Just as Quine has noted that it is conceivable to adjust basic or analytic commitments to make a theory accord with experience when its initial formulation encounters "recalcitrant experience," Scriven suggests that optimization in value fulfillment or, by extension for cases in which disputes are involved, optimization in keeping value systems open to relevant experience, requires that we also be prepared to adjust primary goals, where this is psychologically possible, in the light of constraints of external and in reality limitations." This position accords well with Quine's suggestion that one can resist the psychological tendency to regard analytic components of a theory as unchangeable when a theory confronts "recalcitrant experience," adjusting only the so-called synthetic components to make the theory accord with experience. It is possible, as Quine noted, to adjust "analytic components" to bring about the accord. To regard them as untouchable is a consequence of an oversimplified notion of how any component relates to experience. Theories can be thought of as hierarchical if we focus on their syntax, but it is disabling to think of them as hierarchical from the viewpoint of the relationship between different kinds of statements and the theory-data interface. In like manner, rejecting the traditional hierarchical tree or "pyramid" model of a value or moral reasoning structure leads Scriven to suggest that such structures are better regarded as "webs," "stretching across the ground of experience, serving as one of the structures that unifies it."[21] In such a web, basic or primary values serve as intersections or points of termination. Although their relationship with experience is less direct than that of other value components, which, in Quine's terminology, are closer to the "sensory periphery," they help coordinate and organize the value system in its overall relationship with experience. As changes occur in the relationship between experience and any of the points in the web (usually those with a more direct reference to experience) tremors are set off in the web that may ultimately change a basic value or, as Edwards defines it, a fundamental moral judgment.

Scriven's perspective therefore provides multiple channels through which a moral calculus becomes permeable to the world of experience. In a perspective in which experience is regarded as registering throughout a moral justificatory system, the distinction between fundamental and nonfundamental moral judgments loses its cogency. If we regard moral justificatory systems as complex structures having multiple connections with experience, it is no longer necessary to abandon moral reasoning when one reaches a "fundamental" or noncontingent moral judgment. Within the framework of Scriven's model of the relationship between value systems and experience, moral judgments can be viewed on a continuum of more or less basic commitments, and all moral judgments can be regarded as bearing on experience. Because this perspective invalidates the firm distinction between fundamental and nonfundamental moral judgments, it is fatal to even the modified version of emotivism suggested by Edwards. One caution about Scriven's argument arises from the discussion thus far, however. Scriven makes an overly sharp distinction between values and experience and therefore emphasizes only one direction of impact, that of experience on values. But clearly, what is taken as "experience" is the result of interpretation that is guided by values and standards. Scriven's web metaphor can be salvaged by attending to the web–experience relationship, noting that the web influences the interpretation of the experience over which it hovers. This addition to Scriven's model prepares us to consider what normative discourse becomes in the context of the functional approaches to language and meaning.

The Functional Approach to Moral Discourse

As was suggested above, the traditional distinction between normative and nonnormative (empirical) discourse is based on unsupportable theories of meaning. Objectivist approaches to normative discourse fail, as we have seen, because of their exclusive focus on the referral function of utterances and because of their oversimplified notion of what it means for a term or expression to refer to something. As Wittgenstein and Austin, among others, have shown, the relationship between speech and phenomena is complex. The positions on normative discourse discussed thus far break down because words—ethical terms and expressions among others—cannot be understood outside of the rhetorical context in which they are used. We must therefore consider approaches to normative discourse that take account of the multiple functions performed by utterances. There are at least two that attempt to transcend the inadequacies of previous approaches by building on Austin's conception of a speech-act or performative utterance. One is prescriptivism, a position taken and elaborated by R. M. Hare, and another is descriptivism, adopted by a variety of ethical theorists, including John Searle, whose contribution is especially worth considering.[22] Searle has made a controversial assault on Hume's is–ought distinction, arguing that one *can* validly derive an "ought" statement without the benefit of initial normative premises. Although, I hope, the discussion thus far has sufficiently impugned the very enterprise of emphasizing different kinds of statements, Searle's suggested derivation provides a convenient vehicle for considering the descriptivist and prescriptivist positions on normative discourse.[23]

1. Jones uttered the words "I hereby promise to pay you, Smith, five dollars."
2. Jones promises to pay Smith five dollars.
3. Jones places himself under (undertook) an obligation to pay Smith five dollars.
4. Jones is under an obligation to pay Smith five dollars.
5. Jones ought to pay Smith five dollars.

Searle points out that the derivation does not operate under a situation of strict entailment, but, he asserts, the statement after the first could be logically derived from prior statements that are not evaluative. One would, for example, add an assumption about English usage that would go between statements 1 and 2. This is offered by Searle as statement 1a, "Under certain conditions anyone who utters the words (sentence) 'I hereby promise to pay you, Smith, five dollars' promises to pay Smith five dollars."

There has been a considerable response to Searle's derivation, some of which helps to elucidate both the descriptivist and prescriptivist positions. Here, I shall focus on selective aspects of the arguments involved. It is important to note, first, that statement 1 should be understood in the context of Austin's notion of a speech-act. Accordingly, Searle considers the statement a performative utterance, that is, the emphasis is illocutionary (what the speaker is doing *in* making the statement). So the promise mentioned in the statement is to be regarded as an action, not as a description of a mental state or of some noises that came out of Jones's mouth. Second, the conditions mentioned in statement 1a are those that must obtain for the statement to be felicitous, that is, because as Austin has shown, saying something does not make it so, the words must be uttered under the appropriate circumstances for the action (promising) to take effect.

Given, then, the Austinian account of statement 1, and the implication that the action does not misfire—that it was executed under appropriate circumstances—the derivation has to be valid as far as Jones is concerned. When he produced the speech-act (statement 1) he committed himself or placed himself under an obligation. When he issued the utterance, he constituted a promising game and is therefore bound by the rules of the game. A disinterested reader of the derivation, however, might ask if it is necessary for anyone besides Jones to accept statement 5, the ultimate ought statement in the derivation, on the basis of nothing but what is internal to the derivation. Searle's critics have argued, for example, that an acceptance of the 'ought' conclusion requires the additional acceptance of the institution of promising. But Searle rejects this contention, arguing that the derivation is valid whatever one's opinion is of the institution of promising. In his defense, Searle emphasizes that statement 1 is not merely a description of Jones's behavior. Rather, it is a statement of an "institutional fact" (note the discussion of Anscombe's distinction between brute and institutional facts in chapter 2). Searle's point is that as soon as we agree that the *meaning* of statement 1 involves the action by Jones of constituting a promising game, we must accept the rest of the derivation. This is no more than what is involved when we accept any statement of fact, that is, we presume that the rules which constitute something as a fact are correct or appropriate. Hare, nevertheless, in a critique of Searle's derivation, argues that the interpretation of statement 1 on the basis of the notion of institutional facts, does not obviate the need for the additional prescription that promises ought to be kept if the derivation is to work.[24]

The controversy between Hare and Searle on this issue reflects the general disagreement between prescriptivists and descriptivists over the meaning of moral judgments. Hare's prescriptivism is based on his distinction between the prescriptive and descriptive meaning of an utterance. He views the descriptive meaning of an utterance as being governed by criteria of application because of its referral function, while the prescriptive meaning is based on the referral to standards of the statement, which, according to Hare, cannot wholly be defended by reasons. Descriptivists argue, against the Hare position, that descriptions are not the only linguistic functions having criteria of application. They regard all the elements in moral terms and expressions as having a meaning and application that depend on the context or game they evoke (as, for example, Searle's promising game). Therefore, they argue, the understanding of moral discourse must be based on a search for the appropriate games which the terms and expressions in moral arguments constitute. They argue, further, that one need not simply relate the moral judgments to standards for which one cannot evince cognitive support, as does Hare.

But Hare's position is not based on the kind of psychological theory of meaning employed by emotivists. Like descriptivists, he rejects emotivism because it is based on an inadequate theory of meaning. He regards moral judgments as rule-governed, linguistic performances not simply as persuasive utterances. The primary performance or action involved in a moral judgment, according to Hare, is the act of prescribing. To understand his notion of prescribing, we must consider his distinction between what he calls the 'neustics' and 'phrastics' of an utterance. The phrastic in a sentence is the phrase that refers to what the sentence is about, and the neustic is the indication of what is being said about the phrastic. For example, in the statement "The United States ought to keep out of the domestic affairs of other nations," the phrastics refer to the objects and situations involved in the utterance, that is, the United States, other nations, and domestic affairs. The neustic element in this case is the structure of the relationship between the phrastic elements which produce the prescription about how the United States should act. For Hare, then, moral judgments, taken as a whole, are prescriptions, and prescriptions have criteria of application because of their phrastic element.

Descriptivists disagree with Hare in that they see the nonphrastic element of an utterance as having criteria of application also. The descriptivist has been defined by Hudson as "one who holds at least these two opinions: (i) that it is not always logically possible to separate the descriptive and evaluative meanings of a moral judgment; and (ii) that the criteria applied in moral judgments are *not* in the last analysis merely a matter of free choice."[25] Descriptivists are not ultimately arguing that there is an objective basis for moral judgments. They are, in effect, locating their subjectivism or, better, their interpretive element, in a different place than either emotivists or prescriptivists. They locate it in the selection of games or contexts for interpreting and giving meaning to moral judgments. They emphasize, however, that the rules which give utterances meaning are not pragmatic in the narrow, psychological sense, that is, arbitrarily or purposively employed by the speaker making a moral judgment. Rather, they are semantic rules that function in the context of a linguistic community as a whole. Descriptivists agree with prescriptivists that moral judgments refer to principles or standards among other things, but they argue that ordinary descriptions also refer to principles or standards in the same way that moral judgments do. So descriptivists like Searle take the position that moral arguments can be distinguished from nonmoral, descriptively oriented utterances or sets of utterances in the *way* that rules or principles are stressed, not because they are involved.

Whatever position we adopt on whether Searle's derivation is successful, and, as we have seen, such a position must be based on a complex interpretation of the role of standards, the descriptivist position underlying his interpretation of the meaning of the statements in the derivation brings us toward an understanding of moral discourse that accords with contemporary functional theories of meaning. In arguing for the validity of his derivation, Searle, armed with Austin's critique of descriptive statements, notes that the traditional view of arguments beginning with purely descriptive premises fails to take account of the extent to which prior principles underlying such premises are involved. When we say, for example, that someone has made a promise, we are not merely denoting an object or situation by selecting the words that go with or correlate with the appropriate observation. Rather, we are making a judgment about conditions under which it is reasonable to ascribe the idea of promising to a particular series of behaviors and thereby to regard those behaviors as constituting the act of promising. From Searle's perspective, then, it makes no sense to be concerned about deriving an "ought" from an "is" because the boundary between the two is a matter of emphasis. The conclusion about Jones's obligation in statement 5 of the derivation follows from the rules we evoke in a statement like 1, which is an institutional fact about what Jones did in making the utterance which involved promising. When we move to statement 2 and call the speech-act, the making of promise, we are using rules or standards to ascribe the action of promising to Jones's utterance.

In effect, then, Searle's approach to speech-acts, based on Austin's notion of performative utterances and Anscombe's notion of institutional facts, accords with C. I. Lewis's position quoted above, which concludes with the argument that the question is not whether we can derive an "ought" from an "is" but whether it is possible to establish any position on "what is" without, at the same time, affirming the validity of prior normative principles.

What kind of metaethical position remains? It is clear that the moral judgments common to normative discourse cannot be understood by reducing them to statements of fact, whether the facts are natural, as in the naturalist metaethical position, or nonnatural, as in the metaethical position of intuitionists. It is also clear that a psychological or causal interpretation, such as that supplied by emotivists, is inadequate. The foregoing analysis has shown that moral judgments, like any kind of utterance, must be understood in terms of the functions they perform, on the basis of what is being done *in* and *by* making the utterance as well as on the basis of the content and/or referents of the utterance. Moral judgments contain various different levels of meaning. They involve an action on the part of the speaker, they refer to both objects and situations and to principles (in a complex and interconnected way), and they have affective significance, that is, depending on their context and emphasis, they produce attitudes in the hearers as well as expressing those of the speaker. In addition, their meaning is controlled in part by the other utterances to which they are related in a justificatory system of statements.

Because moral judgments and other kinds of statements such as descriptions differ in emphasis rather than kind, that is, they are all related to experience through the prior prescriptions involved in normative standards, the relevant question is, Why are some utterances expressed in a descriptively oriented mode whereas others are expressed in a more normatively oriented mode? To understand this we can reflect on the fact that since all meaningful statements, whether normative or empirical in their orientation, involve at least implicit norms, what must therefore distinguish a normative statement or moral judgment is the *explicit* reference to a normative standard or an obligation. When a speaker selects a normative mode for an utterance, he or she must therefore be doing so on the basis of an assumption that the norms or principles involved are controversial or ought to be regarded as controversial. Thus, for example, when someone says, "You ought to put that on the table over there," a variety of normative principles is involved, but the speaker is selecting only some of them out for emphasis. There seems to be a presumption in such a statement that there is a problematic choice of rules about where the thing referred to by 'that' should be put. The speaker could amplify the normative orientation of the statement by treating other implicit norms explicitly. For example, the thing identified as a table is so identified on the basis of a norm or set of norms that distinguish various objects as tables or nontables. Were the speaker to assume that *these* norms could be regarded as problematic in this case, the statement might go as follows: "You ought to put that on what we should regard as a table over there." So normative discourse is discourse containing an explicit recognition of potential disagreement over standards for both regarding and for acting. All empirically oriented discourse is thus potentially normative in that the norms implicit in the identification of objects and situations can be selected out for special emphasis; they can be treated as controversial.

This analysis of normative discourse points to a need for thinking anew about the relationship between normative and empirical political inquiry and theory. When one is involved in what would ordinarily be regarded as a wholly empirical analysis of political relationships, i.e., when no normatively oriented statements are used, the presumption is that the theorist is treating the image of persons and of society and the polity that provide the context for the analysis as unproblematic and is treating the norms implicit in the measurements or concept–data linkages as similarly unproblematic (except from a technical standpoint). The theorist, in such an analysis, is thus committed to the idea that the rules governing the formation of both the concepts which are involved in the analysis and the norms or standards involved in indicating what aspects of experience should be regarded as being referenced by those concepts, are not a part of the subject of analysis. A justification of any or all of these norms would ultimately involve one in a moral argument for a way of life, including images and models of persons and of interpersonal relations.

One can always extend or reorient analysis and treat the rules or norms that underlie the concepts in the analysis as part of the subject matter. This is the case for Michel Foucault, who orients his inquiries almost exclusively toward the political significance of the implicit rule structures that gives rise to the identification of various objects and situations which receive attention by a particular discipline, profession, or administrative grouping. In his analysis of the development of clinical medicine, for example, he has shown how the objects emerging in the discourses of professionals were based on the political decisions prescribing relationships among guilds, universities, public assistance, doctors, and more.[26] Thus whether it is explicitly recognized or not, someone doing a typical empirical political analysis of the relationship between, say, the activities of a legislature and the public interest selects a conception of the public interest, based on implicit norms that prescribe what are to be regarded as the legitimate boundaries of the public as opposed to the private domain. Such normative boundaries inevitably emerge from various past political decisions about relationships among various individuals and groups within the society. Were the theorist to assume that the norms regarding how to conceive of the public domain are controversial, the analysis might begin with an explicitly normative argument about where public versus private boundaries ought to be drawn and what aspects of persons should be assumed in the development of those boundaries. In the context of such a normative interest, the theorist might then be encouraged to ask a Foucault-type question about *why* various objects and events tend to emerge in given periods as foci of analysis, as well as being concerned with what they ought to be. One way to highlight the conventions that constitute prevailing models of public life in the United States is to examine changes in the structure of the public–private distinction over time. For example, throughout most of American history, the dominant model of public life for economic, sociological, political, and even to some extent psychological, disciplines has been based on economic productivity as the major attribute of persons' public existence. An alternative or complementary attribute that might best be termed "emotionalism"—the tendency for one's empathic responses to push out exchange- or economically oriented (or more generally rational in the narrow, economic sense) motivation—is almost never regarded as a "competence," that is, as an attribute of a person that ought to be publicly taken account of as a social, psychological, or political resource. To view the significance of this in the policy process, imagine a situation in which public funding for education is under consideration. In such a case, an argument about how to enhance a person's future productivity would be regarded as relevant, whereas one about how to enhance a person's emotionalism would not. The discourse within which improvement of person's capacities is embedded, moreover, might all be empirically oriented, because it is unlikely that there would be, in any American public forum, a controversy about the value of economic productivity or any doubt that such a 'capacity' was the major reference of general terms referring to persons' enhancement.

Perhaps as there becomes a significant increase in the prestige and demand for therapeutic processes, persons with an abundance of emotionalism will be regarded as possessing a public commodity. At least, during a transition period in which structural changes, such as increasing urbanization and its attendant alienation and social dislocation, affect conceptions about what should be regarded as requiring collective, public attention, what was once empirically oriented would become normatively oriented. In such a period, one would expect to see the concept of the public domain involved in more normatively oriented arguments.

The normative dimension of political inquiry thus lurks beneath any supposedly empirical analysis, for any political theory, whether or not it is expressed in normatively oriented language, relies on norms or principles providing the boundaries that shape the reality toward which the theory is directed. The metaethical position known as descriptivism is a framework within which we can understand the way that normative and empirical discourse blend into one another. A useful way to regard political theories is to consider them as articulated at two levels, implicit and explicit. The substance of the theory at the implicit level is the set of rules or norms that constitute the concepts and experiential identifications whose interrelationships are treated in the explicit statements of the theory. To analyze a theory at this implicit level might, among other things, take the form of raising questions about the social, political, and economic conditions which give rise to and support such norms. Such an analysis is directed, in effect, toward the question, Why do these things mean what they mean? and involves reflecting back on what we say rather than treating what we speak about, as though it is found rather than constituted by our discursive practices. By raising questions about the constitutive norms for the concepts in an empirical theory, one shifts the emphasis of the inquiry in a normative direction and, at the same time, comprehends additional aspects of social and political relationships. When, on the other hand, one's attention is focused exclusively on the explicit statement in a theory, the theoretical inquiry becomes altogether empirically oriented. To be so oriented is to decide not to reflect further on relationships or data of human experience presupposed in what is said in the statements of the theory.

Thus the discourses employed in normative and empirical political inquiries are very similar. To the extent that we can distinguish them, we must rely on the emphasis, not the particular terms employed. The value of this insight, which is made to emerge after an inquiry into various metaethical accounts of the status of normative discourse, amounts to more than simply being in a position to evaluate various models of moral judgment or various positions on the normative–empirical distinction. We should now be able to see that there is an important level of human relationships (sociopolitical relations) that we can treat as a subject of inquiry. This level is sequestered in speech–phenomena relationships, whatever the kind of discourse those relationships are in. In the next chapter on human action, the significance of this level should be more apparent. In subsequent chapters, the focus will be increasingly on how to orient political inquiry to exploit this level of human relationships so that it contributes to our understanding of politics.

The Problem of Human Action

The Symmetry of Natural and Social Science

For decades, social scientists and philosophers who are interested in metascientific issues have regarded as fundamental the question, Are the norms of science, particularly those related to the problem of causal inference, the same for the natural and the social sciences? A major tenet of the Vienna positivists was that they are. Otto Neurath, for example, argued that nothing inherent in the subject matter of a discipline like sociology marks it for different explanatory treatment from how one would approach problems of explanation in physics. Whatever the discipline, said Neurath, the task is always to "predict individual events or certain groups of events." For Neurath, as for other positivists of the unificationist persuasion, to explain something is to establish correlations, irrespective of the particular subject matter that yields up the variable to be correlated. As he wrote, "No matter whether one is investigating the statistical behavior of atoms, plants or animals, the methods employed in establishing correlations are always the same."[1]

There is a variety of arguments deployed against this position, which is still defended by contemporary empiricists. One of the most common is also the most easily dismissed. It is the argument that a science of human behavior similar to the sciences developed to explain the behavior of inanimate objects cannot be successfully established, because we can never be sure of predicting the behavior of individual persons. According to this position, persons can make a variety of unexpected choices, thereby fouling up any theory invented to account for their behavior. Neurath and others have pointed out that this argument is based on a misconception of the way that ordinary scientific theories in the natural sciences perform. He noted that a piece of paper blowing in the wind is unpredictable, but we have, nevertheless, well-developed sciences of kinematics, climatology, and meteorology. They account for the behavior of the paper, even though they do not always provide a way to predict its precise movement.[2] Similarly on the basis of well-established scientific theories, we can account for aspects of human conduct, even though the precise prediction of the behavior of each person eludes us. It should also be noted that whether a scientific theory is predicting "successfully" can only be reasonably assayed in the context of some level of prediction that a given theory provides. For example, we can accurately predict the temperature at which the water in a kettle will begin bubbling, for a given altitude, on the basis of scientific theory, but we cannot predict the precise movements of each of the bubbles. And, finally, some theories in the sciences provide very powerful explanatory accounts even though they cannot be used to predict anything, as in the case of the theory of evolution that accounts for what has happened but leaves the future to the interaction of what Monod has called "chance and necessity."[3]

What makes a science a science, in short, whatever its subject matter, is not its degree of predictive success—prediction is only one important kind of validating device and only one kind of use to which scientific theories are put—but the standards governing its structure and application. A social scientist is no less a scientist because of failing to predict precisely the behavior of every person to whom his or her theory applies. If, on the basis of a theory, a social scientist claims to know that persons engaged in moralistic social movements (e.g., prohibition groups) are more likely to accept a symbolic victory (e.g., the passage of an unenforceable law) than those engaged in interest-oriented social movements (e.g., civil-rights groups), the claim would be based on inductive and deductive inferences, attention to problems of reliability, validity, and so on, not on the expectation that the attitude of every individual involved in a social movement can be correctly predicted.

There is a second, not easily dismissed, argument against the symmetry thesis. This is based on the observation that human beings, unlike the kind of entities whose behavior is explained by theories in the natural sciences, have their own accounts of what they are doing. Some argue that these accounts that persons have of what they are doing are more than a post hoc rationalizations. They are, rather, what must be included in any valid explanation of what people can be observed to do. The model underlying this position on explanation is that persons' actions depend on their "intentions," which account for their resulting behavior or, preferably, "actions" (behaviors that are intended). Moreover, those with this position argue that this kind of account in terms of purposes or intentions is incompatible with the kind of causal accounts used in the natural sciences to explain inanimate objects. Some thinkers who have supported this incompatibility thesis have argued that because the understanding of human conduct requires interpretation in order to comprehend what persons do, the human sciences are essentially interpretive, requiring a Verstehen or interpretive-understanding approach rather than an Erklären or causal-explanatory approach in the inductive generalization mode that is familiar in the natural sciences.[4]

This second attack on the symmetry thesis focuses on the problem of the *meaning* of a person's behavior. Max Weber called attention to the problem of meaning in the explanation of human action by distinguishing what he called "direct observational understanding of the subjective meaning of a given act" from "explanatory understanding," which is the meaning that an actor attaches to what he or she is doing.[5] Following Weber's discussion of "explanatory understanding," both those supporting the symmetry thesis and those supporting an asymmetry thesis have tended to distinguish actions from mere behaviors, agreeing that human action is behavior in the context of the 'motives' the actor has for behaving in a particular way. For example, May Brodbeck, who is generally considered a naturalist (one who regards causal explanation in the natural sciences as the appropriate model for the social sciences), calls an action "any bit of behavior whose complete description requires, in addition to manifest behavior, either of such things as the persons' motives, intentions and thoughts or of such things as moral, legal, or conventional standards or rules."[6]

What distinguishes the position of antinaturalists, who also regard human action as behavior in the context of motives or intentions, is their insistence that any valid explanation of human conduct *must* include an account of the motives or intentions involved, and their position that such an account differs in structure from ordinary causal accounts used in the natural sciences. This leads many of this persuasion to argue that different methods are appropriate for the human sciences, since the observational and experimental approaches developed in the physical sciences cannot discern the in-process motivations that give meaning to behavior. These motivations they understand not as effective causes of behavior but as reasons for behaving that represent the actor(s) goals or ends-in-view.

In general, then, the disagreement is not so much over the validity of distinguishing action from behavior, at least on the surface, as it is over the role that the meaning of behavior must play in an understanding of why persons do what they do. Part of the issue can be clarified if we note that different kinds of "why" questions can be raised about human conduct and, correspondingly, different senses of the notion of understanding conduct.[7] Those leaning toward the naturalist or symmetry thesis have argued that there are many situations in which motives are causes in the ordinary sense.[8] They have argued, further, that there are acceptable explanations of human conduct that do not take account of the motives or intentions of the participants involved. Ayer, for example, has asserted that motivated action is rule following, that is, that there are normative criteria applicable in recovering the meaning of the conduct involved. But this presents no problem in explaining what has been done, contrary to the suggestion of various antinaturalists. Ayer suggests that it is simply a matter of explaining something first, and then, if one is interested in the motives and therefore the meaning of the conduct, one can judge it once it is explained.[9] Brodbeck argues similarly than an explanation of something need not address the rules giving it meaning. Like Ayer, she implies that we can explain something independently of its meaning, as in her example of explaining the simple behavior of a person walking down a street. This can be explained, she states, "without taking note that the person walking is doing so in order to mail a letter," for what is presently observed is the same. To speak of the intention in such a case, according to Brodbeck, is to speak about what is to occur later as the action is concluded.[10]

But the problem is more complex than either Ayer or Brodbeck suggests. Reconciling a standard causal account with the concept of human action involves more than simply a careful separation of present and future times in the action process as Brodbeck suggests, and it is misleading to separate explanation and evaluation as Ayer suggests. When a person's movement is observed, it is a matter of problematic interpretation to determine *what* is being observed. Even in the physical sciences, for that matter, observation is not construed as record sense data. For example, a different causal explanation is probably warranted for understanding why a person is walking down the street rather than taking public transportation than would be appropriate for understanding why a person is walking down *this* street rather than some other street. A choice of what is to be explained, moreover, might not involve the walkers' intentions (reaching a destination or otherwise), because one can construct the "meaning" of walking down a street within frames of reference whose defining norms are not affected by the perspective of the actor. Therefore, because describing and interpreting are always conjoined, meaning and explanation are interdependent. Ayer and Brodbeck were thrown off, no doubt, by the overly mentalistic accounts of what gives meaning to conduct, for many argue that the meaning of human conduct resides in the subjective experience of the actor. If we are concerned with this kind of meaning (experiential meaning), Ayer and Brodbeck are correct in asserting that this can be dealt with as a separate issue, at least with respect to the kind of explanatory accounts that interest them. But if we treat the meaning of human conduct as residing in the rules that persons are following, that is, as a matter of rule-governed interpretation, whatever the actors' subjective experience may be, meaning and explanation cannot be separated.

Some approaches to the concept of action distinguish observations of behavior or movement from the interpretation of the meaning of that behavior, but to do this is just as misleading as it is to separate explanation and evaluation because, as Shwayder has pointed out, the reporting of observed movements "incorporates explanations." He notes that even the seemingly simple report than an animal "twitched" incorporates the idea that the movement was made involuntarily, in response to an internal neurological stimulation. Interpretation is thus omnipresent, rendering it inappropriate to separate out a special case of mere behaviors or movements as though they are not actions because they have no meaning. Not everything a person does, however, is an action. Shwayder notes, for example, that "stumbling is not an action, though pretending to stumble is."[11] To regard an agent as involved in an action is therefore to ascribe responsibility to the agent. This action–responsibility relationship is complex, however, and will be treated at length below. At this point it is important to understand that interpretation is inextricably linked to any observation of what is done.

We can often see the kind of role that interpretation plays in the explanation of conduct by examining a controversial case. Such a case is exemplified in Freud's essay on Michelangelo's Moses. Most interpretations of the statue before Freud's assumed that Moses is portrayed at the moment that he had seen his people worshiping the golden calf. This assumption was based on the facial expression and the position of the body. It appeared to these observers that Moses is shown to be about to leap to his feet in anger and dash the tablets bearing the Ten Commandments to the ground. Freud's "observations," however, are quite different from this standard version. Judging from the position of the body and the way that the tablets are being supported, he argues, Michelangelo's Moses is portrayed at the moment *after* a movement has already taken place. "What we see before us," says Freud, "is not the inception of a violent action but the remains of a movement that has already taken place."[12] What Freud saw before him as he viewed the statue was based on his knowledge of where the statue was to appear (as one of the many figures adorning the tomb of Pope Julius II), on the position of the tablets being held (upside down, an aspect not noticed or mentioned by other commentators), as well as the position of the rest of the figure, on the character of the pope for whom the sculpture was being executed, and finally, on the relationship that had obtained between Michelangelo and Pope Julius. So what the statue was "doing" or was about to do is more than a matter of unproblematic observation.

The same case must be made with respect to the conduct of "real" people. We must invoke a variety of rules or conventions to determine what we are observing, because what we observe is a "that" by virtue of a complex interpretation. Even when what is seen appears to be relatively unproblematic, for example, the biting of a thumb:

> "Do you bit your thumb at us, Sir?"
> "I do bite my thumb, Sir."

One must identify what has taken place in the process of deciding how to explain it. One might employ a causal explanation that is either anatomical or psychological in content to account for the biting of a thumb—it could be treated as a reaction to pain in the former case or a satisfaction of oral needs in the latter—whereas if the thumb biting is interpreted, as in the above quote from Shakespeare's *Romeo and Juliet*, as the delivering of an insult, the causal explanation could be historical, sociological, and so on. Clearly the appropriateness of one versus another explanation, in the ordinary causal sense of explanation, depends on *what* is observed. This reveals that the shortcoming of the naturalist approach to explaining social phenomena is not that ordinary causal explanation is inappropriate for dealing with the subject matter of human conduct. The problem is that naturalists have failed to deal adequately with the rules or norms constituting what is there to be explained. These rules, as the above example suggests, must be constituted as a guide to applying a causal explanation, not supplied post hoc as additional interpretive material.

The Phenomenological Alternative

We can now ask how inquiry into human conduct must be reoriented if one accepts the view that interpretation and causal explanation are compatibly interrelated in producing comprehension of human action. One answer is suggested by Schutz, who argued that the explanation of human conduct must be based on an interpretation of the motives (in the sense of reasons) that a person has for doing what is done. From Schutz's perspective, the thumb-biting incident in *Romeo and Juliet* constitutes the delivering of an insult if the thumb biter intended or planned the insult. Schutz therefore elevates the interpretations of the actors themselves to an epistemologically privileged position. Methods of inquiry that follow from this position must therefore be oriented toward recovering the motives of the actors. As has been noted above, Schutz states this methodological norm as the "postulate of subjective interpretation." "In order to explain human actions the scientist has to ask what model of a human mind can be constructed and what typical contents must be attributed to it in order to explain the observed facts and the result of the activity of such a mind in an understandable relation. The compliance with the postulate warrants the feasibility of referring all kinds of human action or their result to the subjective meaning such an action or result of an action had for the actor."[13]

Schutz's reference to the "subjective meaning of an action" is somewhat misleading, because what constitutes human action for Schutz is conduct "devised in advance," and he carefully distinguishes conduct from behavior, regarding conduct as involving subjectively meaningful experience. Thus, for Schutz, the defining characteristics of action are its being (1) subjectively meaningful and (2) oriented toward a future, preconceived goal or state of affairs (in Schutz's terms, a "preconceived project"). To determine, therefore, what an action *is* within Schutz's framework is to determine, among other things, its subjective meaning for the actor. The social scientist seeking to explain human conduct is thus faced with the interpretive task of determining what the action is. To say that the social scientist must determine the "subjective meaning of the action" is inappropriate, for the concept of subjective meaning is immanent in the interpretation of what the action is. The action does not, therefore, stand apart from its subjective meaning.

Schutz's emphasis on subjectivity appears to be a highly psychologized perspective on action, for he frequently invokes mentalistic metaphors when referring to meaning. He speaks, for example, of what the actor "has in mind" by way of a preconceived project. But in such places, Schutz is not referring only to experiential meaning, that is, the feelings that persons have which accompany what they do. Rather, he is referring to the thought objects or constructs that persons have which preselect and interpret their experience. These thought objects are the above-mentioned "motives" that the social scientist/observer must interpret to understand human action. For Schutz there are, however, two kinds of motives. The projected thought objects, which represent the meaning of conduct "devised in advance," are what Schutz calls "in-order-to motives." These he contrasts with "because-of motives" which he views as antecedent conditions that account for the kinds of projects the actor selects.

So, for example, if we say, "He is offering you a ride in order to have a chance to speak to you privately," we are speaking of "in-order-to motives." If instead we say, "He offers people rides because his parents taught him to be generous," we are speaking of "because-of motives." To develop an adequate explanation of human action, according to Schutz, the social scientist must invent "typifications" of the in-order-to motives that the actor(s) use to constitute their experience, and, select among alternative courses of action as well as understanding the because-of motives which motivate the action(s) in a causal sense. Having emphasized the importance of the *two* kinds of motives, however, the major orientation of Schutz's discussion of social inquiry is on the interpretation of in-order-to motives. These motives constitute what Schutz calls the "subjective meaning of action" (even though, as noted above, this is redundant). The because-of motives, which involve events prior to the action and are not directly cognized by the actor, constitute, for Schutz, the "objective meaning" of the action.

In developing the subjective significance of action, his primary interest, Schutz distinguishes two ways of looking at the world. In the first, the meaning of one's experience is abstracted from its genesis. The world as preconstituted is thus taken for granted, so one does not see that it is constituted as it is by one's "intentionality." This position is obviously influenced by the Husserlian development of the intentionality concept, but Schutz, unlike Husserl, is primarily concerned with the sociology of consciousness rather than with a philosophy of mind. His emphasis is therefore not on the acts of imagining by which, according to Husserl, persons constitute a world of meaningful objects but rather on the "typifications" through which persons experience others. Because he regards these typifications, whereby one interprets the conduct of others, as the basis for one's sharing a world in which there are typical modes of conduct, he ends up constructing a model of the social science observer as one who must construct typifications that accord with those of the actors whose conduct is to be explained.

The second or reflexive look at the world, of which Schutz speaks, is but another element of his *social* phenomenology. In the first look at the world, the actor is not conscious of typifications. He or she takes the world as pre-given and formulates action projects in the process of living through experiences. In the second look, the actor turns consciousness inward, reflecting on his or her own intentionality or reality-constituting process. This look illuminates the subjective genesis of the meaning of experience, just as the intersubjective meaning of experience is illuminated by the social scientist/observer's conscious attention to the typifications she or he uses to interpret the conduct.

What, then, is the contribution of Schutz's approach to human action? Accepting interpretation as a necessary complement to the understanding of human conduct, Schutz illuminates the standpoint of the actor, showing how it provides evidence of what the action involved *is*. To study social behavior as a lived-through process one must, according to Schutz, interpret its subjective meaning in the individual's intentions. This emphasis on the subjective grounds of interpretation including both the typifications of the observer and the perspective of the actor(s) offers a radical contrast with the positivist/empiricist approach to human conduct. For positivists, subjective perspectives, whether the observer's or the actor's, are sources of bias rather than relevant data. Emphasizing the importance of objectivity, empiricist treatments of social science methodology place a premium on nonreactive or unobtrusive measurement devices. The meaning of what is observed should not be contaminated by the perspective of those who are being observed, for meaning, in the positivist tradition, is exhausted by the relationship between the concepts employed in the analysis and the observations to which those concepts refer, when they are given measurement criteria. Schutz, and others who advocate the phenomenological approach to human conduct place a premium on methods that involve empathy (in the sense of shared interpretations or typifications) between the investigator and the actor(s) whose conduct is to be explained or accounted for. The standpoint of the subject thus becomes an important part of the analysis rather than a potential bias to be avoided. This tradition, which yields methods oriented toward eliciting the subjective understanding of conduct, clearly rejects some aspects of the objectivity favored by positivist metascientific positions.

There is an important limitation to Schutz's perspective, however, particularly for one interested in the political significance of human action. His emphasis on the subjective grounds of action makes it difficult to construct a model of social/political reality that captures the conflicts of value, interest, and authority which are involved in legitimating a particular standpoint on human action and thus a particular meaning account of conduct. By insisting, through his postulate of adequacy, that the social science theorist must provide a perspective on action that is congruent with the subjective perspective of the actor, Schutz neglects the various structural/ideological perspectives from which one could discuss the meaning of conduct with attention to its *consequences*.[14] This limitation is especially evident in Schutz's discussion of equality. There he explicitly notes that the social science observer must construct a philosophical anthropology to create a standpoint on the human condition on which to predicate a discussion of equality. But rather than indicating how one could justify a position on one versus another model of equality, he becomes enmeshed in the subjective standpoint, arguing that even if, from the observer's standpoint, equality of opportunity seems to exist in a society, persons' subjective chances may be unequal because of the kinds of typifications they use to understand.[15] This may be a valid "empirical" point, but the *meaning* of equality relates to structures and justifications of human association that go beyond the perceptions of the individual. To ascribe equality or inequality to a given social system involves interpretations based on the prejudgments and standards of the ascriber, not just on what one thinks is perceived by the citizens.

In the ethnomethodological approach of Garfinkel, whose perspective was also influenced by Husserl's phenomenology, there is a withdrawal from Schutz's almost exclusive emphasis on the subjective meaning of action. Influenced by both Husserlian phenomenology and the Wittgensteinian approach to language, Garfinkel approaches the meaning of a person's conduct from the standpoint of subjectivity. His concept of rationality, accordingly, is understood as the relationship between persons' behavior and their "accountability projects" (a process rather than a means-ends rationality).[16] But at the same time, he focuses on the *situations* of actions, the situations that give actions their meanings as publicly interpreted linguistic forms. Like Wittgenstein, Garfinkel approaches the meaning of statements in terms of their location in ordinary speech. Departing from the tradition that seeks meaning in the logical and structural properties of language, Garfinkel sees meaning as inhering in the context within which statements and actions are produced, that is to say, in the location of the speakers/actors, the life situations within which they find themselves.

But Garfinkel's approach to meaning, while departing somewhat from the Schutzian preoccupation with the standpoint of the ego, still fails to address the standpoint of the observer and the problems of interpretation attaching thereto. He explains decision making, for example, as "the process whereby actors produce and manage settings of organized, everyday affairs."[17] In this process, he argues, their management is identical with their procedures for making those settings "accountable." But Garfinkel's emphasis on this process neglects an external standpoint from which one could characterize what is happening with this or that aspect of human conduct. Ethnomethodology ends up providing an elucidation of various islands of conduct that have meaning with respect to various individual, process-oriented rationalities. But Garfinkel's norm of ethnomethodological indifference explicitly rejects a standpoint on collective rationality that we as observers can use to create implicitly an archipelago of the individual islands and to impute significance not only to episodes of purpose behavior, that is, situations in which actors regard themselves as involved in decisions, but also, and more importantly, to episodes of nonchoice in which persons are continuously involved by virtue of their affiliation with the symbolizing system that constitutes their world of objects and situations. In Garfinkel's model of human conduct is a keen appreciation of the social context within which individual actors understand themselves and their projects. The accountability models that actors evoke are not merely personal constructs. They are selected from the collective context in which they function. Although Garfinkel's insights help us to understand human decision making and emancipate us from a misleading and restrictive construal of rationality, they nevertheless fail to provide us with a self-understanding of what we, as investigators, contribute to what we understand.

To understand better the limitation of phenomenological social science, at least as it has been developed under the influence of Schutz and Garfinkel, we can use a distinction that Schutz has made between action and act. Acts, for Schutz are accomplishments. They are, in effect, completed performances. "Action is the execution of a projected act."[18] This "action" is what Schutz focuses on almost exclusively in his analysis of the meaning of human conduct, which accounts for his emphasis on subjectivity. When one becomes interested in acts, in meaningful accomplishments, clearly it is necessary to deal with meanings other than what the actor has projected as the end-in-view. Schutz himself recognized this. He simply failed to promote an analysis of the meaning of acts that would complement his fascination with the subjective meaning of action as conduct carried out with projected acts in the minds of the actors. In the final analysis, Schutz's position is as ideologically obtuse as that of the empiricists in that he shares their commitment to a construction of the social scientist as a disinterested observer. If one focuses, as Schutz does, on intentional action, understood as how the actor typifies his or her conduct, it becomes necessary to see the observer as one who must invent typifications that accord with those of the actor(s). The observer can have an "objective" view in such circumstances because, as Schutz notes, there can be only one subjective meaning for an action. When one is interested in acts, however, it becomes a problem to select an interpretation or meaning to ascribe, for the meaning must be embedded in an ideological model of consequences, a view of what a society is, a view that therefore involves commitments to rules for individual and collective rationality.

The difference between Schutz's approach to human action and the analysis of human action offered by language analysts hinges on the difference between actions in progress (what Schutz calls the lived-through experiences oriented toward the subject's projected act) and acts (accomplishments). As linguistic analysts tend to understand it, the problem of action is concerned with what Schutz calls acts. They emphasize what might appropriately be said about what has been done, recognizing that ascriptions as to what has been done are not controlled by the intentions or plans of actors. The issue of what controls the meaning of action in progress as compared with actions that have been completed has been illuminated by Ricoeur,[19] who predicates his analysis on the difference between speech and writing. In speech, which Ricoeur regards as "discourse" (the actualization of language), the subjective intention of the author/speaker coincides with the meaning. Once we have a "text," something that has *been* said, the author's intention is no longer controlling. As Ricoeur puts it," the text's career escapes the finite horizon lived by its author." "Action-events", according to Ricoeur, can be distinguished similarly. There are actions which are ongoing, intentional processes with subjective meaning, but one can also ask how action is "fixed" the way that speech is fixed once it has been written. Once action is "inscribed," says Ricoeur, we have a problem of interpretation that transcends the subjective interpretation of the actor, just as texts outdistance the intention(s) of the writer. "In the same way that a text is detached from its author, an action is detached from its agent and develops consequences of its own."[20] Ricoeur refers to the "inscription" of actions as "depsychologizing" the action, carrying the action outside the interpretation of the actor into a field where multiple interpretations are possible. Like texts, human actions are subject, he states, to plurivocity, that is, one can linguistically construct them in a variety of ways. But the field of possible constructions is limited in that some interpretations are less valid than others. One can argue for some norms of ascription as being more plausible and reasonable than others.

It is especially important to note, however, that the procedure one employs to validate an ascription of action has a polemical dimension. To fix an interpretation, as Ricoeur points out, is to affirm what he calls a "possible world." This is yet another way of saying, as Wittgenstein did, that our statements have meaning within the context of a way of life or, in Heidegger's terms, a mode of being-in-the-world. So, as we move to the linguistic analyst's understanding of human action, we encounter a concern with the meaning of conduct from the viewpoint, not of the actors, but of a model of how the social world should be viewed as a context for constructing what has been done *after* conduct is deployed. Although linguistic analysts themselves have paid this issue little heed, I shall ultimately concern myself with a useful way of examining the content of the norms one can use to interpret human action, for the constitutive rules of actions are part of the rules by which collectivities are organized and are represented in the interpretations that constitute what we observe and what we say in constructing references to what we are speaking about. Persons do not move about in a field of meaning that is self-constituted. They engage in meaningful behavior (action) to the extent that they behave in accord with preexisting or preconstituted practices. Charles Taylor has said it well: "It is not just that people in our society all or mostly have a given set of ideas in their heads and subscribe to a given set of goals. The meanings and norms implicit in these practices are not just in the minds of the actors but are out there in the practices themselves, practices which cannot be conceived as a set of individual actions, but which are essentially modes of social relation, of mutual action."[21]

In summary, the subjectivism of some of those implementing their interpretation of the phenomenological approach to social inquiry does not provide an antidote for the positivist/empiricist failure to deal with the rules that give various behaviors meaning or significance as action. To clarify the issues involved in the explanation of human conduct, we must interrogate the linguistic meaning as developed by ordinary-language philosophers more closely, therefore, for the analysis of ordinary language developed by Oxford philosophers provides a framework for understanding the relationship between rules or conventions and meaning as it constitutes action.

Linguistic Analysis and Human Action

In his "Plea for Excuses," John Austin provides an important insight when he discusses the problem of speaking about what has in fact happened when, for example, we observe a man taking a woman's purse and walking off with it. Austin asks, "Should we say, are we saying, that he took her money or that he robbed her?" How can we decide what the action is? Here is clearly a situation in which the perspectives of the participants do not wholly, or even slightly, control the way we can appropriately speak about the episode. As observers, our ability to translate what we see into a finished statement that ascribes an action or actions to a sequence of behaviors depends on *our* acquaintance with the rules or conventions that produce actions within the social and cultural frame of reference of the participants. Of course there can be disagreements about what set of rules or norms should be employed to consitute an episode as involving one or another kind of action. Linguistic philosophers, relying on common or stock use of expressions, have tended to neglect the extent to which there is an "ownership of the means of enunciation,"[22] for there is a variety of interests implicit in the ordinary uses of expressions. One can use alternative rules of use that assume alternative ways of life that one might wish to promote rather than affirming an official ideology by accepting ordinary usage. This theme will be developed at greater length below. For present purposes, it is important to note that actions, in the sense of what we interpret as having-been-done, are determined by rules that do not necessarily coincide with what actors or participants think they are doing, and what rules are used involves an important political problem.

In Austin's example of the "purse snatching," although the participants' attitudes or motives and intentions are often part of the subject matter of these rules and conventions, we would rarely, if ever, decide, in a case like the one Austin suggests, what the purse taker was in fact doing simply on the basis of his report about what he thought he was doing or what he thought he was experiencing at the time he was doing it. We would, rather, determine what was done on the basis of the extent to which the behavior followed rules. If one of the rules necessary to call the episode a case of robbery happened to be a rule about intentions, an interrogation of the purse taker might be relevant but certainly not controlling as to whether we ascribed intention and thereby determined robbery as the appropriate characterization of the event.

When people do something, just as when people say something, what has happened or been said, as the case may be, is a product of more than what the actor or speaker has willed or intended to have happened or been expressed. This point was emphasized above in relation to the meaning of the concept of 'use' in theories of meaning developed by Wittgenstein and Austin, which locate the meaning of utterances in the use to which they are put. To speak of the ordinary use of a term, for example, "Priesthood," is to refer to the standard meaning it has, irrespective of the term's particular user. If the term is used in a standard way, it is used to designate a particular level of leadership in a religious organization. The particular aspect of the meaning of utterances is what has been explicated above as semantic meaning. However, an individual speaker, in given circumstances, might intend to produce an extraordinary effect with a term and might therefore employ it in a nonstandard way. So, for example, someone might use the expression "the medical priesthood." Those who use such expressions are not trying to identify religious leaders who used to be doctors or vice versa. They are probably using the idea of a priesthood to model a leadership situation that is extremely hierarchical and unsusceptible to claims from followers. In modeling medical leadership in such a fashion, they are undoubtedly using the term "priesthood" to argue that leadership in the medical profession has illegitimately removed itself from a positon whereby it might be reasonably responsive to its clientele or other groups who might seek to regulate medical or potentially medical issues. This latter use of a term or expression corresponds to what was described above as the pragmatic meaning of a term or expression. Pragmatic meaning is based on the individual use to which an expression is put by virtue of the particular intention or purposes of a given speaker. This kind of meaning of language that arises when the speaker uses terms or expressions in a nonstandard way has also been referred to as the occasion as opposed to the timeless meaning of utterances.[23]

Therefore, just as most speech is best understood by assuming that the terms are used in their ordinary way—that well established semantic rules are being followed—so most actions are best understood by assuming that they are the actions they are by virtue of the participants' following rules of conduct, whether or not they have the rules "in mind" as they engage in the activity. Most action is thus not purposive in a conscious, deliberative sense, just as most speech is not nonstandard pragmatically oriented utterances designed by the speaker to produce special effects. As Melden has pointed out, "most of the actions we perform are done without deliberation or choice."[24] They are actions (behaviors with meaning or significance) because we have learned to follow rules without having consciously to debate them, just as our speech has meaning because, having learned the semantic and syntatic rules for meaning discourse, we can be intelligible to others without weighing the possible meanings and positional structure of each term or expression we employ.

If we pursue the idea that what actors plan as their accomplishments does not wholly control what their actions become, we must reconstrue the concept of intention, for intentions are conceived by many as deliberate plans. Intention as it relates to the concept of action becomes clarified if we realize that the interpretation of someone's conduct, such that it becomes one or another kind of action, does not involve treating intentions as mental causes of the resulting behavior. Intention is ascribed as part of the interpretation that creates actions.

We can better understand what is involved with using intention ascriptively rather than causally to understand actions if we turn back to more of Austin's argument in his "Plea for Excuses." He pointed out there that sometimes we use modifications of expressions such as "He kicked her *on purpose*" (the "on purpose" here being a modification used to suggest intention) or "he left the room *impulsively*" (the "impulsively" being a modification also used to ascribe features of the kind of intention or choice involved in the action). We use such modifications, according to Austin, only when the action in question can be considered usual or untoward. Austin states the principle as, "No modification without aberration."[25] If Austin's observation is correct, there must be a role for intentions as a concept other than as a cause of behavior. Austin's analysis indicates that we take note of intentions in order to ascribe them to some kinds of behaviors, because we regard some behaviors as the kind of actions that involve the responsibility of the behaving agent, and we cannot decide what has been done without an attendant ascription of intention.

Thus our using intention to interpret and understand human action does not treat intentions as psychological causes of conduct. Psychological processes—motives, intentions, attitudes, and so on—can nevertheless, be treated as causes for persons' doing things. When they are so treated, the structure of explanation involved is the same as that which is familiar when we explain things in the physical sciences. But when we become interested in action, behavior that has a meaning by virtue of being embedded in a cultural, social, and political context, our interest can only be realized by our raising contextual questions in order to analyze or account for the action. Because we are never interested in pure behavior (in meaningless movement of persons), we are always making contextual assumptions, even when our analysis is wholly causal, because without such assumptions, it is not clear *what* we are explaining. To the extent that we want to regard the *what* (the action) as problematic, it becomes an explicit part of our analysis and we then must use a variety of concepts (intention among others) in a noncausal way before any kind of causal explanation can be usefully begun. When we treat concepts like intention in order to account for what action is involved in our analysis, we are concerned with mental events not as causes but as criteria for determining what rules should be involved to account for what has been done.

This treatment of intention as an ascription rather than a cause is presented systematically in H.L.A. Hart's controversial discussion of responsibility and rights. Hart's original thesis and the responses to it exemplify the solutions that come out of the ordinary-language tradition, which highlight the problems in understanding human action. Hart begins by discussing the role that ascriptions play in discourse, noting that "There are in our ordinary language sentences whose primary function is not to describe things, events or persons or anything else, nor to express or kindle feelings or emotions, but to do such things as claim rights ('This is mine'), recognize rights when claimed by others ('Very well, this is yours'), ascribe rights whether claimed or not ('This is his'), transfer rights ('This is now yours'), and also to admit or ascribe or make accusations of responsibility ('I did it,' 'He did it,' 'You did it'')[26] Hart notes that prior philosophical inquiry into the concept of human action has been inadequate because sentences of the form "He did it" have been treated as simple descriptions. They should, he argues, be seen as ascriptions wherein responsibility is ascribed as part of the interpretation of an action. In like manner, sentences of the form "This is his" should be seen as ascriptions of rights and should also be treated differently from how one would treat descriptions.

Hart's parallel treatment of the concepts of property and action is particularly illuminating. He begins by showing that both claims to ownership of property and of actions can be defeated in arguments with more or less the same structure. If, for example, someone has a legal interest in a piece of property, the structure of the legal argument supporting such a claim is not positive, that is, it is not a catalogue of the necessary and sufficient conditions required to support such a claim (e.g., evidence that it was transferred to the person lawfully, that he never lawfully transferred it, etc.). Rather, the argument would be negative; it would consist in a presentation of some conditions that would defeat the claim. The attribute of legal concepts that renders them susceptible to negative arguments is referred to by Hart as "defeasibility." If a person, therefore, has a legal interest in a piece of property, that interest can be "subject to termination or *'defeat'* in a number of different contingencies but remains intact if no such contingencies mature."[27] This concept of defeasibility, he points out, can be applied to any kind of contract. If, for example, it is necessary to establish that a particular contract involved "true consent," solving this evidence problem would not entail an attempt to list all the sufficient conditions required for "true" or "full" and "free" consent. Rather, Hart argues, a defense might have to be prepared to show that no undue influence or coercion produced acquiescence rather than consent. In fact, a list of circumstances that could defeat the contract would constitute the boundaries which establish the *meaning* of the legal requirement of true consent.

The important part of Hart's analysis, for purposes here, is its application to the concept of human action. Having explicated the concept of defeasibility as it relates to contracts, Hart moves on to the concept of action, stating, "I now wish to defend a similar but perhaps more controversial thesis that the concept of human action is an ascriptive and defeasible one."[28] In defense of this thesis, Hart notes that the difference between the physical movement of a human body and human action can be understood as parallel to the distinction between a piece of earth and a piece of property. In order, therefore, to establish the validity of a claim like "This is Smith's property," one would have to resort to a variety of nondescriptive or normatively oriented utterances dealing with the rules by which real estate is designated and acquired. Except in extraordinary circumstances, no normative utterances would be expected to support a statement like "This is a piece of earth," or "Smith is holding a piece of earth." But it must be recalled that in this latter case, as in all cases of descriptions, there are implicit standards involved, even when we are dealing with such "brute facts" as hunks of earth.

Moving back to the concept of action, Hart suggests that the statement "His body moved in violent contact with another's" could be taken as primarily descriptive, whereas a statement like "He did it" (e.g., "He hit her") must be *explained* with reference to nondescriptive utterances that ascribe liability or responsibility. And, as is the case with defeating a claim to a piece of property, the "ownership" of the action ("He did it") would be defeated with reference to the rule-governed circumstances which, if they obtain, render the statement "He did it" invalid. This approach to legal responsibility is counterintuitive in that one's ordinary image of how claims like "He did it" are sustained is by showing that the deed was done "willfully" or "intentionally." In his analysis, Hart points out that in practice, legal tribunals do not, as indeed they could not, attempt to measure an event or episode, such as the functioning of will or intention, prior to the human physical movement or movements at issue. When someone is said to have done something, courts of law refer, not to the evidence of the activity of mental processes directly, but rather to the circumstances which, if they obtain, make it inappropriate to ascribe deliberate action. For example, if someone hits a person with a hammer, responsibility for the action ("He hit her") could be avoided by showing that she walked in front of him while he was hitting a nail into the wall in order to hang a picture. In this case it would be regarded as an accident, and perhaps rather than saying that he hit her, we would say that she got hit while he was hammering a nail (part of what the action *is* rests on where responsibility lies). Or, in a similar circumstance (hitting someone with a hammer) it could be claimed that the person hit was mistaken for a prowler (it was dark and she came in the window, having forgotten her key). Such a case might be called mistaken identity, thereby discharging responsibility for hitting her.

Hart's analysis of action thus accords with what was suggested above about the role of intention or purpose in understanding human conduct as contrasted with understanding behavior. Human action, in short, is understood not by showing that a behavior is intentional, in the sense that a causal relation can be established between a mental process and observable conduct, but by establishing that the action we ascribe is an action by virtue of the rules being followed, that is, by showing that a plausible argument exists whereby the context may be interpreted in such a way that it is appropriate to interpret the conduct in a given way. The implications of this analysis clearly extend to such methodological questions as those bearing on the legitimate location of the data of human action. Developing an adequate or useful understanding of human action requires more than observing the actors and/or inferring from indirect measurement when the actors were thinking, because action cannot be adequately explained with reference to a combination of physical and psychological events. Action is normatively based and is ascribed with reference to rules or norms, some of which are reflected in legal codes and other social control institutions. As Hart put it succinctly, "our concept of action like our concept of property, is a social concept and logically dependent on accepted rules of conduct."[29] Because this is the case, explanation of anything more meaningful than the physical movement of persons requires interpretation, and the more that this is recognized, the more it can become a self-conscious and systematically applied component of social and political analysis. These implications will be developed further in subsequent chapters. There is more to say here about Hart's analysis of action.

It was suggested above that Hart's conception of human action explicated here is controversial. Indeed, Hart himself cut the controversy short by abandoning his argument (or at least part of it—he does not indicate why) after some critiques were written in response to his essay. What controversy there was, however, highlights some important issues in the theory of action. Hart's position is defensible, and that defense will provide a framework for reconciling causal explanation of human conduct with noncausal accounts. Critiques of Hart's position all fault him for choosing examples from legal discourse, arguing that his position on human action cannot survive analysis within a broader frame of reference. One critic, Feinberg, states, for example, "The notion of defeasibility is inextricably tied up with an adversary system of litigation and its complex and diverse rules governing the sufficiency and insufficiency of legal claims, presumptive and conclusive evidence, the roles of contending parties, and the burden of proof. He argues further that fault inputation in everyday life differs from the ascription of faulty performance in legal processes. Feinberg suggests that only *some* fault imputations can be regarded as defeasible, particularly those characteristic of legal fault imputations, which involve "blame above and beyond the mere untowardness or defectiveness of the ascribed action."[30] There are, according to Feinberg, fault imputations or ascriptions that are nondefeasible. These he characterizes as ascriptions which point out that the action is defective without also implying that the actor is reprehensible or blameworthy for the action.

Feinberg's distinction between defeasible and nondefeasible ascriptions is based on the severity of the offense. It should be evident, therefore, that his argument does not touch Hart's, for Hart was concerned with the *meaning* of action sentences and the analysis of action that follows from a position on meaning, whereas Feinberg's analysis focuses on the *implications* of action sentences. Hart is speaking of the ascription that constitutes a given behavioral episode as one or another kind of action, and Feinberg is speaking about an ascription that comes after the fact, that is, once the interpretation has been made and an action is ascribed.

Feinberg's failure to come to terms with Hart's argument can be understood more clearly if we consider an important distinction that has been noted with respect to kinds of rules. Both John Rawls and John Searle have made a distinction between constitutive rules and regulative rules.[31] Hart's argument focuses on the former; Feinberg's, and those of others, are based on the latter. Constitutive rules govern the meaning of action sentences. So that if, to return to Hart's example, a person swings a hammer and it hits another person's head, the action problem is one of deciding whether it is appropriate to *say,* "He did it." To decide whether such an utterance is appropriate, one must examine the rules (constitutive rules) for such an action, and if the circumstances are such that a reasonable defense (in accord with the rules for such an action—constitutive rules) can be offered, it is inappropriate to make the statement. To speak, as for example Feinberg does, of "the defectiveness of the ascribed action" is to speak incorrectly. If there is defectiveness, in Hart's sense, the action statement "misfires" and there is a question as to what was done. It is not, as Hart has shown, a matter of deciding whether someone is responsible for his or her actions. Once it is decided that there is some kind of action, the responsibility question has also been decided by implication, for actions become actions by virtue of the responsibility interpretations used to determine them, among other things. What Feinberg and other critics of Hart have focused on are regulative rules.

Once an action is ascribed in accordance with the constitutive rules for such actions, it is another matter to decide where that action fits within the system of regulative rules which prescribe and proscribe rules of conduct and suggest penalties for various kinds of actions and inactions. So, to suggest, as Feinberg does, that one can distinguish between acts that are merely defective and those for which someone should be held responsible or to blame, is to confuse constitutive and regulative rules. To call an event an action of any kind is to make an implicit decision on the agency of the act. The issue of "blame" is thus decided when the utterance is made. The remaining decision has to do with the significance of the act—is it one for which severe punishment is warranted or is it merely a breach of etiquette, for example? The extent of blame (inferred on the basis of regulative rules) is thus a matter of the severity of the infraction. It does not provide a basis for distinguishing defeasible and nondefeasible actions. Regulative rules dealing with such things as the extent of blame are merely the tip of the normative iceberg. Action statements are not descriptions to be subsequently subjected to norms or rules. They are norm-laden ascriptions whose meanings depend on a host of constitutive rules that are implicitly invoked when events or movement are considered to constitute one or another kind of human action.

The distinction between constitutive and regulative rules provides a response to part of another well-known critique of Hart's position that is offered by P. T. Geach. In the first part of his critique, Geach states that holding a person responsible for something is a moral or quasi-moral attitude, but ascribing an action to someone does not generally involve taking up a quasi-legal or quasi-moral attitude.[32] He states, further, that only a bad choice of examples makes it seem otherwise. Here Geach's argument, like Feinberg's, rests on a confusion over types of rules or norms. Social control over human conduct can be thought of as being deployed in two stages. The first stage involves the operation of attitudes that are quasi-moral or quasi-legal (as the case may be), but they are only implicitly so. They are not attitudes in an immediate cerebral sense that belong particularly to the ascriber, for they are embedded in the language used to characterize behavior and render it as action. The attitude(s) involved can thus be quite unconscious or at least unreflective. So when, for example, a person is observed grabbing a child roughly by the arm and pulling it into a car, anyone seeking to state simply what has happened must draw on several institutionalized moral/legal attitudes belonging to the society in which the event has taken place.

The question that now arises is whether the event witnessed is a case of "kidnapping," "child abuse," or simply a normal exercise of "parental or guardian duty." Those witnessing the event may, accordingly, have to be tentative about interpreting what has happened, not knowing, for example, the relationship between the puller and the pullee, or perhaps other relevant contextual factors. A selection (assuming one is ultimately in a position to determine) from among these three ascriptions (and perhaps others) of the action depends on prevailing rules about interpersonal relations. For example, it is not a case of kidnapping if the grabber is a parent or guardian who has not for some reason lost legal responsibility for the child. Whether or not it is child abuse would probably depend on (a) the condition of the child after the episode (as compared with before; a little muscle soreness would not create entry into the abused condition, but a dislocated shoulder might), and/or (b) other circumstances at the time of the grabbing (a resulting serious arm injury might not qualify as abuse if the child was being pulled from the path of another oncoming car at the time).

Now we do not usually think of the function of using traditional or current rules to ascribe actions as the taking of a moral position, because we tend to think of moral positions only in the context of controversial attitudes. But clearly, any person witnessing the episode described in this example has a choice of attitude and thus of ascription, even if it means they must employ terms in a nonstandard way to express their attitude. A witness can save cognitive energy and rely on traditional norms. For example, if the puller is a parent and the pulling results in no serious injury (of a physical sort), the ascription would

probably be the third alternative suggested (the normal exercise of parental or guardian duty). But all the rules that are used in such an ascription have moral components. Because they are institutionalized and
well known and accepted, we do not tend to regard compliance with
them or employment of them as involving a moral posture, but a moment's reflection on how such an incident is likely to be discussed
makes clear that morals guide the categories employed. In this case, the
morals involved relate to the duties and responsibilities of parents and
perhaps the status of families as compared to other social groupings in
the placing of responsibility for children's welfare. In a discussion of appropriate and inappropriate occasions for using the word "inadvertently," John Austin made a point that is especially relevant here. He
noted that while it is commonplace to say "we trod on the snail inadvertently," it is difficult to get away with using the same plea for stepping on a baby.[33] When, in a given situation, we have occasion to resist
calling the stepping on a baby inadvertent, we are resorting to norms or
rules in the process of characterizing the situation, and those rules have
a moral content that addresses issues of responsibility for children.

So moral attitudes govern the first stage of our approach to human
conduct, contrary to what Geach was arguing. This, recall, is the stage
of characterizing what has been done. In the above example, moral
norms regulate what we say has been done when a parent (if it was a
parent) roughly thrusts a child into a vehicle. We, or perhaps other relevant social control agents (e.g., judges and juries), then resort to the
second stage in the response to the conduct involved. Having decided
what the conduct *is*—having ascribed various rules to determine the action in question—we then decide what collective response, if any, is appropriate. Thus when we speak of "holding someone responsible for an
action," (e.g., "kidnapping a child"), we are involved in the application
of regulative rules. In this case, responsibility would have been already
implied if the action is interpreted as, for example, kidnapping. The next
step is the application of other, officially sanctioned moral attitudes,
choosing the correct or appropriate societal response. This might range
from a severe punishment (one form of "holding a person responsible")
to no societal response at all. Perhaps the person could be regarded as
having performed the action "kidnapping," but in the context of other
circumstances (e.g., being blinded by grief over having lost custody of
the child), there might be no punishment. In such a case, the person *is*
responsible for the action (it was judged to be kidnapping) but would not
be *held* responsible. The regulatory mechanism relevant to such responsibility would be aborted because of the circumstances.

This brings us to the second part of Geach's critique of Hart's position. According to Geach, Hart's type of argument, common to ascrip-

tivists, is like tantamount to claiming that to say "X is happy," is not to describe a characteristic of X but to call X happy. Again, Geach refers to this "calling" as the expression of a pro or con attitude, and he then goes on to point out that there are cases in which we use a term (P) when we are expressing no attitude toward it, for example, when we "predicate P of a thing" as in "If gambling is bad, inviting people to gamble is bad"). We can say this, Geach argues, without expressing an attitude toward gambling.[34]

This second part of Geach's critique also fails. Ascriptivists in general and Hart in particular are not claiming that what appear to be descriptive statements about person's conduct (e.g., "Henry hit her on purpose") actually involve calling someone or something a thing of one sort or another in the ordinary sense of calling or labeling. To analyze the statement "Henry hit her on purpose" as Hart would, we would not treat is as a causal description, that is, we would not search for the mental event (motive or intention) that triggered the physical event (the swinging of a fist). Rather, we would treat it as a rule-governed utterance and consider the rules about what circumstances must obtain if the person (Henry) is to be able to offer a reasonable defense against a charge of willful battery. Even though saying "Henry hit her on purpose" in certain circumstances might be a serious charge, making the utterance is not really calling someone something nor does it make someone something (except in rare circumstances when the speaker has a special, official role). Using the semantic rules involved in the utterance does not even involve, as was indicated above, expressing an attitude in an immediate, self-aware sense. The attitude expressed in such an utterance is implicit, because it is already there, embedded in the semantic rules used. So it is possible to say "Henry hit her on purpose" without a view toward taking sides, even though the statement, if believed, makes it look bad for Henry. Geach's gambling example is a hypothetical condition and not a description, that is, there are no identifications of a case of gambling involved. Whenever a concept has to be coordinated with an event or, more simply, with some experiential data, a norm is involved and thus we have a case of attitudes that are at least implicit, even though the statement is not what one ordinarily regards as the taking of a stand.

The question that can be raised here concerns what roles these seemingly disparate kinds of analysis (causal and noncausal) have in explaining social and political phenomena. All of what has been said above is not meant to discredit what is known as ordinary causal explanation, even for cases of intentional conduct. People often do things because they want to, and thus we can often understand much that they do by paying attention to their hopes and plans. But human "action," as the expression is ordinarily understood (by philosophers and social scientists), involves more than what individual actors try to do and think they are doing. A person who performs something usually has limited control over what that something is or will become. If we understand this, we can sort out the seemingly incompatible approaches to the explanation of action. Donald Davidson has argued that explaining an action by giving a reason for it (the actor's reason) is a causal explanation in the ordinary sense. One of his examples involves a person turning on a light, an action, he claims, that can be explained by pointing out that the person wanted to turn on the light.[35] Davidson contrasts his view with Melden's. Whereas Melden would explain the behavior of raising an arm as constituting the giving of a signal (because of the rules governing the act of signaling), Davidson, as in his light-turning-on example, would reinterpret this as a causal explanation.[36] In Davidson's framework, the "action" (raising the arm) would be explained by "the desire to signal." But this is precisely the confusion that can be sorted out by considering the agent's degree of control over what the action is. Although one *could* explain the raising of the arm by a causal antecedent (like desiring to signal), such a causal explanation would be inadequate as an account of signaling. It might be, for example, that a person would wish to produce a particular kind of signal, but what the person does in fact produce is partly a function of social conventions about what constitutes a signal.

We could go back a step in this analysis and regard as problematic the question of whether one's intending to raise an arm is an adequate account of raising an arm. Even though a person might intend his or her conduct to achieve the simple accomplishment known as "raising an arm" rather than a more complex one such as signaling, to say "He raised his arm" is to interpret the conduct, and other interpretations are always possible (e.g., his arm went up involuntarily), interpretations that may not coincide with the plans and self-interpretations of the actor. Thus, it is a matter of the interpretation and not just psychological cause as to the kind of action constituted when someone raises an arm (or whatever it is that happens—there is no neutral way to describe it). Thinking about or desiring to signal may explain why an arm is raised and/or a signal is made, but only if the causal account is complemented by an interpretive one. We can imagine many different circumstances in which a person engages in an action despite what they may intend to do (intention here being used in a causal sense). Going back to Davidson's turning on a light, for example, imagine a person turning on a light in a photographer's darkroom, just as a picture to be used in a court case is being developed, thereby "destroying material evidence." Should we say that the person merely turned on a light, or should we say that he or she did much more, up to and including obstructing justice? This would be determined by criteria extending well beyond what the person "had in mind." It may be that the person planned to do more than turn on a light, not even knowing he/she was in a photographer's darkroom. Nevertheless, the person could be engaged in a serious act of negligence if there is reason to argue that he/she should take greater precaution, given the setting of the room, and so on. If there is such a reason, given prevailing norms, the description of what was done would include reference to responsibility for negligence. Only in very limited circumstances, therefore, do intentions, in a causal sense, control or constitute what the action is for the meaning of utterances and conduct is established in the context of the social and cultural norms in which the statements or conduct are located.

Explaining Human Action

We can now clarify the issues raised at the beginning of this chapter, the symmetry or asymmetry of explanation in the physical and social sciences. The patterns of inference involved in causal explanation in the physical sciences apply to the social sciences. Things like wants and purposes account for what people do, much as the operation of celestial processes accounts for the succession of night and day. But just as "days" and "nights" are events that have meaning only in the context of the human rules that constitute their boundaries, so human activities like voting, affirming, loving, and ignoring, though produced in part by consciously formulated plans, achieve the status that their names imply by virtue of their conformity to the rules which constitute the meanings of those names. For example:

CHILD: You're ignoring me.
FATHER: That's funny, what I thought I was doing was paying special attention to you. I took you out to lunch (JUST THE TWO OF US), and here we are at the ball game.
CHILD: Yes, we are together, but every time I ask you a question, you just say, "eat your lunch," or "watch the game," you won't listen to me.

Clearly in such a case, the interesting questions that arise relate to the concept of ignoring; does ignoring involve physical distance, the degree of listening to the other's statements, both? Given the ordinary use of the verb "to ignore," it is probably reasonable to agree with the child in the above scenario and say that the father *is* ignoring him or her. In making such a judgment, we are comparing the scenario with what we would consider a case of nonignoring in the same kind of circumstances. Although the norms that apply to the kind of attention a parent is expected to pay to a child are not associated with elaborate social control mechanisms, that is, the penalties for violation of them are diffuse and deferred or, one might say, prophetic rather than profane, they are nevertheless relatively familiar. So to explain what the father is doing, we would probably not be content with focusing solely, or even largely, on the causal process that links purposes with behavior. Indeed, in this case, the father did not intend (in a causal sense, i.e., "plan") to ignore his child. A causal explanation at the level of intentions of the verbal behavior would thus not address itself to most of the questions one might formulate about why the father has ignored his child. (Although there are certainly interesting social or social-psychological causal explanations one could explore.) Intention, as a concept, is involved in some way here, but it is problematic to determine just how to apply the concept.

John Austin seemed to be highlighting the difficulty of properly identifying the role of intentions in human conduct when he said (I am now extending a quotation I employed above): "Should we say, are we saying, that he took her money, or that he robbed her? That he knocked a ball in a hole, or that he sank a putt? That he said, "Done," or that he accepted an offer? How far, that is, are motives, intentions, and conventions to be part of the description of actions? And more especially, here, what is *an* or *one* or *the* action?"[37]

Whether or not an intention or motive is part of the description of an action has to do with the rules that govern the boundaries of what *the* action is when someone does something. In the above example, the father regarded his action, which consisted of taking a child to lunch and a game, as "paying attention," while the child added up the same behaviors and came up with the action of "ignoring." What are the boundaries that push the sequence into one category of action versus another, and how can one determine them? The problem of identifying such boundaries has often been discussed in connection with the role of intention in the law, as we saw in the analysis of Hart's position on responsibility and rights. In another analysis of intention and the law, Anthony Kenny raised a useful question about whether it is reasonable to assume that persons intend a consequence which they foresee but do not necessarily desire to bring about.[38] Acts, he states, have "results" and "consequences." The result is the "end state of the change by which the act is defined," whereas consequences are other things that follow from the act. Within this model, then, an act is related to its results intrinsically and its consequences causally. Kenny decides that what we attach intention to should be restricted to the results of a person's actions and not the consequences, even when the person can be reasonably expected to be able to foresee the consequences. So for

Kenny, the description of the act would be limited to results and intentions would be treated as part of the act that is constituted by the results.

This does not, however, solve the problem of how to relate intentions to action: causally, noncausally, or both. The issue can perhaps be best understood by considering, again, the extent to which a person can be said to control his or her actions. Kenny has obviously decided that control attaches to what he calls the results of an action and not the consequences. For example, a person may decide to dam up a stream on his property in order to create a body of water sufficient for recreational use. A consequence of this, which he might clearly foresee, could be the destruction of a business enterprise downstream that uses the stream to cool its machinery. Under the circumstances, those involved, that is, those about to be unemployed, would like to regard the action, and thereby the rules for responsibility, as one that includes the destruction of the business in the act itself. It would be in their interest to have the property owner be responsible for helping to maintain their livelihood or at least be responsible for not removing it. They would thus want to be able to say that damming the stream should be an action called destroying the business, among other things.

Thus, in this case, how could we speak correctly about what the property owner plans to do and therefore about what he is liable for if he goes ahead and dams up the stream (which the property owner might claim is all he intends, even though he knows it will destroy the business)? At a minimum, he obviously would not want to leave the boundary between the results and consequences of the act to the actor. The question is clearly not causal alone. Whether the action ends up as just damming the stream (which then causes the factory to go out of business) or damming the stream *and* forcing the factory out of business depends on the rules for responsibility within the society or community where the property owner resides, to the extent that there is a noncontroversial body of rules to which one can turn. As was noted above, linguistic analysts have tended to neglect the extent to which the "rules" one locates constitutes a choice of power constituencies. Kenny's boundary between results and consequences is simply a matter of convention. Nothing that can be observed about human conduct or the interaction between persons and their predicament is going to yield up such a boundary. Whatever the property owner thought he was doing, or wanted to do (intended to in a causal sense), we will say that he intentionally put the factory out of business if our rules for responsibility make it expected that he should plan his use of his property with the existence of the factory in mind. If we do have such rules for responsibility we will then include the effect on the factory of damming up the stream as part of the action, rather than simply looking at what happens to the factory as an unintended consequence of the stream damming. Thus rules of responsibility can often include, as part of an action, outcomes that people have an obligation to avoid.

The idea of human action, then, introduces a complexity which exceeds that of explaining people's behavior. To the extent that persons have control over their behavior, we speak of purposive behavior. When we use this concept, we are thinking of intentions, purposes, and plans in the ordinary causal sense. Some conduct is not purposive but has meaning nevertheless (we do not plan to jump when we are surprised by a loud noise), and some conduct *is* purposive, (we stand up and start walking, usually because we are planning to leave one location and move to another). If someone is driving a car and sticks an arm out the driver's window, it might not be clear what kind of action it is. The person may have intended (planned) to signal but will not have, in fact, signaled unless the gesture conforms to the rules for signaling in such circumstances. Or, in the reverse situation, the driver may stick an arm out the window not intending (planning) to signal, but will have, in fact, signaled if the gesture conforms to the rules for signaling in such circumstances. In both these cases, the intentions are not causes of the action known as signaling. When we are concerned with human action, then, we are concerned with conduct that exceeds the control of the individual actor. This makes it logically impossible to account wholly for action within a causal framework. Persons cannot invent rules for their conduct every time they do something and hope that their inventions suffice to cover their behaviors with meanings so that they end up in the action categories they desire. Meanings are, however, sometimes negotiable so that claims about intentions by the actor *can* affect the interpretation that is ultimately controlling. Persons, of course, differ in how much control they have over their and other's conduct in terms of the meanings that the conduct has. To point this out is simply to note that power and authority tend to be unevenly distributed. The utterances of judges and legislators are more likely to constitute various behaviors as actions than those of farmers and mechanics.

When we speak of "behavior," therefore, it makes sense to ask if it is voluntary or involuntary, purposive or aimless, and so forth. It is not clear that we can speak of action this way. People, as has been noted, do not wholly control their actions because when someone does something, the resulting action is a function of the norms which provide the context for it. These norms are the social, political, legal and/or administrative rules by which conduct is defined and regulated within a human community. In some instances the definition of an action depends on whether those engaged in it planned (in a causal sense) to do it, and in some instances it does not. An example of the former is the action of becoming a party to a contract, and an example of the latter is an action known as criminal negligence (e.g., failing to service an amusement ride adequately—an action that is not planned). There is no such thing as mere behavior, because to look at the world and see conduct is to make an interpretation. For this reason, a solely causal account is never adequate. Causal explanations are always inextricably linked with interpretation.

Voting, for example, is an action. When one speaks about research on "voting behavior," one usually means research oriented toward developing causal explanations of the choices that persons make when they decide whether or not to engage in the act of voting or how to vote. Such explanations usually involve causal sequences with sociological or psychological variables. Because voting, as an action, is, as political acts go, a fairly trivial and uncomplex one, relatively little attention has been focused on noncausal explanations of voting, for example, it is unusual to find explanations of the rules which stipulate that a given sequence of activity has come to be regarded as voting rather than something else. There are, however, some concepts (ordinarily referred to by political scientists as dependent variables) whose explanation simply on the basis of causal antecedents, however rigorous (syntactically elaborated and carefully validated, etc.), would not satisfy one interested in political phenomena. "Political participation," "political development," and "equality" are among these. To articulate rules about what constitutes political participation, for example, is in effect to make a normative argument about the boundaries of the political culture in a society. And to stipulate what a situation of equality *is,* whether social, economic, or political, is to establish rules or norms about what attributes of persons ought to be regarded as relevant to public life. For purposes of denoting situations of equality, should we focus on persons' needs, their abilities, their demands, their ethnicity, their group members?

Much of the emphasis in the discussion thus far has been on what I have termed two stages that must be involved in the explanation of human action. Quentin Skinner has conceived of the explanation of human action problem in a similar manner, arguing that after one has accounted for an action on the basis of the agent's intentions in performing it, we can then go on to provide relevant causal explanations for the same action.[39] Although the meaning dimension of human action has been developed here in a different manner from that suggested by Skinner's focus on intentions, his claim about the compatibility (indeed the complementarity) of non-causal and causal accounts of the same action is one implication to be derived from this chapter. It is possible, however, to go further. The emphasis on meaning and its contribution to understanding human action presented thus far has served to indicate that we should note that *what* things or conduct mean, be they utterances or movements, is a function of the rules that govern the situation within which they are deployed. Once this is pointed out, however, another kind of question arises, the question of *why* things (utterances and behaviors) mean what they mean. When we speak about children and adults (to pick up a theme inaugurated in the first chapter), we are identifying constituents that are not (a) a matter of mere observation (as some positivists would have it), or (b) a psychological commitment on the part of persons using the distinction. A person becomes a child or occupies that status not simply by dint of some physiological or chronological factors but because of the application of the constitutive rules of childhood. A person is thus a child because of the rules, derived from the social, political, and administrative organization of the society that identifies some humans as children. We therefore do more than speak about objects and events. Our speech is constitutive of objects and events, even when it is unself-consciously constitutive. The characteristic ways of speaking which constitute the objects and situations that gain our attention are what Michel Foucault has called discursive practices. In the next chapter, then, I shall analyze his notion of discursive practices in order to suggest that a mode of political inquiry emerges from the analysis of those practices. This is an analysis of the political processes that inhere in the way we speak, which takes us beyond stipulating the rules for what things mean to an analysis of how and why they mean what they mean and of the political relationships that reside in the meanings that various discursive practices represent.

However, before turning to an examination of how discursive practices constitute phenomena—persons, objects, events, actions, and institutions—we must clarify two questions: (1) what is it that is constituted? and (2) what role is played by what persons in this constitutive process? The answer to the first question is that constitutive rules constitute things—children, adults, hysteria, workers; they constitute actions—murder, playing, working, judging, deciding; they constitute institutions or collective phenomena—education, medicine, law enforcement. The "things" and activities that we speak of emerge with the help of rules which prescribe distinctions we make, distinctions that reside in our language in general and speech practices in particular. As has been noted above, moreover, the distinctions or commitments to meanings that we make have the effect of allocating power, authority, and legitimacy. The constitutive rules that general individual roles (child), actions (work) and collective interactions (education) are thus part of a society's political culture. Although they are not part of statutory law, they legitimate kinds of control by kinds of persons. "Things" like property reflect rules about who can control activity in various geographic domains. "Things" like children reflect rules about who is responsible for protecting whom and about who may rightfully participate in various public processes. Similarly, actions like "working" reflect rules about what set of behaviors engaged in by what kinds of persons are to be regarded as legitimately remunerable, and institutions like a society's system of "education" reflect rules about what set of activities carried out by what set of persons are to be legitimately regarded as contributions to learning or as preparations for other activities.

There are two dimensions to the answer to the second question— "what role is played by which persons in this constitutive process." The first dimension relates to the persons who are the objects of particular social or political inquiries. Although what persons are and what they can do is, to a large extent, preinstitutionalized, the norms or standards that create roles for persons and produce what are understood as persons' actions are always in a process of development. Because it is misleading to assume that all social behavior is regulated by a preexisting set of rules, it is important to appreciate the activities whereby members of a society, in varying degrees, negotiate their social order in the process of being a part of it. Persons sometimes participate in the process wherein things, actions, and institutions are constituted or given meanings. Although most activities are best seen as rule-following activities whose interpretations are pregiven, some activities actually do produce the rules that constitute the social world within which activities in general have meaning.[40] An appreciation of this process provides a valuable domain for the investigation of human conduct. For example, traditional social science approaches to the decision-making behavior of a given group—foreign-policy decision makers, family planners, welfare agencies—ordinarily take the decisional context (the set of roles, objects, and actions legitimized as relevant to the decision-making task) as given. However, an appreciation of the role that persons play in constituting the decision context makes possible another level of analysis. One can investigate the process by which actors constitute the situation within which what are regarded as "the decisions" are made. With respect to understanding political kinds of decision-making behavior, this kind of question will necessarily alter the time frame of a study. Foreign-policy decision makers and administrative agencies, for example, usually inherit the frames of meaning within which they operate, so one must locate the crucial episodes in the past that have created the interpreted worlds within which the decision makers function in order to understand the constitutive process. In other cases, the decision-making situation is, from the viewpoint of the actors involved, sufficiently ad hoc so that the decision making must involve the development of a preliminary self-understanding before choices are made.[41]

The second dimension to what role persons have in the constitutive process relates to the social science investigator/observer. Traditional, causally oriented investigations of social phenomena proceed with the assumption that the set of categories for social phenomena which belong to the investigator's self-understanding are fixed. The limitations of this view, however, are well known. Many have pointed out how it fails to comprehend the extent to which interpretations of the meanings of some persons' activities requires an appreciation of their self-understanding, particularly when it is foreign to that of the investigator. Nevertheless, as has been noted above, the actors' view of what they are doing is not necessarily epistemologically privileged. An investigator might legitimately want to go beyond the self-understanding of the group under investigation and, for example, speak of as a form of social control what the group may regard as a health practice. Whatever understanding an investigator might wish to bring to an interpretation of a given group or to a society's practices as a whole, however, it is useful to recognize that the investigator's rules or norms can also be thought of as negotiable or subject to reinterpretation. What may begin, therefore, as the study of an exotic culture with the goal of making intelligible what seem to be exotic practices may become a reflexive analysis in which the investigator, finding his or her frame of reference inadequate, changes his or her own self-understanding to accommodate the unfamiliar practices. The very process that Peter Winch has described as necessary for the effective interpretation of exotic practices—the jettisoning of some of our sophistication in order to understand another "primitive" culture—can be the beginning of a new self-understanding. We can thus treat the rules constitutive of the investigator's frame of meaning as a fit domain for investigation. In so doing, we can reinterpret the significance of the study of exotic phenomena such that the study of the "other" becomes the study of the "self."

Michel Foucault and the
Analysis of Discursive Practices

Language and Human Conduct

Oxford philosophers or, if one prefers, English linguistic philosophers, have rarely said much of substance about the social and political relations of a society, at least not directly. Their attention has been on more abstract matters such as meaning and truth, and their approach—the analysis of ordinary language, which is designed to illuminate questions of meaning and truth—has been focused on questions of the order, What can properly be said about X? or, What does one mean when one says that the meaning of an expression is related to the use to which that expression is put by the speaker? Not surprisingly, those interested in "explaining" or understanding human conduct find these kinds of questions and the answers they produce unsatisfying. It is not at all obvious to those who wish to get on with the work of analyzing sociopolitical relations how to move logically or practically from the analysis of language to the analysis of human relations. Yet a move from the analysis of linguistic or discursive practices to the analysis of human conduct requires little more than the exercise of a perspective, one that rejects a radical distinction between discursive practices and nondiscursive (real, actual, what can we call them?) practices. Before scrutinizing how such a perspective is realized in Michel Foucault's work, however, it is worth retrieving some of the political analysis that emerges from linguistic analysis almost inadvertently.

In his "Plea for Excuses," John Austin begins by analyzing what appears to be a nuance of language use: the occasions on which it appears to be relevant to modify a statement about an action with an adverb which indicates mood or intention or the like, i.e., the adverb "inadvertently," as it appears in the last sentence in the above paragraph.[1]

Although his attention is mainly on the language-oriented question, Why do certain kinds of actions take certain kinds of adverbs? Austin ultimately analyzes the dominance patterns of human relations in his subculture.

Austin points out that "to examine excuses is to examine cases where there has been some abnormality or failure: and so often, the abnormal will throw light on the normal, will help us to penetrate the blinding veil of ease and obviousness that hides the mechanisms of the natural successful act." As was noted in chapter 4, Austin suggests a number of principles for the use of modifiers of actions, the foremost of which is, "No modification without aberration." This principle is based on his observation that only actions that are untoward or are done in unusual circumstances are accompanied by modifiers. We would not, he notes, add the word "intentionally" to a statement like "He sat in a chair," whereas we would add such a modifier to a statement like "He sat in a puddle" [intentionally]. How, then, do we learn about human conduct in general and political relations in particular by examining excuses? We learn, as Austin's principle suggests, what actions are regarded as untoward and thus the ones about which we are prone to raise questions of responsibility. This becomes very evident when, at the end of the essay, Austin discusses what psychologists call "displacement behavior," which is the generating of apparently meaningless activity when a goal-directed activity is thwarted. Here he notes that, for both displacement behavior and "compulsive behavior," there appear to be no satisfactory adverbial expressions that highlight the circumstances under which such activities are witnessed. He then observes, "This is understandable enough, since compulsive behavior, like displacement behavior, is not in general going to be of great practical importance." One is tempted to think that here Austin dismisses compulsive and displacement behavior as unimportant and thus unworthy of analysis. But, rather, he argues that their apparent unimportance, signified by their lack of accompanying modifiers, tells us something about human conduct.[2] Their lack of familiar adverbial modifiers indicates that they are generally regarded as not relevant enough to the public domain to evoke a sanctioned social control response. If they were, they would carry the appropriate tags to indicate where responsibility is lodged for the behaviors.

It is possible to imagine a society with alternate norms that would be reflected in the use of adverbial modifiers for these kinds of behaviors (displacement and compulsive). If, for example, we habitually say, "After that happened, X displaced his energy desperately," the implication would be that we expect such behavior under such circumstances, that is, we regard the situation as beyond the control we expect of people. If, however, we say instead something like "After that, he displaced his energy deliberately," this would imply that the action was untoward or aberrant, that is, we would expect people to control that kind of response. What we would say under the circumstances would thus reflect our political culture. If we chose the second rather than the first locution, this would mean that we have politicized a process (displacement) that is ordinarily (as reflected in the first option) regarded as a psychological phenomenon without public, political significance. To say that something has no political significance is to say that we do not have responsibility to others associated with it and no corresponding authoritative, social control response to it.

Thus, analyzing the use of "excuses" does more than tell us about how a given linguistic community habitually speaks. It also provides a partial mapping of the political culture that resides potentially in a society's system of signification (language and other meaning systems) and is actualized in speech. Discursive practices therefore *are* political practices, which is why John Austin more or less backed into a theory of action in the process of dealing with a particular style of speaking. One need not, therefore, restrict one's analysis to the field of statements commonly designated as "the language of politics" itself in order to inquire into the political relations represented in discourse.

The idea that speaking is a form of activity is therefore a major contribution of English linguistic philosophers to the understanding of human conduct. In developing the idea that various kinds of utterances have a meaning in relation to the situation of the speaker, however, they never comprehensively addressed the relationship between language and speakers. This kind of concern has been more apparent in the writings of Continental philosophers, who have explored the way that a society's language or system for making meaningful utterances sets the boundaries for what persons can meaningfully and appropriately say and, in so doing, structures the kinds of relationships persons have with each other. In the discussion of Heidegger's approach to language in chapter 2, it was suggested that in some respects it is inappropriate to speak of persons having a language. Heidegger suggests that, rather, language is something that has human beings. To speak, according to Heidegger, is to enter the flow of activity that is already constituted in the language. The French tradition in language philosophy incorporates Heidegger's suggestion.

Influenced by the linguist Saussure's distinction between language and speech (*langue et parole*), French philosophers, linguists, and historians have elaborated on the language–speaker relationship, showing how language contains the field of possibilities from which speakers select. Barthes, for example, demonstrates, with various analogies, how.the language system contrains speech. Regarding food as a signifying system analogous to language, he suggests that "the 'alimentary language' consists of i) rules of exclusion (alimentary taboos); ii) signifying oppositions of units, the type of which remain to be determined (for instance the type *savory/sweet);* iii) rules of association, either simultaneously (at the level of a dish) or successive (at the level of a menu); iv) rituals of use which function perhaps, as a kind of alimentary *rhetoric.*"[3] Speech, within the context of Barthes' food analogy, becomes "alimentary speech." To understand the selections of individual speakers/eaters we must consider the possible variations in "usage" that are constrained by the alimentary language, for example, the menu of a particular family.

What does this explication of the relationship between language and speaking suggest? It indicates the way that speaking (and acting by implication) in its ordinary or common form is not an originating or innovative activity. In their common use of language, persons enter a system that already contains the objects one can speak about and the relationships one can invoke. Reinforcing this idea, Jacques Lacan has suggested that the common use of language is like the exchange of a coin, "whose obverse and reverse no longer bear any but worn effigies, and which people pass from hand to hand in silence."[4] What people say is therefore usually a matter of giving voice to discursive practices that represent a selection from a fixed set of practices permissible in the language. The language or system of signification is the system of the constitution of objects and events that emerge in speech as language is actualized. When persons engage in conduct, that conduct takes on a meaning or meanings as a result of the interpretations that are available in the language from which the interpreters select. When we therefore review the set of constructs relating to conduct that exists in a language, we are viewing not only the horizons of possible speech but also the horizons of possible actions. The possibilities of action, then, exist in the language of a culture, and the actions that actually emerge are presented as a result of the controlling interpretations, those with general legitimacy. When we are speaking about those interpretations of conduct that produce and affirm actions and their concommitant subjects and objects that are institutionalized because the interpretation is oft repeated and accepted, we are speaking of "discursive practices." Discursive practices, according to Foucault, who treats them as his primary unit of analysis, delimit the range of objects that can be identified, define the perspectives that one can legitimately regard as knowledge, and constitute certain kinds of persons as agents of knowledge, thereby establishing norms for developing conceptualizations that are used to understand the phenomena which emerge as a result of the discursive delimitation.[5]

If language can be viewed as the container of possible practices within a society or language community, and if speech represents selections within that language or system of signification, what are the implications for the conduct of social and political inquiry? Most significantly, this view implies that we must go beyond the idea of human action as consisting of a series of disconnected episodes of behavior that can be analyzed separately. As Culler puts it, "the cultural meaning of any particular act or object is determined by a whole system of constitutive rules; rules which do not regulate behavior so much as create the possibility of particular forms of behavior."[6] To understand and analyze conduct, then, we must uncover the system of constitutive rules that creates different meaningful episodes and objects, or, if they are controversial, the contending systems of constitutive rules that create alternative objects, events, and kinds of conduct. Because these systems reside in various discursive practices, the discourses selected in a society can be the data whose interpretation would reveal policies that allocate and legitimate various kinds of control. The systematic study of various discursive practices, for purposes of understanding political relations, has not been undertaken, but in the work of Michel Foucault, which has been influenced by both English and Continental traditions in language analysis, there is an inchoate model for such an undertaking. Foucault has focused his analysis of discursive practices primarily on the statements that comprise practices of various disciplines, professions, and administrative agencies. But although he has never addressed himself deliberately to political theory or political inquiry, he has stated that his mode of analysis could be addressed to the field of statements comprising political knowledge. After analyzing the discursive practices involved in various disciplines in his *Archeology of Knowledge,* he stated: "It seems to me that one might also carry out an analysis of the same type on political knowledge. One would try to show whether the political behavior of a society, a group, or a class is not shot through with a describable discursive practice."[7]

Although not explicitly focused on political behavior, Foucault's analysis comes across as manifestly political, for, as was suggested above, discursive practices in *any* domain are at least in part political practices. To appreciate how one can understand political relations by employing Foucault's analysis of discursive practices, then, we must inquire into what a discursive practice is and why it evokes the archeological metaphor that Foucault applies to his method of analysis.

Locating Foucault's Archeological Method

Foucault's approach involves asking a question like, What in fact are medicine, grammar or political economy?[8] A profession, discipline, or any similarly bounded activity *is,* for Foucault, constituted as a discursive practice, that is, its exclusivity derives from the mode and substance of its statements. One can thus analyze such statements to understand the practice of the named activity or group of activities (e.g., medicine) that they represent. Foucault calls this kind of analysis archeological to contrast it with what he sees as the traditional approach of intellectual historians who are involved in interrogating "documents" in order to recover a silent past, an exercise in refreshing our memories. Foucault treats discourses not as something to be deciphered in order to determine what lies behind them but as "monuments," something whose very description provides an understanding of the relations and objects that are constituted in the discourse; hence, the archeological metaphor. There are a variety of approaches to inquiry which, like Foucault's, raise primarily noncausal or interpretive kinds of questions about the subject matter of human interactions. Among these, the hermeneutical and structural approaches provide significant contrasts with his archeological method. A brief discussion of these approaches should place Foucault's assumptions about inquiry within a field of possibilities, particularly with respect to the problem of the investigator's standpoint, a problem for which Foucault's solution is especially radical.

Hermeneutical schools of thought emphasize the understanding of symbolic systems (texts, human cultures, etc.) through the raising of questions about the meanings that those systems convey. The hermeneutical approach to meaning involves elucidating not only the symbolic system that is the subject matter of analysis but also the interpreter's frame of reference. Interpretation for hermeneuticists is thus often diachronic (longitudinal through time) inasmuch as it involves mediating symbolic systems from one period to another. Gadamer, for example, speaks of understanding the utterances and actions of others in terms of our own system of prejudices, which he sees as the bases through which we experience our world.[9] Similarly, Ricoeur speaks of the "receptivity structure" through which we understand others.[10] What both Gadamer and Ricoeur see as the essential aspect of understanding through interpretation, as opposed to causal explanation, is that we understand others in the context of a *self-understanding* and a model of being or way of life. The development of explanations, whose validation require the objectivity or removal of the biases of the investigator, presumes a prior, interpretive commitment which serves to frame the questions that scientific explanatory approaches address. As Gadamer has put it, "The hermeneutical experience is prior to all methodical alienation because it is the matrix out of which arise the questions that it directs to science."[11]

Structuralism, as a method of explaining human association, has a substantially different emphasis. Rather than seeking to unite the symbol system(s) under investigation with the symbol system providing the investigator's self-understanding, the structuralist aim is to "put at a distance, to objectify, to separate out from the personal equation of the investigator the structure of an institution, a myth, a rite."[12] The structural mode of analysis is primarily synchronic, attempting to elucidate the structure of simultaneous relationships among elements. To the extent that structuralists treat events which involve temporal processes, they tie these processes to the transformation of structures, thereby making diachrony dependent on synchrony, that is, they treat change in the context of an elaborated model of structure. As an approach to the human sciences (it is especially popular as a mode of structural anthropology developed by Claude Levi-Strauss), structuralism emphasizes the human relationships that reside in the symbol systems of the persons who are the subject matter and deemphasizes, indeed neglects, the structure of the investigator's mind. Basing its notion of the structure of human activity on the linguistic model—primarily that developed by Saussure and elaborated by others, like Barthes and most notably Levi-Strauss—structuralism interprets human conduct as the surface practices emanating from a deeper structure that represents the constitution of human thought. As Ricoeur has written, structuralism is predicated on a Kantian rather than a Freudian unconscious, on structural imperatives that constitute the logical geography of mind.[13] Structuralist inquiry into human conduct therefore is an attempt to explain human practices by showing how they are expressions of structural aspects of human consciousness, just as structurally oriented linguistics interprets speech or various discursive practices as applications of the rule structure that constitutes language. No historical relationship is posited between the observer/investigator and the system of human interaction being analyzed. There is no attempt, as in the case of hermeneutical analysis, to relate the meaning of the present (the predicament of the observer) to the past.

Now where does Foucault fit within these traditions of inquiry? Foucault's archeological method of interpreting human conduct is certainly much closer to the structuralist than to the hermeneutical persuasion. For Foucault, an analysis has no place for the investigator's self-understanding. In fact, the individual speaker or author of a statement has no such place, whoever the speaker/author is, investigator or investigatee. Speaking (or writing) for Foucault, as for structuralists in general, is an event: the actualization of language in the form of discourse. But the production of discourse in the development of the particular speaking practices or "verbal clusters" which are the "events" that Foucault studies, is controlled by the language system from which the symbolic events emerge. That system contains what Foucault calls the rules that are responsible for the objects and events that are produced by discursive practices. Whatever significance a speaker/author has for Foucault is in the way that a subject of a statement is used in the statement. Rather than separating the speaker from the utterance, Foucault, much like Heidegger, notes that the individual speaker or author rarely adds anything significant to a statement. The meaning of a statement, which depends on the discursive practices within which the statement has a place, includes the rules that create a particular kind of subject of a statement. These rules provide boundaries that determine who can speak about what. Author functions, Foucault notes, are part of particular discourses; they do not stand apart from them. "The author function is tied to the legal and institutional systems that circumscribe, determine, and articulate the realm of discourses; it does not operate in a uniform manner in all discourses, at all times, and in any given culture; it is not defined by the spontaneous attribution of a text to its creator, but through a series of precise and complex procedures; it does not refer, purely and simply, to an actual individual insofar as it simultaneously gives rise to a variety of egos and to a series of subjective positions that individuals of any class may come to occupy."[14]

Foucault thus sounds a lot like a structuralist inasmuch as the role of the individual speaker or actor is diminished in significance and the structure in which persons have a place becomes the focus of analysis. But Foucault's archeological metaphor is designed to dissociate him from an important aspect of the structuralist orientation. Whereas structuralists deal with speech or texts as the surface events that have meaning as a result of the deeper structure—the signification system—from which they arise, Foucault argues that the rules which give speech or conduct meaning are on the surface, that is, they are represented by discursive practices; they inhere *in* discourse rather than lying beneath it. Foucault writes, "Archeology tries to define not the thoughts, representations, images, themes, preoccupations that are concealed or revealed in discourses; but those discourses themselves, those discourses as practices obeying certain rules."[15]

So while structuralists, and to some extent hermeneutical analysts, treat the content of the statements of a culture, society, or subsocietal grouping as the surface expression of a deeper level of meaning, Foucault insists that the meaning lies on the surface of a discourse. Like structuralists (and hermeneuticists), he argues that the meaning of terms or expressions is not intrinsic but rather is to be understood only in the context in which they are found: in the relation of each term or expression to the others in the set of statements, to the speaker, to the style of the utterances involved, and so on. But he rejects the structuralist commitment to the notion that each discourse one analyzes contains an underlying structure to be discovered. Hence Foucault's archeological metaphor and his search for "monuments" rather than texts.

The archeological method, as used by Foucault, has been applied to the group of statements that comprise a discipline or profession. For example, Foucault's analysis of the practice of medicine in the Nineteenth Century is essentially an analysis of medical discourse in that period and of the rules of formation that constitute that discourse. The "rules of formation" are the rules or norms that are responsible for the objects which emerge in a discourse, the distribution of enunciative modes or speaking styles available (e.g., kinds of speakers and kinds of statements involved in particular discourses), the set of concepts involved in the statements, and the themes in the discourse which serve as strategic frameworks for combining concepts into an interpretive system.[16] These rules can therefore be construed as part of the prescribed relationships in a society that are represented in particular discursive practices. This somewhat recondite notion will be explicated more fully below.

In order to provide a preliminary purchase on these social/political relationships implicit in discursive practices, consider what is now commonplace in medical discourse. Doctors in contemporary industrialized societies frequently speak to their patients using the passive voice. We would not be surprised, for example, to hear a doctor say, "An angiogram is indicated in your case" (this is a diagnostic test to locate clogged veins and arteries). This enunciative modality (the passive voice) has emerged as a result of a changed relationship between doctor and patient. Whereas before the development of medical *science,* the doctor, practicing the medical *art,* fixed his gaze directly on the patient in order to engage in a diagnostic interpretation. The gaze became partly averted in the transition to scientific (i.e., laboratory-assisted) medicine. The doctor–patient relationship is now mediated by the doctor–lab technician, doctor–drug company, doctor–medical science, and doctor–public health regulation relationships. Among other things, the use of the passive voice represents a diminished responsibility of the doctor for diagnosis and treatment. A statement that "X is indicated," sounds less as though a doctor is responsible for choosing than a locution like "I have decided to try X."

The statement "an angiogram is indicated" is, in Foucault's language, based on a different set of rules of formation from that of diagnostic statement in the active voice. The rules of formation, as Foucault calls them, are "conditions of existence (but also of coexistence, maintenance modification and disappearance) in a given discursive division."[17] The rules responsible for the formation of the enunciative mode used by doctors in diagnoses are those that organize the medical profession and relate it to the rest of society. Doubtless, therefore, these rules must be understood as products of broad-based social and political change. But another aspect of understanding them emerges when we recognize that whatever brought them about, they *are* the system of responsibility reflected in the doctor's drawing back from the role of sole decision maker in diagnostic and therapeutic processes. When we notice how the various enunciative modalities discernible in medical discourse represent rules about how the objects (and subjects) of medical discourse relate to each other, we see the way that discursive practices are political practices.

Foucault and Epistemology

Before moving on to a fuller treatment of the implications of Foucault's method for political analysis, it is useful to place his analysis in the context of the contemporary developments in epistemology that have been treated in previous chapters. Foucault can be viewed as a neo-positivist. Traditional positivists such as members of the Vienna Circle regarded the meaning of statements as governed primarily by the objects to which the statements refer. Foucault, rejecting a radical separation between speech and phenomena, locates the meaning of a statement in the rules that give rise to the objects and relationships involved in the statement as well as to the rules governing the enunciative form of the statement and its conceptual and thematic structure. In the context of traditional positivism, we speak *about* things and events, while, according to Foucault's model, our speaking is constitutive of things and events. For this reason, Foucault's method is not to decipher statements in order to discern more perspicuously what they are about. For him, the statements themselves are the data of analysis. His approach, like that of the positivists, therefore purports to be strictly empirical; it is simply deployed on a different empirical domain, one that can only be seen as an empirical domain on the basis of an altered view of meaning. As Foucault puts it: "The field of statements . . . is accepted in its empirical modesty, as the locus of particular events, regularities, relationships, modifications and systematic transformations; in short . . . it is treated not as the result of something else, but as a practical domain that is autonomous (although dependent), and which can be described at its own level."[18]

Foucault's neo-positivism is thus more than a subtle shift from the positivism developed by the Vienna Circle in the early twentieth century and subsequently refined by two generations of "logical empiricists." His position, in fact, builds upon the critiques of positivism embodied in the analysis of the English linguistic philosophers. Foucault, like the English linguistic philosophers, views the context and function of a

statement as constituents of its meaning. Inasmuch as he therefore regards the speaker's status as a contribution to the meaning of a statement, Foucault is adopting a position that is quite similar to that of Austin explicated above. Whereas Austin (among others) has spoken of
"speech-acts," Foucault refers to "verbal performances." For Foucault
as for Austin, the act that is actually performed when a statement is
made depends on the role or location of the speaker. For example, the
statement "You are legally in the clear" is an absolution if said by a
jurist under the appropriate circumstances, but it is something else (perhaps bad advice) if uttered by a next-door neighbor. What Foucault adds
to this analysis of speakers—owing to his intellectual debts to the
French linguistic tradition—is the idea that rather than simply viewing
speakers as persons who use language to do various things, we should
be aware that there are kinds of persons that exist in language generally
and in various discursive practices particularly. In Foucault's terms we
would elaborate the above example by noting that juridical speech practices provide a place for judges that is exclusive. It is one within which
next-door neighbors cannot take up residence.

Foucault has therefore gone beyond the mere stipulation, which
comes out of the Anglo-American linguistic philosophical tradition, that
word–object relationships are ruled governed, whether those rules are
regarded as mere observational procedures (the empiricist position) or
norms for the use of statements in varying contexts (the linguistic philosophy position). Foucault has suggested that given the relational quality of those rules, i.e., that they place persons in the network of social,
political, and administrative arrangements, they are worth examining as
data. When we do so we can raise questions about how those social,
political, and administrative relationships in a society give rise to rules
in accordance with which various kinds of objects emerge as a focus of
attention for particular disciplines, professions, and other, similarly
bounded, collectivities.

In asking this kind of question, Foucault stands athwart epistemology
and the sociology of knowledge, for he is concerned with both the question of what a statement means (epistemology) and with why it means
what it means (sociology of knowledge). The two concerns come together for Foucault because his treatment of the epistemological question, as should be evident from the above discussion, raises the sociological one (not to mention the political ones). The implications of
Foucault's kind of position and the questions it raises thus lead to a
wholly different kind of assessment of statements than that pursued by
empiricists. For empiricists, the *value* of a statement must be based on
whether it is true or false or at least confirmable in principle when confronted with relevant evidence. For Foucault, however, since the mean-

ing of a statement is determined by the rule-governed "discursive formation," statements are to be evaluated on the basis of their significance for social and political relations. He claims that "to analyze a discursive formation . . . is to weigh the 'value' of statements. A value that is not defined by their truth, that is not gauged by the presence of a secret content; but which characterizes their place, their capacity for circulation and exchange, their possibility of transformation, not only in the economy of discourse but more generally, in the administration of scarce resources."[19]

The methods of analysis involved in testing the truth of statements, which derive from empiricist epistemology, depend on the commitment to a radical separation between statements and that to which the statements refer ("evidence," as it is sometimes called). In Foucault's position, however, the objects referred to in statements are partly constituted by the rules governing their meaning. Their truth value is therefore contingent, for the evidence of their truth is not 'out there' as independent validity criteria. Foucault's approach to the concept of truth is not unlike the position adopted by Habermans, who, like Foucault, rejects a correspondence theory that informs empiricist approaches to truth. Influenced by the English analytic tradition, Habermas has claimed that statements are not true or false on the basis of their correspondence with "things," because a "fact" (that which is regarded as true) is not the same as a "thing." As Strawson put it, "facts are what statements (when true) state; they are not what statements are about."[20] Facts are facts, moreover, in connection with what Strawson and other linguistic philosophers call conventions (interpretive norms). Habermas makes this point referring to "standards" instead of conventions, noting that "the facts are first constituted in relation to the standards that establish them."[21]

The importance of this approach to truth, which could be called "conventionalist," as it is based on a rejection of the separation between discourse and facts, is that it alters by implication the relationship between ideological commitments and knowledge. Habermas uses the concept of "interests," arguing that the theoretical attitude productive of knowledge cannot be separated from interests, because interests are the source of the standards or conventions that control the interpretations from which "facts" are constituted. Habermas might back away from my use of "ideological commitment" as a synonym for interests as he conceives of them, because for Habermas, interests are more cognitive and universal than are ideologies. The ideology notion would fit better in Foucault's framework for dealing with truth.

Foucault thus takes a similar but somewhat more radical position on truth than does Habermas. Whereas Habermas seems to regard the "interests" behind the standards that are constitutive of facts and therefore productive of knowledge as universal or natural, Foucault treats them as strictly ideological or partisan. Instead of mentioning the dependence of knowledge on interests, he speaks of how knowledge is dependent on power. Similar to Habermas's claim that it makes no sense to regard the suspending of interests as a necessary precondition to developing knowledge is Foucault's claim that it is misguided "to imagine that knowledge can exist only where the power relations are suspended and that knowledge can develop only outside its injunctions, its demands and its interests."[22]

Foucault explicates this claim in relation to "knowledge about bodies," showing how the operation of certain powerful interests in a society creates the condition for such knowledge. This becomes clear when we ask about the content of the standards that would contribute to knowing a "fact" about a body such as whether it is healthy or not. Foucault notes, for example, that societies are so constituted that bodies are more or less useful to the extent that they are both productive and subjugated. How does this relate to claims about the health of a body? Whether a body is judged as healthy or sick is not a matter of observation. The "facts" of health and unhealth become facts only in connection with some standards about how a body should perform. The political context of the standards implicit in attributions of health and illness will be addressed again below. Here it should suffice to note that when power in a society is exercised by requiring certain performances from bodies (e.g., both ability for productivity—defined in a particular way—and subjugation so that bodies are *willing* to produce), what comes to be regarded as knowledge about bodies is knowledge in the context of standards for those performances, standards that are controlled by the powerful and implemented by their servants. It is thus the case that in an important respect, knowledge of the body is closely linked to the ability to conquer it, to exact certain performances from it.[23]

Foucault's linking of knowledge and power does not imply that hypothesis testing has no role in a knowledge enterprise; it remains important to weigh a statement's ability to reflect correctly the situation it purports to constitute and describe. This implies, however, that standards other than those identified with science are involved in deciding that a hypothesis has been confirmed or disconfirmed. It suggests, in addition, that there is another significant dimension of value in statements, a value other than that of a statement's truth or falsity.

The interplay of the ordinary empiricist approach to evaluating statements and Foucault's approach is evident when we try to evaluate two completing discourses that purport to illuminate the same domain. For example, one could compare the discourses of liberal and Marxist eco-

nomics on a variety of criteria, one of which could be their relative predictive capabilities. Although it may be true that we can do better at predicting the growth rate of certain industrial economies with the liberal
theoretical system, it is not possible to speak about the relationships
known as political economy with the liberal discourse, because the two
domains (the economic and the political) do not meet in the discourse.
Thus part of the *value* of the Marxist economic discourse is that political
and economic relations meet within it. More specifically, the subset of
statements that comprise the "labor theory of value" derive the kind of
value referred to by Foucault by creating a relationship between labor
and the price or worth of goods in a society. One can derive the economic value of goods by deriving that value from the worth of goods in
exchange instead of evaluating those goods based on the labor that produced them. But when the worth of goods is calculated on the basis of
the labor input, workers achieve an importance or a place that they do
not have in alternative economic models of the worth of goods.

Thus the "value," in Foucault's terms, of the statements comprising
the labor theory of value resides in the position within the discourse of
persons who work. When Marx promoted the labor theory of value, he
was therefore delivering an asset to a class of people, not simply trying
to build a "better" theory (in the scientific sense). It is precisely this
kind of asset that Foucault is focusing on in his approach to discourses.
He is, in fact, explicit in regarding a discourse as an "asset," one that
"from the moment of its existence . . . poses the question of power; an
asset that is, by nature, the object of a struggle, a political struggle."[24]
If, following Foucault, we view discourses as domains within which
power and authority are conferred on some and denied to others, as political analysts and theorists our approach to language must shift. Rather
than regarding language and speech practices as denotational tools for
discovering aspects of experience, we can regard them as representations, in themselves, of political relations. What Foucault therefore
brings to this kind of conventionalist view of language, meaning, and
truth that has hitherto been only obliquely suggested is a highly politicized consciousness, which has led him to analyze discursive practices
for purposes of retrieving the politics within which we reside unreflect-
ing as we construct our worlds of domination and submission with our
utterances.

Foucault is certainly not the only one who seeks to attack structures
of domination through a radical rejection of the prevailing, empiricist
epistemology. The critical-theory school associated with writers such as
Adorno, Horkheimer, and Benjamin, the primary influence on the work
of Habermas, engages more directly the empiricist philosophical tradition that Foucault implicitly dismisses. Foucault, like others who reject

empiricist epistemology, avoids the radical distinction between the subject and object in the knowledge relationship. But his view of the subject, is Nietzschean; it is radical to the point of being nihilistic. Like Nietzsche, he sees the pursuit of truth to be predicated on a misguided externalizing of the object and source of truth. For Foucault, truth is conventional, as it is for Habermas, but the conventions extend to the constitution of subjects as well as objects and object relations. There is no nonconventional arena exterior to discourse within which subjects can transcend convention and pursue universal interests (as in Habermas's ideal-speech situation). Foucault's position thus implies something different from the phenomenological and critical-theory views that because persons constitute their object worlds, a theory of knowledge must allow for the activity of knowing subjects. He argues that subjects *exist*—acquire identities—within prevailing discursive practices. It would be appropriate, within his view of the subject, to reverse the familiar notion that persons make statements, and say that statements make persons.

Foucault's radical position on the subject therefore implies a radical approach to understanding human relations. To understand how human actions and practices are constituted—to apprehend the rules that give them meaning—is to understand not the activities of knowing subjects or the interests they pursue but the practices embedded in discourses that create subjects, objects, and relationships among them. It should be noted in addition that Foucault's historical analyses are more applied than are those of other, contemporary continental thinkers (e.g., the critical theorists) who focus on power relations in society. To appreciate the possibilities that Foucault's mode of analysis portends for political understanding, we can first examine his various applied investigations and then turn to his methodological writings in order to contrast his philosophical self-understanding with that of other schools of thought.

Foucault's Applications

Given Foucault's view that knowledge of any kind is politically predicated, it is not significant for our purposes that he has not applied his method of analysis to political discourse, i.e., to discourse that purports to be explicitly oriented toward political relations. Indeed, discursive development within a society provides insights into that society's political structure, in that a discourse of any kind provides at once for both the emergence of objects and for kinds of subjects who have the legitimacy to speak and act in such a way that they control those objects. Foucault demonstrates this in his first well-known investigation, a history of the phenomena that have been included in the category of "madness." Specifically, in *Madness and Civilization* he examines the uses of the concept of madness from the end of the sixteenth century through the eighteenth century. In keeping with his commitment, to be examined more fully below, that knowledge of various phenomena are historically discontinuous because of the dependency of knowledge on power relations in a society, he demonstrates that madness is not the same phenomenon from one historical period to another.[25] The change from the "ship of fools" to the "hospital of madness" (the change from treating persons regarded as mad by exiling them to treating them in hospitals) is not for example, simply a change in technique for dealing with *a* phenomenon; it is also a change in phenomena. The madness of the ship-of-fools period (sixteenth century) is constituted in an era of religious dominance. When a religious hierarchy is the primary authority in a society, what becomes madness or any kind of deviance becomes so in the context of a moral discourse that distinguishes good from evil—the operating standards of an ecclesiastical authority. Because "moral education," a primary social control method for maintaining such an authority, produces its effects through the demonstration of exemplary behavior of such education's targets, deviants must be sent away lest they pollute the moral environment, for the coexistence of rule followers and rule breakers in a society where moral solidarity is prescribed is intolerable. Madness in the sixteenth century was thus seen as an otherworldly representation of vice, and as such, it was "sent out of the world." In contrast, the madness of the hospital period—houses of confinement were built for the "mad" in the seventeenth century—coincides with the growing dominance of economic interests as a result of the industrial revolution. It is a worldly phenomenon that provides and reflects standards for measuring reason, a reason that is compatible with the emerging socioeconomic structure.

What, then, constitutes the way madness is conceptualized and then treated in given historical periods? Foucault's analysis of the genesis of confinement in the classical age suggests an answer. Foucault sees confinement in this period as "condemnation of idleness" brought on by "a new sensibility to poverty and to the duties of assistance, new forms of reaction to the economic problems of unemployment and idleness, a new ethic of work, and also the dream of a city where moral obligation was joined to civil law, within the authoritarian forms of constraint." The answer, then, is that madness takes its definition and produces its response within a framework of economic, social, and political change. The rules of formation of the madness phenomenon arose primarily from the need for a large labor force, given the developing economic system in France and its attendant social, administrative, and ideological developments. These developments "explain in part the mode in which madness was perceived, and experienced, by the classical age."[26] Briefly, then, madness as a phenomenon is constituted on the basis of norms for performance. Because of the growing dominance of industrial or entre- preneurial interests, as opposed to ecclesiastical interests, being mad becomes being unable or unwilling to perform occupationally in contrast with its earlier connection with being unable or unwilling to perform morally.

With confinement, madness thus changes its locus in the administra- tive structure, for confinement is a police function, having become "an economic measure and a social precaution." Whereas prior to the sev- enteenth century madness was constituted out of a religious structure that functioned by measuring itself with respect to an other worldly do- main of vice and virtue, with the confinement of the classical age, "mad- ness was perceived on the social horizon of poverty, of incapacity for work, of inability to integrate with the group." Foucault's answers to the formulation of madness as a concept in any period is in terms of the organization of collective life in that period. To summarize what pro- duced madness, as it was experienced in the classical age, for example, he states, "The new meanings assigned to poverty, the importance given to the obligation to work, and all the ethical values that are linked to labor, ultimately determined the experience of madness and inflected its course."[27]

The analysis of madness, as it is pursued with Foucault's archeologi- cal method, thus involves questions about the discursive formations in which madness appears. Madness was not, for example, medicalized— not constituted as a kind of phenomenon in medical discourse—until the seventeenth century. Thus the question, What is madness? pursued with the archeological method, produces responses about the process by which social control agencies in a society shift their loci of control as other material changes affect the demands that persons and groups make on each other. The question implied in Foucault's method of analysis can be posed somewhat differently, however. One can focus on a phe- nomenon like madness and then examine the various discursive prac- tices in which it is located in order to find out what it is and why it is what it is. Or, one can, as Foucault has done on *The Birth of the Clinic,* focus on a discursive formation within the practice of a particular col- lectivity (the medical profession) and ask questions about the kinds of objects and relations that emerge within that discourse.[28]

In *The Birth of the Clinic,* Foucault applies his already more refined archeological method to an analysis of medical discourse from the end of the eighteenth through the nineteenth century, and he provides a more self-conscious treatment of the mode of analysis implied by the ar- cheological metaphor. One way of describing what Foucault says about his mode of analysis in *The Birth of the Clinic* is to note that in his analysis of medical discourse/practice, he begins to systematize the step he has taken beyond the Anglo-American position on meaning that emerged from critiques of positivism. It is one thing to note, as contemporary Anglo-American language analysts have, that the meaning of statements is contingent on the context within which utterances are made, and quite another to analyze that context. To the extent that utterances convey a way of thinking, one can look at that way of thinking in terms of how the context controlling the means of utterances involves dominance patterns in the society. Persons do not simply express their individual thoughts in words; they enter the flow of language and particular discursive practices which contain preconceived ways of thinking that are predicated on rules with a content, a content involving modes of interpersonal relations. As Foucault notes, "What counts in the things said by men is not so much what they may have thought, as that which systematizes them from the outset"[29] Foucault thus brings the word–object debate in contemporary epistemology full circle, back to a form of positivism by giving substance to the rules or conventions that correlate words and things and by demonstrating the origins of some of those rules in collective life.

The Birth of the Clinic is, among other things, a powerful treatise on the politics of medicine, revealing the political undergirding of the developing of medical concepts. Applying a spatial metaphor to the concept of disease, Foucault speaks of the primary, secondary, and tertiary spatialization of a disease. Primary spatialization is the position of the disease with respect to other diseases that it *resembles*. In this sense, a disease takes its place in a nomenclature and is measured by its distance from or degree of resemblance with other diseases. Secondary spatialization places a disease in the body. Although a disease is not constituted by its place in certain organs, "the organs are the concrete support of the disease."[30] Tertiary spatialization is described by Foucault in his characteristically recondite manner. "Let us call tertiary spatialization all the gestures by which, in a given society, a disease is circumscribed, medically invested, isolated, divided up into closed, privileged regions, or distributed throughout cure centers, arranged in the most favorable way." Although it is less than obvious from this quotation, tertiary spatialization is the most politically significant division or location function. The tertiary spatialization of a disease locates it in the sociopolitical and administrative structure—places it in the locus of "political struggles, demands and utopias, economic constraints, social confrontations. In it, a whole corpus of medical practices and institutions confronts the primary spatialization with forms of a social space whose genesis, structure, and laws are of a different nature."[31]

The spatialization metaphor thus functions for Foucault to illustrate the role that social relations and political and administrative practices play in establishing a concept and giving it meaning. In the case of medical discourse, the concepts it contains are partly constituted by and thus reflective of relationships between medical functionaries and other authoritative roles in society. Analyzing the concept of an epidemic, for example, Foucault points out that it is predicated on relations between doctors and police, because "A medicine of epidemics could exist only if supplemented by a police: to supervise the location of mines and cemeteries . . . to control the sale of bread."[32] Throughout *The Birth of the Clinic,* Foucault shows, in effect, how ideology and medical technology are intertwined to constitute the objects of medical attention and to constitute the norms that give various signs significance as medical symptoms. His analysis of the development of modern medicine thus demonstrates his thesis that knowledge (in this case medical knowledge) is predicated on power and authority.

Another important dimension of Foucault's mode of analysis that becomes more clearly highlighted in *The Birth of the Clinic* is his theory of change. He argues that medical discourse is altered as a result of changes that are external to that discourse, showing, for example, that the development of "a conceptual mastery of probability"—probability theory became available as an instrument of medical inquiry as it did for other kinds of inquiry—helped to produce a medical science which turned from the analysis of individual cases to the analysis of classes of disease. Such a change produced the need for a single, controlled domain for analysis (the hospital) rather than a variety of domains (patients' homes) which complicate the inference processes central to a science, and it also produced a different discursive mode or style, as illustrated in the above example of doctors' use of the passive voice.

Some other insights into Foucault's approach to social inquiry that may be derived from his recent treatments of punishment and sexuality will be discussed below along with an elaboration on the implications of his work for developing a mode of political analysis. At this juncture, we can turn to his writings on inquiry both to comprehend better his specific historical studies and to confront some relevant issues of the social sciences with which his approach consorts.

Foucault on Inquiry

In considering Foucault's methodological-oriented studies, perhaps most noteworthy in his radical approach to the relationship between language and consciousness, which begins to emerge in *The Order of Things* and is more thoroughly developed in *The Archeology of Knowledge* in his essay on language.[33] Foucault argues, as do others in the French linguistic tradition, that language uses persons rather than vice versa. Discourses, the various forms in which language is actualized for particular purposes, are responsible for the deployment of both objects and subjects. Phenomena like madness emerge as objects in certain discourses, and discourses provide status and sites for various kinds of subjects (e.g., those who are mad and those who deal with them as professionals or bureaucrats). Rather than thinking of subjects using language, we can think of forms of speaking (various discursive practices) as offering places for various kinds of subjects. This position on language has its adherents in various kinds of writing. In addition to the similar position developed by Heidegger, for example, we can find this notion of language in Samuel Beckett's work (to which Foucault refers occasionally). In Beckett's *The Unnamable,* for example, the narrator, frustrated by an inability to speak about himself with anything but a language created by others, says, "I am walled around with their vociferations, none will ever know what I am, none will ever hear me say it, I won't say it, I can't say it, I have no language but theirs." Similarly, speaking of the persons engaged in scientific discourse, Foucault says, "I should like to know whether the subjects responsible for scientific discourse are not determined in their situation, their function, their perceptive capacity, and their practical possibilities by conditions that dominate and even overwhelm them."[34]

Or, speaking of medical discourse, Foucault says, "Medical statements cannot come from anybody; their value, efficacy, even their therapeutic powers, and generally speaking, their existence as medical statements cannot be dissociated from the statutorily defined person who has the right to make them and to claim for them the power to overcome suffering and death."[35] Medical discourse, like any discourse, creates subjects because the actualization of such a discourse requires a certain kind of speaker. This provocative position, developed in *The Archeology of Knowledge,* is worth considering at greater length, but before that, one aspect of Foucault's earlier methodology work, *The Order of Things,* is worth developing, particularly because it bears on issues provoked by Thomas Kuhn's influential study of scientific revolutions.[36]

There is a surface similarity between Foucault's analysis in *The Order of Things* and Kuhn's *The Structure of Scientific Revolutions.* In *The Order of Things* Foucault develops the idea that language controls and directs consciousness and presents a historical framework relating what he calls "epistemes" to the substantive or reigning theories of various disciplines. Epistemes are essentially metalinguistic orientations, theories of the meaning of statements or of word–object relationships. Foucault's analysis suggests, among other things, that the development of the "human sciences" has been discontinuous (a position of his intellectual predecessors Bachelard and Canguilhem) as a result of having developed within different "reigning epistemes." These have determined the structures of the different human science disciplines such as grammar, political economy, and natural history (or biology as it later became) in various historical periods.

In assessing Foucault's position that knowledge systems which evolve from one period to another do not follow a developmental pattern but rather represent radical ruptures often provoked by "events" outside the frame of reference of a given knowledge system, one is inevitably drawn to a comparison between Foucault's idea of reigning epistemes, with the conceptualizations which they comprehend, and Thomas Kuhn's conception of "paradigms." Although Kuhn's notion of what a paradigm is remains ambiguous despite his clarifying statements developed since his original statement of his ideas, his initial definition is useful for discussion. Kuhn stated that paradigms are "universally recognized scientific achievements that for a time provide model problems and solutions to a community of practitioners."[37] The achievements to which Kuhn refers include, he states, "law, theory, application and instrumentation together." What has been both controversial and attractive to some about Kuhn's notion is his account of the process by which paradigm shifts occurs. It has seemed to some that Kuhn rejects a positivist model of science that radically separates theory and data and scientific interests from political interests. Cited in this respect is his claim that the choice among competing paradigms "can never be unequivocally settled by logic and experiment alone." Kuhn adds, "As in political revolutions, so in paradigm choice—there is no standard higher than the assent of the relevant community."[38] In response to critics on the "right"—mainly empiricist philosophers of science—Kuhn has elaborated on what he means by the "assent of the relevant community," stating that because paradigms being with different premises, one cannot fall back on standards of inductive and deductive inference in selecting among them. But Kuhn assures us that by persuasion he means "rational persuasion," the kind one would expect to have currency in a community of scientists which is cognitively oriented, that is, who evaluate knowledge frameworks on the basis of enlightenment criteria that purport to be universal (freed from particular interests). Thus, as Richard Bernstein has recently argued, Kuhn's account of persuasion leaves him squarely within an essentially positivist position.[39]

Unlike Kuhn's position, Foucault's commitment to a nondevelopmental model of the production of knowledge is based on a rejection of positivist/empiricist models of science. In the first place, Foucault's level of focus is different. He conceives the objects of knowledge as emerging from the relationships in a society that produce the discursive practices within which the "objects" are embedded. Foucault then seeks to highlight these relationships ("rules of formation"), which produce what empiricist language would call both the theory and the data. Therefore the important characteristic of a given knowledge framework is the model of interest and power relations that informs it and therefore gives it meaning as well as the meta-level commitments about what meaning is—Foucault's "epistemes." A Foucaultian analysis is therefore interpretive in its orientation; it seeks to elucidate the meaning foundation of knowledge. Kuhn focuses in his discussion of paradigms more on the laws and theories that represent the syntax of conceptualizations than on the underlying semantic structure. Preoccupation with syntax implies a trivialization of the problem of meaning which is characteristic of positivist philosophy of science and is especially likely to occur when one emphasizes the history of physics, as Kuhn does, as opposed to the human sciences, as does Foucault.

Secondly, given Kuhn's exclusive focus on the knowledge community comprised of practicing scientists and his emphasis on the structure of knowledge systems rather than their meaning and significance (on the rules that link knowledge systems with the way of life within which they emerge), his notion of transformation from one paradigm to another is highly cognitive, that is, dependent on "rational persuasion." For Foucault, in contrast, ruptures and transformations in knowledge systems, whether these constitute academic disciplines or professional and/or bureaucratic functions, are not cognitive. They are not actively debated but emerge as a result of changing interests within a society that locate persons in various roles and distribute authority and responsibility differently. This focus clearly comes out of Foucault's concern with the relations that *create* knowledge systems rather than the syntax and justificatory structures of those systems themselves.

Thirdly, Foucault brings a much more highly politicized understanding to his account of changing knowledge systems. Kuhn's understanding of the knowledge community is one in which no dominance patterns exist. He conceives of a world of scientist/scholars who seek to build models oriented toward comprehension but not action. He has no model of the relationship between ideology and science and employs the concept of persuasion to comprehend everything that is not inductive or deductive inference arguments, which are presumably self-persuasive. If, with Foucault,we consider knowledge structures in a broader sense than what is involved in theories in the physical sciences, we have a more significant interpretive task to understand the context within which one can speak about knowledge. The purposes embraced by a particular scientific discourse oriented, for example, toward cosmology or celestial mechanics are narrow and relatively unproblematic. It is generally agreed that the value of a theoretical formulation is related to such dimensions as its ability to reduce one's surprise about where a given object in the universe appears and to the relationship between such predictions about movement with various other relevant understandings. As soon as we broaden the community of understanding to those with an interest in knowledge about persons, groups, and societies, the "premises" of knowledge, in terms of the kind of assets that particular discursive practices provide, involve more than simple stipulations about initiating assumptions. Predicating socially relevant knowledge involves no less than a comprehensive model of a way of life, a polemical or ideological position on the appropriate structure of the social and political world. Foucault seems to understand, as Kuhn does not, that "knowledge" is contingent not on mere assumptions (understood as simple initiating premises) but on full-blown ideological models of power and authority. How the relationship between knowledge and power and authority produces the need for a particular mode of inquiry is elucidated in Foucault's *Archeology of Knowledge.*

In *The Archeology of Knowledge,* Foucault offers a comprehensive specification of his archeological method and applies it to changing conceptual frameworks in the disciplines of medicine, grammar, psychopathology, and political economy. As his fullest and most recent statement of his method, it merits some explication, particularly because it provides a foundation for the approach to political analysis that I shall develop in subsequent chapters. He begins with the position (which he attributes to G. Canguilhem) that "the history of a concept is not wholly that of its progressive refinement, its continuously increasing rationality, its abstraction gradient, but that of its successive rules of use, that of the many theoretical contexts in which it developed and matured." It is usually the case, asserts Foucault, that one tends to think of disciplines as unities with historical continuity. But why are they thought of in this way? In attempt to answer this question, he examines and rejects four hypotheses that might account for the apparent unity of a discipline. Viewing a discipline as a discourse or group of statements that constitutes a particular practice, Foucault defines the question as, "What is it about such a group of statements that provides a 'discursive regularity' over time?"[40]

The first hypothesis is that the statements of a discipline can form a group because, over time, they refer to the same objects. Upon brief inspection, however, it is clear, as Foucault has demonstrated in both *Madness and Civilization* and *The Birth of The Clinic,* respectively, that madness in one historical period is not the same phenomenon as it is in another, and that even within an historical period, "the object presented as their correlative by medical statements . . . is not identical with the object that emerges in legal sentence or police action."[41] In short, what *constitutes* objects are the discursive formations in which they occur. They do not exist as meaningful phenomena independent of how one speaks. The second hypothesis is that a group of statements of a discipline form a group or coherent whole by virtue of "their form and type of connection." Perhaps it is the case, for example, that "medicine was organized as a series of descriptive statements."[42] But as Foucault notes, clinical discourse contained ethical choices, hypotheses, and several other formulations as well as descriptive statements. Enunciative styles are not uniform within a disciplinary discourse. The third hypothesis is that a group of statements might be established by "the system of permanent and coherent concepts involved." But a brief inspection of the discipline of grammar, as it has changed conceptually from, for example, the seventeenth to the eighteenth centuries, invalidates this hypothesis. The fourth and last hypothesis is that statements can be grouped on the basis of the "identity and persistence of themes." But again the hypothesis is easily invalidated. Foucault shows that the same set of concepts in the discipline of political economy is organized within different thematic strategies in different periods. The concept of the "formation of value," he shows, has been analyzed both on the basis of exchange and on the basis of the remuneration for a day's work.[43]

Foucault concludes that disciplines do not offer or present a unity. There exist simply "systems of dispersion" that can be described in flux as a discursive formation. So taking the dimensions of a discipline that he had formulated as hypotheses accounting for unity, Foucault then analyzes them as aspects of a discursive formation. He shows that psychiatric discourse in the nineteenth century, for example, "is characterized not by privileged objects, but by the way in which it forms objects that are highly dispersed." Through this analysis, Foucault points out the substance of the rules that intervene between word and object in various disciplines, and he traces the origins of those rules. The origins, he argues, inhere in "relations established between institutions, economic and social processes, behavior patterns, systems of norms, techniques, types of classification, modes of characterization."[44] It is such relations, he concludes, that are responsible for the appearance of objects, and, it should be added, are in part constitutive of the meaning of statements about such objects.

This aspect of Foucault's analysis can be explained with reference to almost any publicly meaningful phenomenon. Consider "suicides." It should be evident that a death can become an object known as a suicide only in connection with a variety of norms, institutional premises, values, and so on. The boundaries between suicides and other kinds of death are not "out there" to be observed. They are a consequence of the rules we employ about such things as how much care a person should exercise in self-protection (not smoking or not mountain climbing is *not* expected, but not standing in the middle of a frequently used railroad track *is*), and rules about relations between persons in prescribed roles (a death from a self-inflicted knife wound would surely be classified as a suicide, unless the person involved were a surgeon and there was reason to believe she was acting in her professional capacity).

Suicides thus emerge within the intersections of various discourses (medical, penal, psychological) that create various objects and give roles with attendant responsibilities to various subjects. We confront in Foucault's approach to the speech–phenomena relationship, therefore, an implicit analysis of human action that accords with Hart's position presented in chapter 4. Ascribing an action to a person, such as a "suicide," is a matter neither of simply describing the person's behavior nor of representing the person's "state of mind." It is, rather, a matter of analyzing the norms that constitute what is called a suicide, norms which are embedded in modes of speaking and which create both subjects and objects, that is, persons with particular responsibilities and the phenomena (objects) to which they relate in their activities.

In developing his idea that discourse creates the kind of subjects as well as objects, Foucault is enriching the Oxford/Cambridge philosophical approach to language. If we recognize that among the conventions which give statements meaning are those that determine who must make the statement for it to have a particular meaning, we are in a position to relate the meaning of statements to the distribution of power in a society. To ask about the meaning of the statements that comprise a discourse, for Foucault, is to ask, among other things, "what is the status of the individuals who alone have the right, santioned by law or tradition, juridically defined or spontaneously accepted, to proffer such a discourse."[45] Applying such an idea to a particular kind of discourse, Foucault notes (to repeat a quotation) "Medical statements cannot come from anybody; their value, efficacy, even their therapeutic power, and generally speaking, their existence as medical statements cannot be dissociated from the statutorily defined person who has the right to make them, and to claim for them the power to overcome suffering and death."[46]

So the meanings of statements and of the discourses in which they are deployed create positions for persons. Because of this, the analysis of the development of various discourses is, at the same time, the analysis of the development of various social, political, economic, and administrative institutions and processes in the society in which these discourses occur. The discourses are, in effect, "practices" precisely because they reflect and guide relationships among persons. Foucault's focus on particular disciplines is thus incidental to the important point that his approach to language and speech implies, for in studying disciplines he is elucidating the context that gives rise to them—the social relations, institutional supports, and legitimized practices responsible for the concepts they contain, the objects to which they refer, the modes in which they are enunciated, and the strategic organization that relates one statement to another.

Clearly then, the archeological method, whether applied to particular discourses over time (as in *The Archeology of Knowledge*) or to sets of discourses within particular periods (as in *The Order of Things*), constitutes a form of political analysis, for it reveals the political context that is correlated with the rules of formation for discursive practices. Foucault is even more explicit about the political relevance of his approach in his essay "The Discourse on Language." The important aspects of what Foucault suggests in this essay have already been touched upon, especially in the discussion that compares his position with that of Samuel Beckett on the power of discourse. His major presuppositions there are as follows: "I am supposing that in every society the production of discourse is at once controlled, selected, organized and redistributed according to a certain number of procedures, whose role is to avert its powers and its dangers, to cope with chance events, to evade its ponderous awesome materiality." Language, he continues, operates with rules of exclusion, providing boundaries invested with institutional support and correlated with a variety of social, political, and administrative practices. The prohibitions surrounding speech, he notes, "soon reveal its links with desire and power."[47]

As should be evident from this explication of Foucault's analysis, the archeological approach is deployed in two ways. The first and more comprehensive way is primarily descriptive and static. Foucault demonstrates, in effect, that discourses are forms of practice, and therefore that an attention to certain aspects of discourses, such as, the enunciative modalities, kinds of concepts, and thematic strategies, reveals the structure of relationships in the society that is represented in those discourses. The second and less elaborated way is explanatory and dynamic. Foucault never self-consciously supplies a theory of social and political change, even though superficially it would appear that one could regard his theory as very close to the Marxist version of historical materialism, that is, discursive practices could be regarded as the ideological "superstructures" produced by the "base," consisting of the material productive forces.[48] But Foucault's statements on change defy such facile comparisons. The precipitant for a change in discursive practices seems to vary if one pays attention to his various examples; it can be a technological development, for example the development of probability theory, which Foucault has seen as implicated in changing medical relationships represented in a discursive change, or it can be a change in political practices. For instance, taking the example of a new law of assistance, he explicates the political-practice/discursive-formation causal relationship by noting that the new law "creates a hospital space for observation and surgery (space which is organized, furthermore, according to an economic principle, since the sick person benefitting from the care must compensate through the medical lesson which he gives.)"[49] This new locus of medical practice (the hospital) represents an alteration of the doctor–patient relationship, university–medical profession relationship, and so forth. This altered context gives rise to new rules linking concepts with the objects constituted in medical discourse.

Whether or not Foucault can offer a coherent theory of change, the important part of his contribution to political understanding lies elsewhere. His mode of analysis deployed on discursive practices suggests a way to examine political relationships that are neglected in other epistemological/methodological approaches. This mode of analysis emerges when Foucault compares discursive relations with what he calls real or "primary" relations and reflexive or "secondary" relations. Primary relations are those that may be described independently of discourse. Foucault cites as an example of primary relations those existing "between the bourgeois family and the functioning of judicial authorities and categories in the nineteenth century."[50] Clearly, most of traditional and even contemporary political theory focuses on such relations, relations which, because they are primary or explicit, are publicized and thought to be legitimate relations to inspect or subject to the rigors of analysis.

A political theory about relations between the bourgeois family and judicial authorities and categories in the nineteenth century, for example, might focus on recruitment patterns (on questions such as to what extent judicial authorities are drawn from bourgeois families) or on influence patterns (on the question of to what extent the adjudicative system facilitates and legitimates the economic behavior and interests of bourgeois families).

Secondary or reflexive relations are those within a particular discourse. Foucault notes, in explicating such relations, that there is a difference between the actual relations obtaining for example, between the family and criminality (primary relations) and what nineteenth century psychiatry said about those relations (secondary relations). But the secondary relations are invested with, among other things, the practices and ideologies of a profession or discipline, and they differ from tertiary or discursive relations which, as they relate to psychiatry, contain "the interplay of relations that make possible and sustain the objects psychiatric discourse."[51] Such discursive relations have been largely ignored by political analysts and theorists. Work on the politics of psychiatry by such analysts as Szasz and Laing, for example, has focused on what Foucault calls secondary relations, treating the discourse of the psychiatric profession as the expression of an ideological posture. Foucault's concept of discursive relations suggests a more radical and profound type of politicization of relations that have escaped normal political analysis and theory.

To treat a profession like psychiatry as ideological is to politicize, or treat as politically relevant, what has hitherto been treated as descriptive or scientific. What Foucault politicizes is an anterior step in developing the objects of analysis which comprise a profession or discipline. He politicizes the relations (rules and practices) that give rise to concepts and their related objects in a discipline such as psychiatry, and that create privileged speakers in a discourse like the psychoanalytic or other psychiatric discourse. To understand such relations requires an analysis of such things as professional boundaries and role allocations implicit in concepts and the rules that link them with objects. Psychiatrists, for example, organize themselves around the concept of mental health. Following Foucault's type of analysis, the concept of mental health can be seen as a function of those relations in society which legitimize the statement implicit in the mental health concept: that doctors are in charge of explaining mental deviance (for the terms "mental" and "health" and do not naturally belong together—the meaning of their proximity is to be found in social and political organization). Moreover, the objects that come to the attention of "mental health" related professions are also a function of discursive relations; that is, the "mad" or "insane" are so judged because of the rules which link word and object, and those rules emerge from relations which, according to Foucault, are "established between institutions, economic and social processes, behavior patterns, systems of norms, techniques, types of classification, modes of characterization."[52]

Foucault's notion of a discursive practice thus provides a new domain for the acquisition of "data" on political relations. The exclusive focus on what Foucault calls primary relations, which has characterized traditional social science inquiry, helps us understand political relations between and among those entities that reside on the surface of human relations, those objects and situations which we can speak easily and unproblematically about, ignoring the rules constituting them. Discursive relations are those responsible for producing the rules that constitute the objects and events we speak about. To analyze such relations is to politicize a far broader aspect of human relations than is characteristic of the kinds of analyses directed toward relationships that a society explicitly recognizes as political. It is to analyze not simply what we talk about but also why and how we talk about it.

Toward a Mode of Inquiry

The above analysis suggests that attention to Foucault's approach promises the development of a more comprehensive political understanding than that afforded by an exclusive emphasis on other approaches, notably the empiricist and phenomenological orientations. Nevertheless, Foucault radically rejects an important aspect of the development of political knowledge, that which focuses on the standpoint of the observer/investigator. Foucault is not absolutely silent on this problem; he simply rejects its relevance. This rejection neglects an important aspect of the development of knowledge, one that would help to facilitate the application of his method to social phenomena. After developing some of the implications of Foucault's approach, we can therefore consider what is lost by the disappearance of the observer/analyst, a disappearance that is at least strongly implied if not necessitated by his view of language.

How might the analysis of discursive practices proceed if it is to be developed as a model of political inquiry? The concept or, perhaps better, the ideal of, "health" provides a convenient point of departure. In the context of traditional epistemological assumptions used by most contemporary social scientists, health would be regarded as a "dependent variable." The analyses of what causes health that would follow from such an orientation might include inquiries into how environmental, structural, organizational, professional, and/or psychological conditions affect people's health. From such analyses we might, for example, discover that the level of "health" (perhaps measured by morbidity and mortality rates) is either affected or unaffected by the rank that health problems achieve in administrative budgets. But the archeological method, as Foucault has employed it, suggests a different kind of analysis, which would begin with the deceptively simple question, What is health? The answer to such a question, if sufficiently elaborated, should tell us something about the political culture of a society, that is about the set of rules which allocate responsibility for health, which constitute it in a particular way, and which allocate various control procedures that conform to the way health is supposed to be constituted. In modern industrial society, the concept of health has been, to a large extent, medicalized. So if we regard What is health? as partly a question about where the concept is located in the network of human relations, we learn something about who has authority to speak about the kind of wellbeing referred to. To the extent that health is "medicalized," the most privileged speakers are doctors, and they speak about objects emerging in a medical discourse over which they have disproportionate control. As was pointed out in the explication of Foucault's notion of discursive practices above, the concept of "mental health" tells us, given the authority system that prevails around the health concept, that doctors seem to be in charge of the "mental phenomena" that are regarded as deviant. It is of course a commonplace to regard as controversial the authority that the medical profession has acquired to explain mental deviance. There is, for example, a body of theorists called "antipsychiatrists," who have demonstrated convincingly that psychiatry rests upon ethical, social, and political premises and that we should therefore evaluate it as a discipline not simply on a technical, efficiency basis—that of a care ratio or similar performance norm—but also as a social control agency that is involved in allocating power and legitimacy in the society. The antipsychiatrists have shown, in short, that the meaning of the concept of mental health derives in part from social and structural imperatives and that psychiatry therefore performs social and political functions by reinforcing the norms of some subcultures and groups in the society by allocating control measures in their behalf.[53]

Unfortunately, the sophistication displayed in the analyses of the antipsychiatrists has failed to establish an effective epistemological and methodological base for analyzing the political significance of health discourse in general. Some antipsychiatrists have premised their analyses of mental health as a sociopolitical phenomenon on a rigorous distinction between mental and physical health. Szasz, for example, states that in the case of physical illness, "the notion of a bodily symptom is tied to an antomical and genetic context," whereas, he argues, moral-or social-value-based contexts govern psychiatric judgments.[54] And Goffman states, "The diagnoses of physical medicine refer, on their showing, to objective features of human antomy or physiology; whereas diagnostic operations of the psychiatrists are subjective, value-judgments, impregnated with normative and prescriptive elements which are absent from the clinical appraisal and treatment of bodily maladies."[55] Thus, while the antipsychiatrists have been busy politicizing the psychiatric profession, showing that what appear to be technical judgments actually contain implicit prescriptions about social control, they have at the same time been depoliticizing the rest of the medical profession. Ordinary medical diagnoses are also subject to similar controversy in that they are informed by the same social and political contexts as are psychiatric judgments. The norms involved in medical judgment have heretofore simply been regarded as less problematic than those involved in psychiatric judgment. The fact that health is medicalized to a large extent means many things. Among them is the presumption that health is a biological concept, a commitment reflected in the views of the anti-psychiatrists. It is, however, just as problematic to speak about physical health as it is to speak about mental health. The process of ascribing a state of health to a person is subject to the same kind of analysis whether that ascription is directed toward what are regarded as mental or physical processes. Just as we cannot see mental processes by look-ing inside the skull, we cannot see physical processes by making a sub-cutaneous inspection.

Any attribute ascribed to a person is not a description, governed by something intrinsic to the person or to persons in general. Attributes of persons are ascribed with reference to norms or rules that constitute so-cial and political expectations. For example part of the political culture of a society is constituted precisely by norms about how political man should be viewed—in terms of 'needs,' 'demands,' 'rights,' and so forth. Whether or not the concept of health, along with other related concepts (related in the sense that they imply action on the part of the same social agencies), is regarded as relevant to the political domain in a society, is one aspect of that society's political culture. Health processes tend to be less politicized in the United States than they are for example, in China.

If we treat "health" from the viewpoint of a nonpositivist theory of meaning and ask how the concept functions, we will be raising questions about the kind of discursive practices that health ought to belong to. As-cribing a state of health to an organism is not, therefore, a matter of un-problematic observation. Moreover, health is not a biological concept. Biological science does not provide decision rules for distinguishing be-tween health and disease.[56] It is concerned simply with the interaction between an individual organism and its environment. The application of the concepts 'health' or 'disease' to any state of that interaction (re-flected in the "condition" of the organism) involves interpretation based not on a study of how an organism reacts to its environment but on our models of good or ideal interpersonal relations. Given the social per-formance expectations we have for persons, we judge capacities or pro-clivities for performance with interpretations along a continuum, an-chored at the ends with the concepts 'healthy' and 'diseased.' Health is thus not a physical or mental concept.[57] It is simpler than or superordi-nate to our concepts of physical and mental processes (similar to G. E. Moore's notion of the concept of 'good' in ethical theory), and, as is noted above, our criteria for applying the concept involve social per-formance norms (in this sense the concept of health is complex rather than simple). This is illustrated in Peter Sedgwick's example. Arguing that "all ascriptions of illness, whether 'physical' or 'mental,' are heavily loaded with social value-judgments,"[58] has illustrated this point by providing the following scenario of a client–doctor interaction.

CLIENT: (Telephoning doctor) Doctor, I haven't consulted you before but things are getting desperate. I'm feeling so weak, I can't lift anything heavy.

DOCTOR: Goodness, when does this come on you?

CLIENT: Every time I try to lift something or make an effort. I have to walk quite slowly up the stairs and last night when I was packing the big suitcase I found I couldn't lift it off the bed.

DOCTOR: Well, let's have some details about you before you come in. Name?

CLIENT: John Smith.

DOCTOR: Age?

CLIENT: Ninety-two last February.[59]

The doctor, Sedgwick points out, would immediately ascribe the patient's problem to age rather than illness because "none of the physical signs would be regarded as symptoms of illness, since we have special expectations about what constitutes normal performance in the elderly."[60] He goes on to point out that a change in our culture of old age, involving mass rejuvenation techniques or the like, would result in the interpretation (from the same scenario) that the ninety-two-year-old man's complaint was a normal medical referral.

Sedgwick's argument notwithstanding, with a few notable exceptions, there exists no vigorous body of antimedicine theorists to equal the size and productiveness of the antipsychiatrists. Perhaps the most comprehensive treatment of the normative basis of medical judgment is that of Georges Canguilhem. He notes that the concept of a disease, as it is used in medical practice, varies in meaning, depending on the ontological framework that is presupposed by any particular nosological system (system of classification of diseases). Diseases can be understood within a framework of a continuing struggle between inner agents (in the body) and foreign agents. Or they can be interpreted on the basis of an equilibrium–disequilibrium model.[61] The most common framework for interpreting diseases, however, still dominates the medical profession. It suggests a quantitative interface between what are regarded as a physiological process and a pathological process.

Canguilhem resists this contemporary model (or ontological commitment), on whose basis maladies are interpreted as simply quantitative variations of physiological phenomena. He argues that there is no objective or empirical method with which one could locate pathology as an exclusively biological phenomenon. Pathological states must be understood within a context of what he calls the "normativity of life." Pathological states are thus interpretations based upon notions about social order, models of man's relationship with man and with his environment. The norms that are used to distinguish pathological from what are regarded as normal physiological process are not merely technical, for, as Canguilhem notes, "a technical norm reflects, more or less, an ideal of the society and of its hierarchy of values." Canguilhem's analysis demonstrates that one cannot refer to the needs of an organism outside the context of the needs or imperatives of social organization. Given that one cannot demonstrate absolute norms for social organization, there can be no absolute norms for the body that would provide a fixed referent for terms such as "pathological."

Merely to state, however, that the concept of health is based on our norms for performance is not to offer a comprehensive political analysis of health processes like those one can develop by raising the Foucault-type question, What is health? How the elucidation of such norms does provide a political understanding has been quite clearly developed in Foucault's recent historical investigation of punishment. There he suggests that our knowledge of bodies is "politically invested" in the sense that it cannot be separated from the attempt to control or master bodies.[62] Looking at punishment as a way that power gets communicated or signaled to those over whom it is exercised, Foucault speaks of the various forms of "penal seminology." To understand why a body is punished in a given way, during a given historical period, is, according to Foucault, to understand how power is being communicated both to the person whose body is the site of the punishment and to the rest of society. Torture took the form that it did because it represented the spectacle of princely revenge.[63] Public execution or torture is, Foucault says, reactivation of the power of the prince. When power is vested in a person, violation of the law is an act against that person's power. Punishment is therefore not the reestablishment of justice but the demonstration of power. The body, when tortured in such a power system, is therefore a placard upon which power is inscribed. In the industrial age, the political significance of the body changes as the wrongdoer becomes the "imperfectly subjugated producer."[64] Imprisonment—as opposed to torture, say, or public execution—becomes a form of discipline to create a subjugated and productive machine. In general, the model of the body that informs penal policy in any period is generalized into other disciplines and practices in the society (e.g. educational institutitions share the model with penal ones). The norms used to judge normality are deployed everywhere so that health education and social work professionals are all part of what Foucault calls "carceral apparatuses."

He states, "We are in the society of the teacher–judge, the doctor–judge, the educator–judge, the social worker–judge; it is on them that the universal reign of the normative is based; and each individual, wherever he may find himself, subjects to it his body, his gestures, his behavior, his aptitudes, his achievements. The carceral network, in its compact or disseminated forms, with its systems of inspection, distribution, surveillance, observation, has been the greatest support in modern society."[65]

Foucault thus enlightens us about the source of the norms for performance that are the standards for the ascription of health or illness, aptitude or ineptitude, or any qualities ascribed to "bodies." That source has to do with the nature of the prevailing systems of power. Although Foucault seems to be suggesting a primarily Marxist interpretation of the system of power, one that locates it in the control over the means of production (at least in the "industrial age"), we can consider the question more generally in an analysis of norms for performance that are sequestered in models of persons, events, relationships. Simply stated, an extremely important aspect of social and political processes is the application and enforcement of norms of performance. The organization of society into institutions, professions, and political, legal, and administrative processes reflects norms of performance. Moreover, the extent of agreement on and benefit from those norms of performance provides, among other things, a measure of the degree of plurality versus dominance among subcultures within the society. In terms of what interests political scientists, one important distinction that can be made about the control of performance norms in a society is the extent and nature of participation in the setting and enforcing of those norms. To the extent that various dimensions of social process—legal, health, penal—are professionalized, the norms for performance become embedded in what is called "knowledge," a knowledge predicated on professional dominance rather than being presented as problematic standards requiring public decision making. Whatever the power structure in a society, to the extent that it becomes deployed through various knowledge-oriented disciplines and professions, it becomes presented in a way that insulates it from political activity. The norms of the "helping professions," for example, are controlled by professionals, not by their clients, because the professionals "know" what to do.[66] This is reflected in the concepts that these professions employ ('multiple problem families' are focused on by the social work profession). The concepts employed in legal processes, in contrast, are explicitly regarded as controversial. The concept of property, often at issue in a legal process, is treated as though its application is regarded as problematic. Questions are raised as to what 'property' *is* as well as the more simple questions about whom it might belong to. Legal processes (like political processes) are thus governed by explicit ideologies. Although some of the ideological commitments in legal processes are masked in descriptive, seemingly noncontroversial language, legal professions employ *some* language that evidences explicit recognition that a decision-making process rather than a series of observations is involved and that the observations upon which decisions are based can bear alternative interpretations. The legal process is thus explicitly recognized to be a social control process, one moreover, involving controversy. Health processes are often compared with legal processes because decisions in each domain result in confinement or separation of the 'criminal' or 'patient' from society.[67] The health process (on-going decisions by 'health'-related professionals) is characterized by noncontroversial, descriptively oriented language. Such a use of language tends to mask the implicit authority relations involved in the professionalization of health processes characteristic of modern industrial societies. This brief inquiry into the question, What is health? thus indicates that the boundary norms which allocate decision-making processes among social agencies are not 'natural' or given in experience. Problems or processes are not by nature biological, medical, technical, psychological.

The experience of our collective actions falling under such rubrics reflects the fact that a considerable portion of the political process in a society is implicit in the language which allocates the control the various agencies in a society have over a variety of kinds of decisions. Occasionally, this aspect of the political process becomes evident when more than one social control agency is competing for the same client or object of attention. Stoll has suggested such an instance in her discussion of the different images of man employed by the police and by social work agencies.[68] In instances where a new object of attention is emerging, and there are questions raised about how to treat it, for example, drug use, the political process literally involves issues about how one can speak appropriately about the phenomena. In many societies, for example, the controversial questions surrounding "drugs" involve whether drug use should be medicalized, criminalized, or otherwise embedded in the discursive practices of one or another social, political, or administrative agency.

But in one important respect, Foucault's conception of discursive practices takes us a step beyond the growing literature relating linguistic phenomena to political practice. Foucault has shown how the structural dynamics in a society—the changing relationships among changing kinds of persons and groups or agencies—present themselves in the forms of discursive practice. The various objects, roles, events, and actions that are part of our everyday discourse are discursive objects; they are phenomena that have meaning within ways of speaking/understanding that *are* the power and authority systems of the society. To analyze language use, within Foucault's understanding of it, is thus to do more than observe the way various groups within a society exercise control over others. Linguistic domination is not a strategy in the self-conscious and immediate sense in which a person or group is said to dominate another with resort to particular categories and rhetorical styles. The strategic dimension of linguistic practices for Foucault is institutionalized. It is already implicit in what the groups and individuals in a society "know" about each other. Murray Edelman's insightful analysis of "the political language of the helping professions" shows how the linguistic usages of a profession disable its clientele.[69] Foucault's mode of analysis goes a step further and shows how helping professionals and their clientele are kinds of persons that are produced by discursive practices. The one dominates the other not so much through the strategic use of language as through the fact that they occupy different places within institutionalized speech practices.

Similarly, Robin Lakoff's analysis of the lexical disparities one can observe in the way women speak and in the way they are spoken of is a significant contribution to understanding sexual politics by the way it clarifies how some aspects of male dominance are implicit in linguistic practices. [70] However, much of her analysis focuses on the attitudinal consequences that result from rhetorical choices, showing how the connotations of various utterances—speaking of "ladies," "broads" etc.—reveal how we think about women. In contrast, Foucault's kind of analysis emphasizes how aspects of our social structure create what we understand to be men and women. In his analysis of sexuality (to be discussed in chapter 7), he shows how such phenomena as the "hysterical woman" are tied to the regulative processes affecting families that are produced by a society involved in harnessing labor capacity.[71] In general, therefore, Foucault takes the language–politics connection to a higher level of abstraction, one that permits us to go beyond the linguistically reflected power exchanges between persons and groups to an analysis of the structures within which they are deployed.

Now where, if at all, must we take leave of Foucault's approach, or if not his approach, at least the self-understanding that accompanies it? The answer is partly in the archeological metaphor, which emphasizes physical collecting of artifacts rather than the interpretive activity of mind. The same reasons for rejecting the positivist construction of understanding, particularly its philosophy of mind, provide an argument for rejecting Foucault's neo-positivism. Foucault has very explicitly denied his own contribution to his analyses. In his recent treatment of punishment, for example, he states shortly before concluding, "I shall now stop with this anonymous text."[72] Ironically, the same commitments which make Foucault's approach a radical innovation illuminating a level of human relations other approaches lack, produce the limitations in his self-understanding. First we can review the gains enjoyed by his approach. Foucault convincingly argues that discursive practices are political and social practices, that to speak within an established mode of speaking is not simply to support some individuals or groups over others but also to reproduce and affirm the existing system of power in the society. But how are we to understand the analyst's mode of speaking? As was noted above, Foucault has recently suggested that his text is anonymous, and on another occasion he stated that we would have liked "to have slipped imperceptibly into this lecture."[73] It would be reasonable to ask how this self-understanding of Foucault's, based on his understanding of language as something that controls and creates kinds of speakers, comports with his designation of some theorists, like Freud and Marx, as "initiators of discursive practices."[74] Foucault emphasizes the effect of what they initiate on subsequent speaker/authors, but what makes them inventors? Clearly it is the analytic standpoints they develop, which lead them to interpret psychological, social, and political phenomena in ways that are radically different from the prevailing modes of their day. However, whether the observer/analyst of social-political phenomena invents a radically new interpretive framework or simply selects from among a variety of familiar ones, there are choices to be made. Foucault consistently employs a politically oriented discourse, emphasizing power, authority, and control to speak of the disciplines of psychiatry and medicine and of the administration of punishment. Some deal with all of these organizations in the context of a therapeutically oriented discourse.

Foucault, like traditional empiricists, has thus rendered the role of the investigator in a passive mode. Although he operates with a radically different model of the relationship between speech and phenomena from that developed by logical positivists and empiricists, rejecting their sharp separation between language and its objects, he shares their neglect of the observer's role in constructing the frame of reference that creates the meanings of the phenomena which are molded and selected. Foucault shows convincingly how those frames of reference are already embedded in discursive practices and thus avoids the overly psychologized view of the observer favored by some phenomenologists. He loses, however, the pedagogy that comes from his own contribution as an analyst who constructs a frame of reference which politicizes phenomena that are treated nonpolitically in other perspectives. In the next chapter, therefore, I shall deal with the implications of Foucault's approach as it relates to the theory-building and modeling problems familiar to standard social science practice. But the Foucaultian position on the author/analyst will be somewhat deradicalized in order to develop an understanding of the modeling or interpretive choices involved in producing explanations and understandings.

6

Language, Theories, and Models

It is appropriate now to consider what implication the discussion thus far has for issues relating to two of the standard forms of political inquiry, interpreting the writings of political theorists (traditional, historical political theory) and theory-building and modeling activities commonly referred to as "empirical theory." Before elaborating on the latter, which is more central to the themes developed in the analysis thus far, I shall briefly outline the former.

There is a variety of kinds of questions that are traditionally raised when a scholar interrogates the political writings of a period. At a minimum, however, any analysis must rest on a position as to the *meaning* of what has been said. Before contemporary philosophical traditions—notably those I have discussed above—had any perceptible impact on traditional, interpretive political theory, attempts to infer the meaning of what "major political thinkers" wrote located their statements in roughly two different kinds of contexts; the context of some interpretation of the historical development of political theory and an interpretation of the social context that obtained at the time the statements under scrutiny were written.

In recent years some political theorists, influenced by the writings of linguistic philosophers such as Austin and Wittgenstein, have developed an interpretive method for analyzing historical political writings that emphasizes the linguistic context in which the utterances or statements have been delivered. Quentin Skinner, for example, has explicitly argued against a social context interpretation of political theory and has promoted a mode of interpretation that treats theorists' utterances, after Austin, as illocutionary acts that have a meaning and a significance within the linguistic context in which they are carried out. We must, Skinner notes, know "how what was said was meant."[1] Skinner's linguistic interpretation does not thoroughly reject the relevance of the social context of utterances to their meaning. Rather, he has utilized the linguistic model developed by Austin to interpret the social context within which utterances take on their intended force. According to Skinner, a society establishes a moral identity by virtue of the distribution of illocutionary acts that reflect the ways various events and activities are regarded.[2] Skinner's position is thus informed by the theory of meaning that emerges from the English linguistic philosophical tradition. He has translated that language philosophy into a method for recovering the meanings in past political writings by giving an epistemologically privileged position to the intentions of the authors, intentions interpreted by construing the speech-acts with which authors convey how what they say is to be understood.

A similar approach to understanding historical political-theory texts emerges in the writings of J.G.A. Pocock. He approaches political theory with an orientation emphasizing the linguistic constraints or paradigms (after Kuhn) that shape the thinking in various periods in the history of political thought. "Men think by communicating language systems; these systems help constitute both their conceptual worlds and the authority structures, or social worlds related to these."[3] Like Skinner's, Pocock's treatment of the linguistic context of historical utterances shows the influence of Austin's emphasis on speech as performance, but his approach to the meaning of utterances is broader than that of Skinner as he goes beyond the almost exclusive concern, characterized by Skinner's approach, with the intentions of a writer as expressed through the rhetorical force of utterances.

He notes, "At any given moment . . . the 'meanings' of a given utterance must be found by locating it in a paradigmatic texture, a multiplicity of contexts, which the verbal force of the utterance itself cannot completely determine."[4]

Pocock's linguistic approach to interpreting texts in the history of political thought emphasizes the institutional contexts that are reflected in the available set of speech-acts from which thinkers select. Reading political thought thus becomes a method for analyzing a political culture. Pocock's kind of analysis therefore combines elements of the philosophy of language from both English and Continental traditions. Although, under the influence of the former, he construes utterances as meaning-creating actions by the speaker/writer, in accord with the latter, he understands that the selection process is constrained. Recall that language for Heidegger is something that speaks to us, and that Foucault offers a similar reversal in his emphasis on the passive role of the author of a statement and in his idea that language creates our identities. Similarly, for Pocock, speech-acts preexist the actors who employ them.

There is a double sense . . . in which the words that perform my acts are not my own, in the first place, they are words used by others and only borrowed by me, and in the second place, they have been institutionalized to the point where they cannot be finally reduced to the speech-acts of known individuals. My acts, therefore, have been preinstitutionalized; they must be performed by institutional means.[5]

Pocock has thus developed a framework for understanding texts in the history of political theory that closely accords with the approach to language I have emphasized in previous chapters, and he has applied this framework in analyses of diverse areas of political thinking.[6] But there is a missing dimension to Pocock's interpretive stance. Pocock (and Skinner), following the orientation that English linguistic philosophers have encouraged, emphasizes the contribution to the meaning of statements made by the linguistic context of the speaker/writer but neglects or neutralizes the context and role of the interpreter. The rich analysis of linguistic contexts that Pocock has developed in his elucidation of historical writings is not turned inward; he provides no analysis of his own discursive choices. Without our delving deeply into a philosophical tradition that would take us beyond the immediate purposes at hand, it can be noted that interpretive theorists such as Gadamer and Ricoeur have developed approaches to analyzing texts that take into account the cultural-linguistic horizons of the interpreter as well as those of the author/speaker.

Gadamer argues persuasively that the prejudices of the interpreter are a necessary, even inescapable, part of our understanding of historical texts. Interpretation, for Gadamer, involves a mediation of the intended meaning that one collects by noting the linguistic context of the author/speaker with the context of the interpreter.[7] The interpreter, in Gadamer's view, thus reconstructs the meaning of a text in the process of interpretation. Ricoeur's understanding of interpretation, which is touched on below, also has a place for the meaning-constituting role of the interpreter. In Ricoeur's view, the meaning of a text escapes the control of the intentions of its author and becomes susceptible to multiple interpretations, depending on the frames of reference within which its interpreters dwell.[8]

What, then, of a methodological nature can be said about traditional political theory if one is to take seriously the approach to language that elucidates the linguistic contexts of *both* the speaker/author and the interpreter? The prescription in its briefest form would be that modern political theory, like modern political philosophy, must escape from linguistic positivism. Elaborating this prescription within the familiar discourse of political inquiry, one could say that an emphasis on data analysis is misplaced, where the data are the written statements of theorists in the case of traditional interpretive approaches to political theory. Within a nonpositivist view of linguistic phenomena, the focus becomes the production of the data. This production, moreover, should be seen as deriving from two sources; the linguistic context of the author that is constitutive of the objects, events, and actions spoken of; and the linguistic context of the interpreter from which discursive selections are made that contribute to constituting the meanings in the text.

This dual focus implies a dual methodological consciousness and makes accessible two domains of understanding. First, to analyze a text is to analyze the linguistic context in which it is produced and thus to provide an analysis of the political culture from which it comes. Second, to analyze the text with the recognition that one is doing something other than passively recording provides for an analysis of what one is doing—the analysis of one's own consciousness. Moreover, because the 'self' of the interpreter has a meaning or location within a cultural-linguistic context, self-consciousness becomes a mode of 'other' consciousness. By analyzing the discursive selections that one makes in contributing to the constitution of the meanings in a text one is implicitly mapping the speech practices in one's own culture. To do this is to record one's own constraints and thereby to analyze one's own political culture. Within the context of an appropriate meta theory of language, then, one can literally read oneself in a text and, having become aware of that self, analyze the processes that constitute that self.

An altered perspective on language can thus afford an altered method of inquiry in political theory. The text identified in one's analysis of political thinking becomes not simply a document in the history of political theory but rather the sign of constitutive processes which give that text various meanings. Interpretation then becomes an analytic inquiry into the meaning contexts that produce the text—including the linguistic context of the speaker/author and a reflexive inquiry into the meaning context of the interpreter. Viewed in this way, the text becomes a document—still in progress—within which one can attempt to read two political cultures and, one hopes, progress in an understanding of political culture, political thinking, and the good society in general.

Turning now to "empirical" political inquiry, we can ask how the altered view of language changes the orientation of methods that are seen as explanatory. One way of summarizing what has been suggested in preceding chapters is to emphasize, once again, the relationships between language and political inquiry that are implied in different epistemological perspectives. As was suggested in chapter 1, the positivist/

empiricist viewpoint embraces a sharp separation between speech and phenomena. For empiricists, logical relationships in language provide a tool of inquiry that allows for the expression and formalization of the data by translating experience into a structured system of communication so that knowledge can be developed and shared. With this orientation toward language, coupled with the view that statements in a theoretical framework derive their value from their correspondence with experience or truthfulness, the positivist/empiricist approach regards language as a potential source of error. In the empiricist view, language must therefore be standardized and pruned of ambiguities. Syntactic and semantic variation, which from some perspectives is a source of information about human conduct, is for empiricists a threat to reliability and validity in the theory-building and -testing process. Seeing the major difficulty in developing knowledge as one of representing the welter of data out there unambiguously and in a manner consistent with making scientific inferences, the early positivists puzzled about how to develop language in a way that would make it a clean and sharp instrument for furthering inquiry. Toward this end, Carnap and other Vienna Circle positivists addressed themselves energetically and in many ways fruitfully to developing valid, reliable, and effective ways of speaking in the process of creating conceptual structures such as theories and assessing relationships between those conceptual structures and the phenomena that those frameworks are designed to elucidate. And modern empiricists have developed sophisticated ways of referring to the relationship between theoretical structures and data, attempting to harmonize the idea of validation with the recognition that some kind of interpretation inevitably intervenes between concept and percept.

Without again rehearsing at length the flaws and limitations that beset empiricist conceits, we can consider, in the light of the kind of analysis introduced in the last chapter, a major problematic premise in the empiricist approach to language and inquiry. If this approach to theory building and inquiry can be charged with unduly constricting the kinds of questions we can raise and the locus of data to be analyzed, much of the problem can be attributed to the principle that radically separates theory and data. By adhering to this principle and thereby viewing language as a medium for expressing conceptual structures and transacting between those structures and experience, the wholly empirically oriented analyst casts his or her gaze outward, peering at the data as though somehow the field of observation or, more generally, apprehension will become perspicuous if we exercise enough care in preparing and employing our linguistic tools.

This perspective on the language–reality relationship is disabling in two respects. First, it discourages us from looking at language and speech as sources of data, that is, as something that bears a responsibility for the entities and relationships we speak about. Therefore, the subject matter that we have been discussing in previous chapters is lost—the subjects, objects, and relationships that emerge in our discursive practices. When we view language in general and various discursive practices in particular as loci of data and the various syntactic and semantic rules of meaningful speech as aspects of human relations, the existence of alternative ways of speaking becomes a fertile field of inquiry rather than simply a threat to the production of knowledge.

Second, the empiricist model of language narrows the range of questions we can raise during inquiry, for if ways of speaking are efforts to reflect accurately the social and political world rather than practices that construct it, we are left to evaluate statements and systems of statements only on the basis of how they prepare us for experience by predicting and accounting for events and not on how they shape, limit, give meaning to, and confer power over experience. To the extent that one denies that language and speech constitute and shape experience as well as providing a transaction medium for sharing it, one will neglect the value that statements have in allocating power, authority, and control. It is both possible and desirable to build scientific theories of human relations, adhering to the scientific norms of inductive and deductive inference and the requirements of reliability and validity, and at the same time selecting the language of theory building and modeling in a way that is sensitive to the constitutive capabilities of language, but it is also important to recognize that the content and styles of language and speech provide the possibility for interpretive inquiries which exploit language as a field data to be excavated rather than as merely a communication medium. Interpretive or reflexive understanding focused on how persons shape the realities they understand, is a dimension of inquiry that can be pursued either independently or as a part of theory building that eventuates in the causally oriented modes of explanation familiar to scientific communities. How these two orientations toward producing understanding, causal and interpretive, fit together will become more apparent when we consider the standard notions of what scientific theories are.

Scientific Theory

The problems raised by a sharp separation between conceptual systems like theories and the domains which they are supposed to elucidate become apparent when, in discussions of the nature of scientific theory, philosophers of science attempt to account for the connections between the "theory" and the "data." The traditional resort has been to the concept of the "rules of correspondence" or the "coordinative definition," concepts that stand for the translation or interpretation of theoretical terms into observational or measurement terms. A coordinative definition is not a definition in the ordinary sense, for defining something is generally regarded as relating (usually by reducing) a concept to other concepts. Coordinative definitions are used to stipulate the aspect of experience represented or referred to by a concept. Using physics as his example, Hans Reichenbach, who originated the term "coordinative definition," says it "simply states that *this concept* is coordinated to *this particular thing*. In general this coordination is not arbitrary. Since the concepts are interconnected by testable relations, the coordination may be verified as true or false, if the requirement of uniqueness is added, i.e., the rule that the same concept must always denote the same object."[9]

The difficulties associated with attempts at moving logically and consistently from statements to "things" have already been rehearsed at length. It should suffice now to note that a substantial interpretive element is involved in relating theoretical terms to experience and that the kind of interpretation is not merely technical. Rather, in the case of social and political theories, the interpretation involves affirming as appropriate a model of human relations within which the coordination has meaning. However, we do not have to search out exotic philosophies of inquiry to find an effective critique of Reichenbach's notion of how theories become coordinated with experience. Even empiricist philosophers of science have shown how Reichenbach oversimplifies.

His discussion of "coordinative definitions" and Margenau's similar treatment under the rubric of "rules of correspondence" have led to a standard way of speaking about scientific theories, which is, as Patrick Suppes has argued, inadequate and misleading. The "standard sketch," as Suppes calls it, is expressed as follows:

> A scientific theory consists of two parts. One part is an abstract logical calculus. In addition to the vocabulary of logic, this calculus includes the primitive symbols of the theory, and the logical structure of the theory is fixed by stating the axioms or postulates of the theory in terms of its primitive symbols. . . . The second part of the theory is a set of rules that assign an empirical content to the logical calculus by providing what are usually called 'coordinating definitions' or 'empirical interpretations' for at least some of the primitive and defined symbols of the calculus.[10]

As an alternative to the "standard sketch," Suppes proposes that the theory–data connection be regarded as a matter of the one blending into the other through a hierarchy of interpretive steps. He points out that it is impossible to show how any concrete application of a theory can be connected logically to the theory, "in any complete sense," and concludes, therefore, that the question, What is a scientific theory? admits of no simple response. In effect, a hierarchy of theories interposes between a theory in the abstract and any experiment that purports to stand as a test of hypotheses derived from the theory such that the experiment can be regarded as a validating occasion. For example, among the interpretive steps involved in testing some theories is the selection of a statistical methodology. Is it appropriate, asked Suppes, to include as part of the theory the statistical methodology employed in a test?

Suppes' difficulty in answering the question he poses at the outset of his analysis, What is a scientific theory? clearly relates to the problem posed above as to the appropriateness of the very distinction between theory and data. As long as we build our notion of what a theory is on an oversimplified distinction between the two, our accounts of the theory-building process will be misleading. As Suppes has suggested, a lot of hand waving and other symptoms of inarticulateness attend discussion about the relationship between "the theory" and "the data" when we fail to elaborate what is involved in that interface.[11]

The beginnings of a more appropriate and articulate way of speaking about the relationship were suggested by Norwood Russell Hanson, who noted, often hyperbolically, that the theory–data distinction is seriously flawed; for example, "The neopositivist model of observation, wherein our sensational data registration and our intellectual constructions thereupon, are cleft atwain is an analytic stroke tantamount to logical butchery."[12] While data are, as Hanson put it, "theory-laden," an approach to social or political phenomena that purports to be scientific is not necessarily futile, as Sheldon Wolin, for example, concludes after citing Hanson's notion.[13] It implies, rather, that the language of scientific analysis must be restructured to reflect the inseparability of interpretation and observation and that modes of assessing theoretical systems must be broadened so as to cohere with that restructuring of scientific discourse. It means, therefore, that the decision-making process associated with theory building in the social sciences should look quite different from what Reichenbach's scenario of the concept–observation interface implies.

The Theory-Building Approach Amplified by the Analysis of Meaning

We can begin to sort the issues out if we initiate the analysis with a simple term or concept and try to embed it in the language of theory building, while recognizing that there are additional political data lurking in the various possible approaches to the meaning of the term or concept, given the frame of reference to which it attaches. So let us begin with the term "work." If one were to begin constructing a theory using the idea of work as a major concept that is to take part in an empirical assessment of the theory, the endeavor would normally be characterized as building a "theory about work." But, we might ask, in connection with the problematic nature of the theory–data interface, Where is work located? Is it, to borrow Znaniecki's distinction, part of the "subject matter" of the theory or part of the "object matter"? Is work a concept or an observation?[14] The phrase "a theory about work" suggests that work is an observable thing, or at least that it stands outside the theory or conceptual system constructed and organized to refer to work in the context of a set of relationships that renders it in some way understandable. Since we are speaking about theories, it is more precise and more in accord with common usage to say that a theory about work is a set of relationships among concepts, including some hypotheses (relationships for which empirical equivalents have been selected) in which the concept of work is featured. Now is seems unclear again where work is to be found with respect to the location of the theory. If we use ordinary theoretical discourse to say things like, "The theory contains some hypotheses about work," we would mean that there are some "empirical statements" containing the concept of work and that this concept is interpreted on the basis of observations or measurement operations.

This leaves us with the question as to how such theoretical discourse elucidates the meaning of work. As has been pointed out in previous chapters, it is misleading to ask about the meaning of an individual word. The rules linking word and object constitute an interpretation that is understandable only in terms of the broader context to which it relates. What is this context? A conception like "work" takes on its meaning within a discourse. Work has considerably different meanings when placed within discourses that are as diverse as those in which the terms are primarily biological and those in which the terms are primarily economic or politico-economic. In the former, the concept of work is almost synonymous with the concept of effort and is judged on the basis of such things as calorie expenditure. Within a biological discourse, to say that something involves a lot of work is to evoke a context in which there exist standards for when an organism is more or less at rest versus when it is exercising reserve capacities. Such standards are not wholly separable from those that play a role in politico-economic discourses, but it is nevertheless clear that the concept of work in this latter kind of discourse develops its meaning from a different kind of context, one in which the standards have to do with rules of authority, exchange, and other social relations. To qualify an activity as work in a politico-economic discourse is therefore to promote at least a partial model of a society which includes norms about who has the right to remuneration for certain activities and about what activities fall within the remunerable set and under what circumstances. Where work is located and thus what it means does, as empiricist philosophers of science have suggested, consist in the linkage between an idea or concept of work and the experiential indicators designated as the referents of the concept; but this linkage is only understandable in a broader discursive context. Unfortunately, this theory–data interface is precisely where discussions in the philosophy of the social sciences tend to be inadequate. Somehow theory and data are to be joined. At times, discussions of this nexus presume that the theorist is standing amid a field of concepts and must select some of them to be involved in hypotheses so as to operationalize that field as a whole, or, as it is regarded in some versions, to operationalize only the concepts in the hypotheses, so that once the rules prescribing measurement operations are developed, data collection and analysis can ensue. At other times, the discussion presumes that the theorist is standing amid the data and knows what "work" is and is interested in constructing a theory to explain some aspect of it. As Suppes has suggested, the connecting process is not a matter of making an obvious, nontheoretical choice. Rather than standing anywhere, the theorist may be better regarded as moving back and forth between the theory and the data, theorizing the while. The theory blends into the data through a series of interpretive steps, or vice versa. Suppes referred to those steps as constituting a hierarchy of theories.[15] For the purposes at hand it suffices to say that it is not clear where the interpretation ends and the observation or apprehension of data begins. It should be added that what is regarded as "theorizing" is going on in this interpretive process. The idea of theorizing, even as Suppes uses it, suggests a wholly cognitive, interest-free enterprise, while it should be evident from the examples above that one aspect of the interpretive part of creating meaning is polemical in that the interpretation promotes some social and political standards.

We can imagine examples of the forms that the interpretation can take. We might observe a man (aged forty approximately) digging a hole with a shovel while dressed in a uniform labeled Water Resources Agency. In such a case, we would probably assume that he was "working." We might look around and also observe a younger man (aged five approximately) sitting in a sandbox across the street, digging a hole with a shovel. In this case we would probably assume that he was "playing," even if he was wearing the same uniform (costumed instead of "dressed for work"). We must infer, if this account is plausible, that digging a hole with a shovel is not sufficient in itself to qualify as work nor, we would discover, is any activity apart from some interpretation we must supply with it, for to identify anything as work is to have a complex conceptual system that organizes social reality in a particular way. To understand, in the present example, why the rules linking the concept of work with some observed behaviors are such that they yield the discriminations between the two cases of digging a hole, one would need to know a lot about the economic, political, social, and administrative organization of the society in which such a discrimination would be made. Part of this context, which constitutes the ordinary use of the word "work," might be explicitly contained in a theory about work, but clearly most of it would not, given the structure of most theories. It is usually the case that a concept like work is part of a theoretical structure emphasizing relationships between work and other concepts rather than elaborating the relationships that are *presupposed* in the meaning one attaches to work. Meaning, in ordinary theoretical discourse, tends to be developed on the basis of the measurement criteria for relating the concept to the data-collection activity. What should be understood, then, is that we do not observe work and that the rules we use to stipulate are more than simple technical-measurement rules. We identify what we see or otherwise apprehend as work through a host of interpretive steps, many of which stand outside of any theory we may explicitly employ as the justifying framework of that identification.

It is therefore at least problematic to identify what is involved when we use the word "work," whatever the function, theoretical or otherwise, of the discourse in which the word is embedded. There is a venerable philosophical distinction, first popularized by Aristotle, which, if not overexercised, assists in understanding what one does in developing the meaning of a concept. This is the distinction between "form" and "matter." As it is traditionally construed, the "matter" associated with something are the characteristics belonging to that thing and may vary without causing it to spill over some boundary and thereby become another thing. One of the characteristics of working, for example, is that some aspect of the working organism is in motion—perhaps the hands ("blue-collar work"), or the mouth ("white-collar work"), or just the generation of brain waves (academics often cite this kind of movement somewhere in their income-tax returns). Of course movement is not a sufficient condition for an organism to be at work. It is merely a necessary characteristic. What, then, is the "form" of work? Closely related to the "matter" or characteristics of work, "form" is the set of standards used to organize the characteristics that provide the necessary and sufficient conditions for using the word "work" appropriately in a meaningful statement. Clearly, such standards vary among human collectivities and change within different collectivities over time. For a given collectivity at a given time they vary from one discursive practice to another, for example, work is constituted as different phenomena in legal and psychological discourses. There are, however, discourses which are complementary in that their intersection helps to locate the meaning of a concept with common currency. In general then, we could say that for a given group at a given time the *form* of work involves efforts (in a biological *and* social sense) that lead to the creation of something to be used at a later time by other persons. This interpretation locates work in an interdiscursive zone created by the overlap of biological, social, economic, and legal discourses. The movement of the organism is understood as a physical phenomenon, but the standards that translate the perceived phenomenon of movement into the idea of work come from legal, social, and economic standards, all of which shade into political standards. For example, a determination that a person is "responsible" for the movements involved so that he or she can claim remuneration for its consequences involves standards that are moral-legal and politico-economic. Thus any attempt to specify what work is involves unpacking a variety of interpretations mingled with identifications of characteristics such that the "form" and "matter" of work emerge as interrelated and just as inseparable as are interpretation and observation.

We can now consider the appropriate way to characterize decision making in theory building, given the intimate relationship between interpretation and other conceptualizing activities and the assessment of experience (what is called "data gathering," "hypothesis testing," etc. in the empiricist frame of reference). To the extent that theory building is to eventuate in some kind of empirical substantiation, obviously it is necessary to temporarily inhibit a process. This process is the sorting through of characteristics and standards (matter and form) so that the identification of something, for example, "work," can be made. To identify is thus to arrest the sorting process. It is to settle on a meaning of a concept like work so that a different, dependent conceptual process—theorizing—can begin. As is the case with so many different kinds of discursive developments, in the building of a theory some questions must be at least temporarily closed so that others can be raised, even though this involved a cost. To close the question of meaning is to close a kind of inquiry and therefore to impede a kind of understanding that might emerge if questions related to that inquiry were entertained more fully. This involves a trade-off.

To appreciate the implications of the kind of decision making involved in such a trade-off, imagine a fairly specific theoretical question about work. One such question, that is probably best regarded as sociopsychological, would be about the relationship between the structure of work settings in a society and workers' attitudes toward themselves (e.g., attitudes that fall into the categories of self-esteem, self-concept, etc.). Decisions at the level of what work is to be—about what activities constitute work—would markedly affect the conclusions one would reach about the relationship. Traditionally, an investigation of such a relationship would not include women who are ordinarily designated as housewives and/or mothers. Yet obviously, one could regard the decision to consider housekeeping and mothering as something other than work as quite politically controversial. Indeed it has recently become politically controversial partly because one effect of not including such activities under the category of work is to deny housewives and mothers such things as social security benefits. A recent piece of congressional legislation in the United States is promoting the inclusion of such activities in the category of work, for purposes of providing social security benefits for persons (mostly women) who have "worked" for years in the home.

Whether or not this piece of legislation becomes law and the definition of work is thereby "officially" expanded, the bill is a symptom of a process. The process of controversy that the legislative effort represents is a process of change in the American political culture. At present, various subcultures in the American society take different positions on whether particular characteristics of persons (e.g., sex) and of activities (e.g., work) ought to be politicized and dealt with as public and problematic. Thus whatever criteria a theorist inquiring into the work setting–attitude relationship adopts, that theorist is implicitly taking sides in the controversy.

There is thus a political theory of culture—a coherent conceptual argument behind the commitment as to what should be regarded as work—implicit in what is called in some metascientific positions the "operational definition" in an "empirical theory" involving the concept of work. But this implicit theory of culture tends not to be the subject of analysis in a theoretical enterprise such as the one modeled here. The theory of the American political culture implicit in the criteria for establishing what the concept of work means in the explicit theory under investigation might be worth investigating in its own right; but, as has been suggested above, one must formulate a different kind of question to approach an understanding of the political imperatives reflected in the way we relate speech and phenomena or theoretical discourses and data. To investigate this different kind of question, the interpretive question, What is work? makes it possible to orient the inquiry toward understanding self-concepts, a major interest in the causally oriented study outlined above. In such a case, the analysis of what gets called work would reveal something about self-concepts, but rather than looking at a causal relationship between something about work, for example, the setting, and the resulting self-concepts, the analysis would show how something about the setting *constitutes* what work is. The investigation would thus be a search for the constitutive rules of work, which prescribe what can be done by whom under what circumstances to qualify as work. The elucidation of self-concepts in such an inquiry does not, as in the causally oriented approach, treat self-concepts as individual, psychological traits. It indicates, instead, the cultural norms about selves that are presupposed in the way that work is located in various discourses and thus the way that norms about selves are institutionalized, creating various system-relevant identities. When one pursues a causally oriented inquiry and therefore focuses on the relationships between concepts rather than the relationships presupposed by each concept, the norms that constitute the meanings are simply stipulated and thus denied status as separate subjects of inquiry.

The seemingly simple question, What is work? is therefore deceptively simply because, as it is conceived in the analysis here, the question is designed to illuminate an interrelated field of data and interpretation which reflects standards that are fugitive in the context of ordinary empirical-research inquiries which focus on only explicit, causal relationships. If this is the case, the problem of the theory–data interface is not dealt with simply in exercising extraordinary care to select operational definitions. To be careful is to follow, a contentless rule, and as should be obvious from the brief speculation about "work," there is a rich content in the word–object relationship to be conceptually shaped and selected by the theorist. "Conceptually shaped" sounds like talk one might encounter in the philosophy of the social sciences, but it implies here much more than what empiricist accounts of the theory-building process mean by such an expression. "Conceptually shaped" here refers to an interrelated set of identities and standards that constitute a political culture. Establishing what "work" is to mean in the context of developing an empirical theory is thus no less than to evoke an image of a collectivity, complete with rules about what persons are and how various activities with social meaning ought to be organized and evaluated.

The implications of this argument become more palpable when presented in connection with some generally recognized ideological commitments about how collectivities ought to be organized, and about what meanings ought to be accorded to human activity. For example, given the set of standards or norms, which is part of the political economy of most western nations, about how exchange value is created, a typical capitalist economist, asked to explain how much work (the contribution of labor) is required to provide living space for one thousand middle-income families, would calculate separately the contributions of those working directly on the project and the equipment or machinery (tools) used to develop the housing units. Given the American political commitment that underlies our economy, namely that private entrepreneurs are encouraged to invest in "labor-saving" devices and then enjoy the proceeds from them individually, except for the taxation levied, this accounting scheme complements the authority system and the dependent-economic relations arising from that system.

A Marxist economist, however, would produce a different accounting scheme, based on a different model of what contributes to the production of those housing units. The context of the Marxian model of political economy is partly provided in the prescription that labor is the source of the value applied to commodities. Anything that saves labor should therefore be evaluated at the front end, that is, in terms of what the labor was that produced the labor saver. Marx, consistent with this evaluational model, referred to machinery as "congealed labor," labor in the past that is presently transformed into equipment. With such a model of political economy, one would thus calculate the contributions of labor to the production of dwelling units without separating persons from equipment.

This difference explains a lot about the perspectives in the Marxian and capitalist models of political economy. And this, in turn, helps us to understand the political commitments underlying the choice of "operational definitions" in empirical research. The process of selecting an operational definition, however technical it may sound, is clearly, therefore, a process involving the affirmation of political principles. The theorist can "go with the flow," think within the framework of predominant discursive practices that represent dominant political authorities, or can fashion a standpoint based on a radical critique of prevailing political practices. To return to the example, to the extent that one's focus is primarily on the explanation of what is required to produce the dwelling units for one thousand middle-income families, one must approach this explanation problem with an altered view of scientific decision making, one that includes the problem of justifying the *kind* of framework (type of theory and content of rules linking concepts to "data") as well as the problem of producing a logically consistent and valid explanation linking labor to the creation of living accommodations. The example shows, then, that different kinds of questions can be raised about political phenomena from those ordinarily raised in empirical theory development and use. The strategy for asking these other kinds of questions has already been introduced in a preliminary way in the previous chapter's discussion of Foucault's archeological method. But, as was noted there, Foucault's perspective diminishes, perhaps even negates, the standpoint of the observer-investigator, suggesting that discursive practices are wholly in control of what we understand of our social and political world. I argued above that although the archeological perspective gives a useful, politicized approach to relationships embedded in discourse, it cannot be denied that we can choose among frames of reference, among different modes of speaking and conceptual content that result in different constructions of what we seek to understand in our common-sense musings and in our theoretical practices. To complement the politicizing of what emerges in our speech practices, we need to develop a political understanding of the decision-making process that precedes the choice of one versus another theoretical discourse in theory building and political analysis.

Social Control Ideologies

The relevant decision-making issues converge conveniently around a relatively recent "object" that has emerged and gained the attention of educational policy makers, the "hyperactive child." I have elsewhere discussed the problems of interpretation that surround this object-concept:

Teachers in primary school classrooms frequently find that their attempts at communicating with groups of children are frustrated by their differing attention spans. They have found that the attention span of a child is markedly influenced by body chemistry and that drugs prescribed by physicians frequently "calm down" what are referred to as "hyperactive" children to a point where they no longer create classroom disturbances by leaving their chairs and moving around while instruction is being attempted. On scientific ground, the empirical explanation employed (in this case a biochemical one) is valid. There is good evidence that the classroom activity of the child is related to his body chemistry. The use of such an explanation, however, takes as given that children should learn while sitting together in groups on a schedule chosen by the school or teacher. The hyperactive child concept is an arbitrary one in that the criterion for calling a child hyperactive is social not biological. The fact that a chemical-biological type of explanation is often relied upon from a "deviant behavior problem" is a consequence of the educational value premise suggested above. From an alternative frame of reference, one could regard the teacher's problem as a strategic one. One could take as given the fact that children have differing interests and attention spans and ask how one might educate large numbers of them nevertheless. If the question is posed this way, the kind of empirical explanation sought would probably not be chemical-biological. One relevant explanation, for example, would be oriented toward understanding why teachers feel that all children in the classroom should have the same daily learning schedule. The concepts in such an explanation would probably be something like past training, current role expectations, etc. Once again the validity of the explanation would be determined upon scientific grounds, but the choice of the type of explanation to be employed and the concepts contained in it would derive from the value premises which precipitated the inquiry.[16]

A variety of frameworks would serve for sorting out the issues raised and partly analyzed in this quotation. One of the most useful and insightful is Michael Scriven's (briefly discussed in chapter 1). In the course of discussing Hempel's covering-law model of explanation, Scriven argues that accuracy is only one criterion for evaluating an empirical explanation. An explanation, he points out, can be accurate or well supported by evidence, but be "inadequate" or "incomplete" as regards what it is supposed to explain.[17] Moreover, an explanation may be both accurate and adequate but irrelevant in that it is not the *kind* of explanation required. Scriven goes on to develop a model of the kinds of justification that attach to each of three different criteria for evaluating explanations. These he calls the "truth-justifying grounds," the "role-justifying grounds," and the "type-justifying grounds." The first involves the ground for thinking that an explanation is accurate, for example, our evidence for thinking that various drugs reduce at the activity level of schoolchildren in the above "hyperactive child" problem. The second involves grounds for thinking that an explanation is adequate, for example, perhaps drugs affect behavior but only in the context of something else not included in the theory. The third involves grounds for thinking that an explanation is appropriate for the person or persons who may use it for something, for example, when drugs are administered to schoolchildren (consistent with the biochemical explanation of their behavior) does the situation meet the requirements of those to whom the explanation is addressed? So here again, as was the case in selecting operational definitions, we find the theorist necessarily making political choices, in this instance the choice of what constituency to serve in selecting the type of explanation to pursue.

It is this third justification problem which stands outside of ordinary discussions of how theories are to be evaluated, that is likely to make us appreciate what is involved in the decision-making process as one constructs an explanation. Unfortunately, Scriven did not develop and elaborate his notion of type-justifying grounds, for if he had, he would necessarily have found himself talking about the politics of explanations. His decision not to do so undoubtedly rests on his narrow view of the pragmatic dimension of an explanation, on the relationship between a theorist and the explanation the theorist constructs. Under the rubric of type-justifying grounds he speaks of the explanation "they need," and "the type of explanation required," as though the problem of the constituency for explanations is never controversial. Such loose talk is understandable because Scriven's focus was not on the political context of explanations but rather on the inadequacy of the traditional empiricist position which emphasizes, almost exclusively, truth-justifying grounds for evaluating theories. It is clear, nevertheless, that a theorist must raise more complex questions in determining the type of explanation to construct than simply asking "what people need," or "what is required." Often, as in the classroom-control example above, what is needed is problematic and controversial (even a "need" model is one among many alternative ones). In such instances, the norms constituting the role of the theorist are also problematic, for the norms of science, which relate primarily to truth-justifying grounds, do not provide guidance as to what constituency (real or imagined) should be served.

Thus we can bring a political consciousness to the problem of selecting a type of explanation and ask questions about the kind of issues that are raised as the theorist makes a choice about what an explanation is going to be. Elsewhere I suggested a framework for analyzing the political dimension of explanations, arguing that the choice of the kind of explanation to employ is guided (usually implicitly or nonconsciously) by a "social control ideology." As I defined it, this is "a persistent orientation toward whom or what should be adjusted when a problem is identified."[18] The functioning of such an ideology is partly described in the above quotation on the classroom "order problem." In that case, the ideological alternatives suggested centered around the commitments to either taking the prevailing organization of primary-school classrooms as given and adjusting students to that (even if this means manipulating their metabolisms with drugs) or to taking the distribution of student attributes (metabolic rates, interests, motivation levels) as given and manipulating the classroom and/or school setting and organization to fit that distribution. Clearly, at the least it is problematic as to what, if anything, is to be explained. The very identification of a problem (how it is named, where it is located, who is thought to be responsible for what) narrows the range of alternative explanations because the identification itself already partakes of a guiding social control ideology.

We can therefore concede the importance of a commitment to valid explanation on ordinary scientific (truth-justifying and, to some extent role-justifying) grounds and still be left with choices as to the type of explanation to employ. It should be noted, however, that contrary to the implication in Scriven's argument, truth-justifying grounds are not completely separable from type-justifying grounds. If we reject a correspondence view of truth and, as was suggested above, regard the criteria for speaking truly as involving substantial interest, power, and authority considerations, we see the validity of an empirically oriented explanation as contingent on the constituency needs and demands that provide the context for validation. What emerges, then, when we connect validity and interest criteria, is a nonstandard model of the relationship between science and ideology. In traditional empiricist approaches to the philosophy of the social sciences, it is presumed that explanations are constructed on purely scientific grounds and that ideological issues, if they occur in relation to those explanations, emerge *after* one ponders the impact of the explanation. This model of science and ideology is a familiar fixture in histories of science that deal, among other things, with changing models of astronomy. For example, the replacement of Ptolemaic astronomy by the Copernican model, seen as a threat to the authority of the Church, had to be facilitated by careful constructions as to what the Copernican system would be used for (e.g., simplyfing calendars rather than describing "the nature of the universe").[19]

But the altered view of scientific decision making discussed here suggests that scientific and ideological issues are intertwined at every stage in the explanation construction process. Since, as Scriven has put it, there is "no such thing as *the* explanation" of anything,[20] the choice of a type of explanation requires presuppositions about who may use the explanation and for what purposes, and, more generally, about what kinds of persons a society is to have. The two alternative social control ideologies discussed in relation to schools—adjusting students versus adjusting schools—are fairly narrow choices out of a much broader possible context. For example, even if we take as given (1) that schools will have to function more or less in their present form, and (2) that the metabolic rates of students are to be a relevant focus of attention, there are choices about what may legitimately be adjusted to affect metabolic rates. If we decide to consider the diets of schoolchildren, it should be evident that a change in what they would eat would affect their behavior in school (the food-drug distinction is, after all, a function of various administrative processes rather than of the nature of substances). What, then, might be the relevant explanation to pursue? Again, there are a variety of choices. One could, for example, develop an explanation of the process by which various industrial and political leaders conspire (consciously or in effect) to control what gets called a food and how that substance is distributed, packaged, and marketed to appeal to either children directly or to those (mostly parents) who select their "food." One could, on the other hand, concentrate on consumer rather than producer decision making and investigate the process by which people develop attitudes toward nutrition and translate those attitudes into the purchasing decisions that are "responsible" at an immediate level for what children eat. In chapter 4 it was noted, in connection with the discussion of Hart's theory of action, that the rules constitutive of human actions, particularly those which relate to the ascription of the agency of actions, are, in effect, rules of responsibility.

Responsibility is thus an important concept for understanding what is involved in a social control ideology, for at least implicitly, the matter of who is to be regarded as responsible for producing the behaviors or situations in question is what guides the choice of an explanation in response to such "problems" as the school–student control one. More is involved than a simple attitude toward who or what should be adjusted. A good way to understand a theorist's choice of a type of explanation is to have a cognitive map of the political culture within which the theorist functions. Such a map is, among other things, an interrelated set of ideas about who or what is responsible for the things that become packaged as events in the society, and these ideas are contained in the predominant discursive practices available. Doubtless, to the extent that buyers of food (parents), rather than producers, are regarded as responsible for what children eat—and that is largely so in countries with market economies—explanations about how adult decision making affects children's diets will tend to be of the consumer-behavior rather than the producer-behavior type. Theorists wanting to link food producers' activities to children's "adjustment problems" are faced with more than an empirical issue (in the traditional sense in which "empirical issues" are construed). They must develop an unusual discursive practice to produce a field of concepts that could then be exploited in a causally oriented investigation. At present there is, no well-developed discursive practice linking nutrition with behavior. Given this, along with other rules for responsibility in societies with market economies, children's diets are unlikely to be implicated in explanations of what are interpreted as adjustment problems.

The same cognitive mapping of a culture can be seen to emerge when we deal with drugs rather than food (to the extent that we can make the distinction). Explanations of drug use, particularly for drugs considered dangerous, tend to focus either on consumer behavior (drug users) or seller behavior. The fact that the largest drug producers—the major pharmaceutical companies—provide enough of the "dangerous drugs" for both medical and nonmedical use is not noted in predominant explanations of "drug abuse," whether those explanations are promoted by social control agencies or social science investigators. This is because the norm that producers are generally not responsible for the effects of what they produce, a norm that is part of the dominant subculture of the American political culture. The acceptance of this norm, which underlies other more explicit ones that serve to organize the legal and judicial systems, along with other related ones, guides the pragmatic dimension of explanation by social science groups.

What has been portrayed as a social control ideology is clearly no less than a highly elaborated model of a political culture—a political ideology—and it is in the context of such models that theorists apprehend objects and events and develop explanations to account for and deal with them. The above examples elaborate on the claim that the currency of explanations extends beyond their scientific validity. Explanations of social and political phenomena, and of seemingly nonpolitical phenomena, enable some and disable others. They serve different constituencies, allocating resources to some and denying them to others. One cannot, for example, charge an economic practice with producing a political malfeasance effectively unless there exists a model of political economy and that model includes relevant attributes. For example, there is no popularly politicized framework (model of political economy) for explicating how that which becomes authoritatively defined as work, as education, or even as illness is connected to production, employment and other economic interests. Or similarly, if "disease" is explained solely on the basis of the microbiological state of the diseased person, clinical practitioners are empowered because such an explanation invites the practitioners, those physicians licensed to dispense germ-fighting drugs, to ply their trade. A broader explanation of disease which focuses on the interaction of persons with their environment and emphasizes such factors as the production and preparation of food, access to clean air and water, and the degree of stress in a person's interaction pattern, is an invitation to others to control the health process. It may even be more than an invitation, for example, a sanction-related expectation. This alternative kind of explanation of disease obviously enables a different constituency, the diseased or potentially diseased persons themselves. It places the responsibility for disease prevention on all individuals and groups within the society, both specialists and nonspecialists, but, at the same time, offers an explanatory framework enabling people to discharge that responsibility if they can operate within an authority framework which allows effective action on the basis of such a model of disease.

It is not surprising that these two alternative explanations of disease describe the orientations toward public health in the United States and China respectively. The Chinese political culture is organized around a concept of power that is collectively rather than individually oriented; power is seen as the ability of a collectivity to control its environment through its system of mutual obligation. The social control model affixed to this power conception is accordingly collective also. Various aspects of mind and body are thus not the exclusive purview of professions whose power is based on their exclusivity and legitimacy for explaining and treating what is regarded as abnormal or deviant, a condition that represents the American model, based ultimately on an individual approach to power (the power of each person over others). The boundaries between medical and nonmedical roles, between professional health functionaries and nonprofessional, health-interested persons are, given the collective conception of power and responsibility, less rigorously drawn than in western societies, where health is professionalized rather than politicized.

This politicization of health is reflected in the nonclinical approach to health problems in China. Whereas in the United States the approach to infectious diseases is for individuals to be treated by doctors or, in cases of widespread contagion, with mass immunization (still doctors, in connection with drug companies, treating individuals), in China the source of the disease is treated by "the people." Schistosomiasis, once a serious and widespread disease of the kidneys, was eradicated in China through the cooperative efforts of villagers who dig up the snail beds where the disease was incubating.[21]

The purpose of this example is not to idealize China's political culture. It is to show, rather, how health decisions in a society are based on the prevailing model of explanation of health problems embedded in the society's political culture, and how models of explanation are of a piece with other cultural and/or subcultural (depending on dominance patterns) norms that guide social and political organization. These norms provide a justificatory framework for the distribution of authority vested in various social control agencies that can vary from individuals to large, quasi-professional groupings, whether they control through biological-, psychological-, or social-intervention techniques. A contrast of political cultures such as that between the United States and China makes these norms evident.

The impact of political culture on explanations is also evident when there exists significantly different subcultures within the same society. Another case of health decision making is illustrative here. Recently, the Australian government noticed a relatively high infant-mortality rate within its aboriginal population. After an official inquiry into the problem, the resulting government report noted that *"the semi-nomadic life of some of the Aborigines,* which has some aspects not compatible with normal standards of health, is a contributing factor."[22] This is a stark example of how an implicit social control ideology guided the explanation of "the problem." The social scientists hired by the Australian government to explain (whose recognition was triggered by the discrepancy between infant-mortality rates in the white, European, and Aboriginal populations), assumed that the dominant European culture would not change its practices. It would therefore be relevant to explore a cultural, psychological explanation of the "resistance by indigenous groups" (Aborigines) to the European-culture-oriented health-care delivery system. Attributes of Aborigines became relevant to the interpretation of their infant-mortality rate only because a particular position on cultural, social, and political integration was accepted as appropriate. The government report was constructed around the assumption that Aborigines would have to adapt themselves to the European patterns of life and abandon their own.

To highlight how particular assumptions about the appropriateness of various possible responses (medical or nonmedical) to the problem of Aboriginal health are organized around a prior assumption of cultural integration, an Australian social scientist (not under contract to the government) suggested an alternative view. His response to the government report was to suggest that, "instead of emphasis being placed on Aboriginal failure to assimilate to our norms, it should rather be put on our failure to devise strategies that accommodate to their folkways."[23] If one adopts his position on how the two cultures might be integrated for such purposes as the development of health policy, the "explanation" sought about Aboriginal infant-mortality rates would focus on the inflexibility of health services rather than the recalcitrance of the Aborigines.

The discussion thus far has emphasized the selection of concepts and conceptual structures which organize the concepts. Clearly, sociopolitical presumptions also guide the constitution of concepts, that is, the development of rules about what data are to provide examples of the concepts employed in the theory. The altered view of scientific decision making thus includes a sensitivity to the assumptions or standards for a political culture (rules of responsibility, social control, etc.) as a guide to both the selection of a type of explanation and of the meanings that the concepts within that explanation are to have. With this extended view of what is involved in theory building and other ways of producing understanding, we can consider a particular strategy of theory building from a new perspective, the strategy of modeling.

Models: Cognitive Functions

The term "model" in the social sciences is so various that it is inappropriate to refer to its standard or stock use (its life in the outside world is obviously even more fugitive), but part of the confusion over what models are dissipates with the recognition that some models are pre- or untheoretic. If, as is a fairly standard practice, one wishes to reserve the concept of a theory for a logically consistent set of statements (verbal or otherwise) that eventuates in empirical propositions, one still needs a term for the various conceptual schemata which, while providing a framework for organizing and rationalizing some domain of human experience, do not qualify, strictly speaking, as theories. "Model" seems to respond to this need. The kind of model used for this purpose can, with some caution, be regarded as a model of "reality," not in the sense that it represents with its structure the structure of the experience to which it refers (it is hard to imagine how it could) but in the sense that it provides a structure designed to illuminate a domain of experience. It is therefore a structure that earns the title of model largely because it is a kind of extended metaphor providing a framework for construing experience by inviting us to view that experience in a familiar way. For example, most pre-theoretical discussions of attitudes in the social sciences involve the employment of a distance metaphor. The implicit model in such discussions is usually a two-dimensional, or greater, Euclidean space in which persons can be thought of as residing at various distances from attitude objects and from each other with respect to those objects. When one is using such pre-theoretical models, it may be that the model can be further elaborated until it becomes a theory, or it may facilitate, in its limited form, a kind of analysis other than the hypothesis testing associated with theories. For example, the distance metaphor is realized in attitude research through the development of various scaling techniques, based on the locations of persons and attitude objects in Euclidean or some other metric space, and often the metric in the scaling technique is complemented with substantive hypotheses to produce a theory of attitudes.

Theoretical models are symbolic representations of theories, or so the saying goes. As is the case with other areas in the philosophy of the social sciences, the discussions of this kind of model are predicated on problematic distinctions. Since the distinction between a theoretical entity and a datum is problematic, it is not clear what is being modeled in the case of theoretical models. Whatever its orientation, that is, whether it is primarily oriented toward modeling a subject matter or a symbolic framework for making inferences about that subject matter (e.g., a theory), a model is a symbolic framework that purports to be homologous or analogous to another structure or structured domain. A model can therefore be viewed as operating at varying levels of abstraction, modeling an abstract theoretical structure in some cases and a minimally interpreted domain of data in others. One could, for example, develop a theory whose entities are purely linguistic and then create a representation of that theory in another way, such as pictorially or physically. In such a case, each representation of the theory is a model of the other(s) in that each exhibits a structural relationship to the other(s). If the relationship is one of structural identity or isomorphism (a condition that social scientists are not troubled with), the models are called homological. Such homologues can be found in cases in which laws from one theoretical domain can be transferred, unchanged, to another. Canguilhem points out, for example, how Fourier was struck by the fact that "the propagation of heat, the movement of waves, and the vibration of elastic laminae are intelligible by means of mathematically identical equations."[24] When the relationship is one of structural similarity rather than identity the models are called analogical. There is a variety of fields in which, for better or worse, analogical models are used. Biologists have developed theories of anatomical functions by modeling them (analogically) on theories of several nonbiological phenomena. Among the more familiar examples is the use of electrical models in understanding the neurological system.[25] In the social sciences, we find the use of analogical models from every conceivable domain. For example, theories of individual attitudes, ideologies, and behaviors are frequently modeled, as was suggested above, on various distance metrics (left-right, etc.) and/ or on energy concepts (strong-weak, etc.). Collective behavior theories are modeled on such things as biological processes (e.g., contagion models of conflict and communication networks (used to explain societies as a whole, organizations, prisons, etc.).

Much of what has been said here about model strategies in the development of scientific theories bears on what is usually regarded as the "cognitive" advantages of such strategies. By "cognitive advantages of modeling strategies," one ordinarily means the assistance that the modeling provides in the pursuit of knowledge. The knowledge-promoting functions of models would therefore be contrasted with the interest-promoting function, and this latter function would probably be called non-cognitive or normative (if collective interests are involved). Recognizing that it is problematic to distinguish cognitive from normative dimensions of knowledge—an issue already addressed at length above—we can nevertheless preserve some sense of what "cognitive advantages" means by restricting our attention to the way that models assist logical, inference-making procedures in both the discovery and justification of knowledge. This allows us to ask about how models function as part of theory-building enterprises. There has been considerable confusion about what aspects of models afford cognitive advantages in the process of theory building. In a discussion that remains influential among social scientists, Abraham Kaplan, refers to a model as a special kind of theory, one that *resembles* the subject matter to which it refers.[26] This idea, which is reminiscent of Wittgenstein's early conception of the language–reality relationship—his picture theory—adds to the confusion. The idea of a model resembling the reality to which it refers is, of course, just as flawed as the picture theory of the language–reality relationship. Because it is impossible to discover a structure or shape to any domain of experience outside the context of the conceptualization used to apprehend it, resemblance makes sense only when one is speaking about relationships between and among models.

A more sophisticated view of the cognitive function of a model is oriented around the idea that models *represent* the phenomena under investigation. But this view is also flawed. Canguilhem makes this clear in his discussion of the decisions involved in the use of analogical models.

> The choice of phenomena for analogical reference depends only on one of the two following requirements: either the knowledge of these phenomena has already reached the stage of being a theory; or these phenomena lend themselves particularly easily to experimental investigation. In neither case does the concrete realization of a model claim to have the validity of a literal representation of the phenomena which the model aims to explain. Maxwell used to say that the physical analogy serves, starting with a partial similarity between laws, to illustrate one science by means of another. Illustration is not representation.[27]

Special care should be exercised in interpreting Canguilhem's use of the term "phenomena" here when he speaks of the "choice of phenomena for analogical reference." Phenomena in this case refers neither to data nor theory but to the combination of the two as they represent the referent domain being used to illustrate the one to be examined and investigated. With this in mind, we can speak sensibly about the cognitive advantages of modeling strategies, some of which are already mentioned in Canguilhem's statement. It is clearly advantageous to investigate a new area by analogizing from one that is both familiar and explicable with a theory whose structure may well apply to a new area. For example, if we wish to study various social and political processes that occur in what are referred to as "totalitarian societies," those where the lines of authority go "down" (leaders to followers) without authority or even communication "upward," it might be worthwhile to model such a society on a prison. We immediately then have a conceptual framework that distinguishes inmates, a custodial staff, a rehabilitation staff, and leadership (the Warden). Because we have notions about relationships between and among these entities in a prison, by analogizing such that inmates become citizens, custodial staffers become the internal security forces, rehabilitation staffers become the socialization agencies, and the warden becomes the political head of state, we can investigate what we would expect to be similar kinds of relationships in a society as a whole that is organized along similar lines. Of course, this kind of analogically aided investigation is possible only to the extent that we already have a well-articulated theory of the relationships in the analogous domain that we are using to model the referent domain, the political system as a whole.

Sometimes, as Canguilhem suggests, the model selected is useful because of the access it affords to experimental investigation. A computer-simulation model of a social or political process, for example, expresses a theory in a mode that renders the theory manipulable. The logic of a verbally represented theory about attitudes, for example, can be examined more fully in a computer-simulated version. If the theory suggests that over a given period interaction among a set of persons with differing attitudes will produce conformity, this can be examined by simulating the interaction process over a representative period, because we can electronically process the theory more rapidly, articulately, and extensively than we can with our own word-making equipment.

Modeling strategies can be especially advantageous in theory building, not only because the model may be a more palpable experimental mode, but also because the model or the mode of expression (system of signification) may be richer than the theory-data domain under investigation, and thereby may suggest extentions of the theory. Contentless formal theories, such as graph theory, can provide models which, because they contain such a rich set of laws, theories, and propositions of their own, can provoke theoretical development beyond the set of hypotheses that are developed before the modeling strategy is employed.[28] One way of talking about extending a theory is in terms of producing "predictive novelty."[29]

Among the means for obtaining predictive novelty with formal models, Braithwaite has suggested two that are particularly worth noting. First, given that one has developed a formal model of a verbal theory, one can examine propositions of the model which, when presented as part of the model's structure, might suggest new propositions to add to the original ones. Moving back to the verbal formulation with these new propositions results in an extended theory with new empirically testable generalizations. Second, the model can be employed to suggest new properties reflecting theoretical concepts in the theory. Combining these new properties with the original ones would yield new initial propositions that could be added to the generalizations in the verbal theory to produce new empirically testable propositions containing new theoretical terms. To see how this might work, consider Harary, Norman, and Cartwright's treatment of the theory of directed graphs.[30]

The primitive or undefined concepts in the theory are:

P_1: A set V of elements called points.
P_2: A set X of elements called lines.

P_3: A function f whose domain is X and whose range is contained in V.

P_4: A function s whose domain X and whose range is contained in V.

The axioms or basic underived propositions are:

A_1: The set V is finite and not empty.
A_2: The set X is finite.
A_3: No two distinct lines are parallel.
A_4: There are no loops.

To these primitives and axioms are added rules for connectedness as follows.

A digraph (directed graph) is strongly connected if every two points in it are mutually reachable. A digraph is unilaterally connected if every set of two points contains at least one that is reachable from the other. A digraph is weakly connected if every two points contain a path (lines connect them but they are not reachable, one from the other), and a digraph is disconnected if it is not even weak.

Finally, the following theorem is added:

The digraph D is strong if and only if every pair of points is three joined; D is unilateral if and only if every pair of points is two joined; and D is weak if and only if every pair of points is one joined.

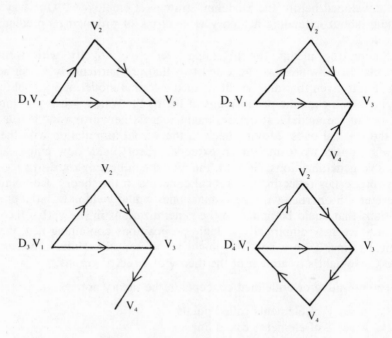

Figure 1. Theory of Directed Graphs

We are now prepared to consider the four digraphs in Figure 1, one of Harary, Norman, and Cartwright's examples. We observe that D_1 is disconnected (note V_4), D_2 is a weak digraph, D_3 is a unilateral digraph, and D_4 is a strong digraph. Utilizing these four digraphs the authors point out how predictions can be made about sociometric relations in housing projects. Assuming that the housing-project residents have answered the question, With whom do you like to spend your leisure time? and beginning with the assumption that two residents will tend to engage in social activities together if, in the digraph of their sociometric choices, there is a line from one to the other, they proceed to derive propositions. The empirical conventions added to the purely formal system represented by the digraphs are simply that the points V_1, V_2, V_3, and V_4 will represent residents and that lines from one V to another will represent sociometric choices. "It is assumed that the absence of a line indicates 'indifferent' rather than active avoidance. Therefore if one V chooses another but the choice is not reciprocated, they will nevertheless tend to associate."

It can be seen from observing the digraphs that any two residents will tend to engage in social interaction if the digraph of their sociometric choices is at least weak as in D, a proposition that is generated from the formal system of graphs without the necessity of our peering in the windows of a housing project. This empirical proposition can then be tested (by such techniques as peering in windows).

It is obvious that one could add Vs or residents in increasing numbers and thereby extend the theory of residential social activities for which the digraphs are models. This would constitute what Braithwaite referred to as adding new properties to the model that would reflect new theoretical concepts in the theory being modeled. Graph theory could also be used to suggest new propositions in a theory. One can use graph theory to model cognitive systems. For example, by beginning with the simple idea that each point in a graph represents a concept or personal construct and that each line represents a belief connecting two or more concepts, one can extend a simple theory about beliefs by paying attention to mechanisms that already exist in graph theory. If, then, a person becomes aware that a particular set of concepts and beliefs is evoked in a situation, what can we expect that person's ensuing explanation of the situation to be, in other words, that person's completely evoked set of categories and relationships between categories after pondering for a while? If we model that person's belief system in a graph-theory mode, we immediately have a useful idea to exploit, that of "reachability." The idea of reachability might suggest a new (and testable) proposition: that the person's ensuing explanation of the situation would include, at a minimum, all the concepts and beliefs that are reachable from those originally evoked.[32]

Models: Normative Functions

Graph theory is perhaps an ideal example for discussing the cognitive functions of modeling strategies, because it is a wholly formal system, uncontaminated by any substantive content or association, and it lacks a specific form that would severely affect its suitability for modeling various kinds of explanations. Often, if not usually, however, analogical models used in the social sciences carry a content as well as a structure, or to use the distinction suggested above, a "matter" as well as a "form." Because analogical models tend to have a content and a restricted form, a selection of a model functions in the context of a social control ideology, in that the choice of a model is often part of the process in theory construction that determines the types of explanation to be used.

The control implications attendant to restrictions in the form of models are evident in a variety of areas. When psychological processes are modeled on the basis of the seemingly content-free stimulus–organism–response theoretical framework, for example, the resultant understanding of decision-making theory organized around such a model of human information processing contains an implicit posture on responsibility. As suggested in an earlier chapter, the traditional stimulus–response theory neglects the role persons play in shaping the stimuli that affect their behavior. If we adopt a different, perhaps more sophisticated model of human information processing, realizing that what is out there is many and varied and does not emerge as stimuli unless it is selected out, we will create an elaborated model of decision making that will include the process by which a person "decides" what is worthy of attention in the world. Such an elaborated perspective on decision making carries with it an elaborated model of responsibility. In the old, stimulus–response framework applied to decision making, it made sense to say such things as "American foreign-policy decision makers, faced with a crisis, decided to send the fleet to blockade Cuba," whereas the elaborated decision-making theory, based on an interactive person-environment model of human information processing, would make such a statement inappropriate. Rather than talking about decision makers being "faced with a crisis," the elaborated perspective on decision making would result in language like "American foreign-policy decision makers decided to construe various things in their environment as events that, given their value preferences, they regard it as a crisis." One could then say that the "decision" to regard events in Cuba as constituting a crisis led to another decision, one to use aggressive means to control Cuba's ability to function in the international system. This second way of speaking, associated with an alternative model of human information processing, then, suggests not only a different understanding of decision making but also an elaborated model of decision makers' responsibility. If persons are faced with situations, then responsibility is clearly diminished in comparison with a construction which suggests that persons create "crisis situations."

In his discussion of what he calls kinds of "model bias" in theories of social action, James March has made a similar point.[32] Beginning with the premise that "Independent of its truth value, a model has a justice value," which concerns the consequences stemming from believing the model, he demonstrates that most individual- and collective-choice models are structured so that purposes must be regarded as antedating action and preferences are seen as exogenous givens that are not to be evaluated. When we are restricted to such a framework, he notes, we end up using language like "finding oneself," "self-discovery," "goal clarification," "revealed preferences," and we have no way to consider how we can act to discover goals and values, to develop a value profile in the process of acting rather than subordinating action to preexisting values.

The content and structure of most analogical models in the social sciences render their control and/or responsibility implications more obvious. In specifying the role that the context of a model has in social science inquiry, however, we must deal with the ambiguity of what is being modeled—the data or another model of the theory. As has been pointed out in several places above, there are no data apart from some model or, more generally, some conceptual commitments that provide the boundaries necessary to package experience in discrete units. In practice, when social scientists employ models in an empirically oriented investigation they use at least two. The first model is usually implicit in the identification of the "data." For example, investigations of "political participation" are premised on implicit models of what the researcher regards as the legitimate and appropriate citizen role. These models are not explict-theory-building strategies; rather, they are sequestered in the identification of some aspects of human conduct regarded as constitutive of political participation. Some discussions of participation refer, for example, to providing "input" to the decision-making process. The use of this increasingly popular information-processing metaphor, to the extent that it is relied on to model participation, reduces the citizen role to an advisory one. Or, consider another popular model often mentioned in political-participation research. Some investigators refer to such things as the flow of information "upward" from citizens to governmental personnel. The up-down model is another one that diminishes the citizen role in comparison with less hierarchically oriented models.

Once the entities or data are identified with the use of implicit models which, as has been noted, carry a political content, the explicit-modeling strategy is then invoked. The explicit analogical models also have an ideological content; they contain ideas about how political relationships ought to be structured. One of the most obvious areas where such models have ideological implications is in the explanations used to deal with various kinds of social deviance. If a particular form of deviance is explained within the framework of the medical model, it is referred to as an "illness." The control implications of such a model are clear. The medical model absolves the deviant of responsibility for the nonconformity by locating the cause in an area which, given cultural values, is beyond the realm over which the person is supposed to exercise control.[33] (In some "primitive" societies illnesses are regarded as the fault of the ill person.) The model also vests control in medical authorities by inviting them to practice their craft on the victims and giving them control over deciding when and if the victim is well. Within the framework of the now familiar way of speaking about the use of various models to explain deviance, we would say that using a medical model to develop an explanation of a particular form of deviance is to "medicalize" that form of deviance, just as the use of a legal model could be spoken of as criminalizing that deviance. Thus the choice of verbal analogical models involves the selection of a discourse within which to embed the phenomena under consideration, and we return to the kind of insight discussed in connection with Foucault's analysis of discursive practices. This selection process looks very much the same whether it is part of theory building in a particular social science or policy making by one or more social control agency. Whether the emphasis is explanation, as in the case of the former, or policy as in the case of the latter, the implications of the choice remain the same. The social scientist may not be planning to guide a particular policy, but the model selected is a form of aiding and abetting, because it provides an action justification that could be exploited.

The discussion of the selection of analogical models thus returns us to the control dimension of discourse elaborated in chapter 5, for to select an analogical model is to place some aspect of interpreted experience in a field of discourse that elaborates that interpretation. Once this is done, the discourse itself takes control in the sense that the meaning of the phenomena under consideration develops only within a discourse, and its relations with other phenomena are constituted within the discursive field. For example, to the extent that "criminal deviance" is explained with psychological models and thus emerges as a phenomenon with meaning in a psychological discourse, the responses to such deviance that can be countenanced will be therapeutic, individual rehabiliative, or in some way aimed at changing individuals. Were criminal deviance to be explained in structural terms e.g. on the basis of such institutions as the class structure of the society, a more social change oriented approach could be countenanced.

In practice the models used in the development of social science explanations tend to be drawn from prevailing discursive practices that embody the authority and responsibility relationships dominant in the collectivity under investigation. Therefore the researcher who places an investigation within a given discursive field may be seen as used by the discourse rather than vice versa. The drug-use example discussed above is illustrative here. If drug use (treating what a drug is as unproblematic for the moment) is medicalized (i.e., studied as a medically understood phenomenon), it emerges as a different phenomenon from what it would if it were criminalized or placed within any of a variety of different discursive practices. Drug users and various other nondrug users have different statuses in the different possible discursive practices as disparate as those of medicine and the law. Responsibility resides differently in the different discourses and the resulting administrative processes are mapped differently.

What remains, then, is to develop an image of political phenomena and political relationships to help evaluate these various discursive practices. This task should not be seen as subordinated to theory building. As has been emphasized, the recognition of the inappositeness of various distinctions and procedures in traditional approaches in the social sciences does not merely constitute a call for greater care in the way we speak. The constitution of political phenomena, for which the researcher is responsible through the use of various models which create entities and relationships, clearly involves ideological commitments, the activation of political biases. Being explicit and precise about what a concept means in a social/political inquiry is thus not only a matter of avoiding ambiguity; it is also a matter of commitment to some image of human relationships which functions as a model that gives a particular inquiry a politically meaningful context. If, therefore, different discursive alternatives constitute different domains of political phenomena, we need a conception of political inquiry that is sensitive to the politics that inhere in discourse, and we need a conception of political relations that complements such an altered view of political inquiry. Although theory building is an important activity in the creation of political understanding, there is more to political analysis than the building of theories. What most fundamentally constitutes a political culture is discoverable in the discursive practices of that culture. The modeling and other verbal or symbolic exercises that go into the theory-building process in a social science are affected and often controlled by those discursive practices. We must therefore step beyond ordinary theory building and ask other than traditional causal questions if we are to pursue a comprehensive understanding of political life, and we need a pre-understanding of political life to provide foundation for our analyses of speaking politics and reflecting on the politics of speaking.

Political Relations

From Metapolitics to Politics

In preceding chapters I have been concerned with elucidating issues relevant to understanding phenomenal domains in general. Nevertheless, running through various parts of the previous discussion have been some relatively elaborated assumptions about one domain, the "political." It is now appropriate to make explicit a response to the question, What specifically ought to be regarded as the political domain? Although this is seemingly a "substantive" question, the appropriate kind of response requires no departure from the conceptual level of focus maintained thus far, for it is misleading to make a sharp distinction between methodological and substantive issues. Because social and political roles, "things" and "events," emerge from what we speak and the way we speak, it is inappropriate as was suggested at the outset, to regard language as merely a tool or medium of communication in the conduct of political inquiry. Language provides the means for approaching, dissecting, and negotiating a subject matter, *and* it provides the rules and commitments responsible for *creating* a subject matter. Because this is so, the problem of language in general and discursive selection in particular in the conduct of political inquiry is not so much a matter of speaking carefully or correctly as it is a matter of ideological self-consciousness, a reflexive concern with the process of constituting the empirical domain through the use of various conceptualizations expressed in discursive practices.

The position I have reasserted here is one that surfaces in several places above, namely, that science and ideology are complementary conceptual systems which are productive of knowledge rather than antagonistic. But such a controversial conception of ideology deserves elaboration. One approach to ideology, which is primarily associated with Marxist thinking, construes ideology as false consciousness and produces an analysis in which ideology is contrasted with conceptual systems that are regarded as more valid on cognitive grounds (e.g., scientific theories).[1] Ideological thinking, within such a framework, is seen as designed to motivate action in behalf of particular interests, while scientific theorizing is characterized as disinterested. Those who promote this view almost invariably regard ideological and scientific conceptualizations as differing in kind because they view the former as value- and interest-laden and the latter as interest- or value-transcendent. There is another orientation toward ideology, however, one which suggests that an ideology is simply a coherent set of beliefs, attitudes, and values on the basis of which persons interpret human relations and construct their own position and choices.[2] Although some with this view of the concept of ideology often see ideological systems as radically different than theoretical systems, others recognize that although ideological and theoretical systems are constructed for different purposes, they differ only in emphasis. Clifford Geertz is among those who have developed the beginnings of a useful comparison between theory and ideology within such a position.

> The differentiae of science and ideology as cultural systems are to be sought in the sorts of symbolic strategy for encompassing situations that they respectively represent. Science names the structure of situations in such a way that the attitude contained toward them is one of disinterestedness. Its style is restrained, spare, resolutely analytic: By shunning the semantic devices that most effectively formulate moral sentiment, it seeks to maximize intellectual clarity. But ideology names the structure of situations in such a way that the attitude contained toward them is one of commitment. Its style is ornate, vivid, deliberately suggestive: By objectifying moral sentiment through the same devices that science shuns, it seeks to motivate action. Both are concerned with the definition of a problematic situation and are responses to a felt lack of needed information. But the information needed is quite different, even in cases where the situation is the same. An ideologist is no more a poor social scientist than a social scientist is a poor ideologist. The two are—or at least they ought to be—in quite different lines of work, lines so different that little is gained and much obscured by measuring the activities of the one against the aims of the other.[3]

Geertz's position on the science–ideology relationship closely parallels the argument presented in chapter 3 on normative discourse. The difference between an action-justifying conceptual system and a knowledge-seeking and -justifying one is not that one is more "empirical" than the other, because they both require the denotation of an experiential domain to specify their meaning. What differs, rather, is the styles of the discourses, as Geertz says or, in the language of chapter 3, the level of meaning selected out for emphasis in each statement. A scientific theory of any social or political domain can therefore be viewed both in terms of what it represses as well as what it emphasizes. To produce a theory that can be used to organize and account for some aspect of experience is to suspend radical doubt about the standards which create and disclose that experience in order to raise questions about relationships *within* the context of that experience. Any knowledge claim that might issue from the construction of experience produced by a social or political theory thus has an implicit ideological element, one that predicates the knowledge toward which the theory aims on an understanding of what persons are and what interpersonal relations ought to be. As a matter of preferred emphasis, theoretically oriented discourse does not tend to reference directly the ideological-moral standards on which its meaning is predicated, hence its lack of normatively oriented statements. Empirical theory building is therefore an outward- rather than an inward-looking (reflexive) mode of creating understanding. Without going into detail, Geertz notes that there are occasions in which scientific and ideological strategies are pursued simultaneously. Here, I am making the more radical claim that there is always an implicit ideological frame of reference without which the scientifically oriented conceptualization could not function, for its propositions would have no meaning.

What is to be avoided is conceiving of ideologies as kinds of conceptual systems to be contrasted with other kinds (like theories). Some conceptual arguments emphasize legitimation (in the case of ideological arguments), some emphasize other functions (explanation in the case of theoretically oriented arguments). Thus ideology should not be opposed to be a theoretical or explanatory-oriented consciousness as it is within some conceptions of the nature of ideology. Ideology is to theory as normative arguments are to descriptions. The difference is a matter of function and therefore emphasis rather than kind. When an argument is proferred in a theoretical discourse with no action motivating or legitimizing emphasis, the interests and values affirmed are simply implicit rather than directly argued. Marx's claim that "The ideas of the ruling class are in every epoch the ruling ideas" thus applies with little modification to the politics of explanation. The prevailing modes of social control within a society or polity are reflected in the meanings embedded in its predominant explanations. The subjects (kinds of persons), things, and relationships constituted in theories and understandings represent a system of power, even when the enunciative mode suggests no legitimating function.

Foucault's contribution to understanding how power operates in a society is predicated on this model of ideology as a set of discursive relations embedded in seemingly nonargumentative discourses. But it would
be misleading to seek to understand his kind of critique by employing
the tradition imagery, that in which ideology is seen as a rhetorical ov-
erlay masking "real" or authentic relations. Power does not function
merely by producing a legitimating ideology in order to divert or distract
those who would seek to grasp its influence. In Foucault's imagery
power is productive; it exists not by hiding something but by producing
something. When we look at existing discursive formations, the question
of power becomes one of looking at the way that persons are locked into
a given set of identities and that things and relationships are restricted
to one set among an almost infinite set of possibilities. To offer a critique of power is thus not to seek what hides beneath power's rhetorical
manifestations but to show power's existence in what lies on the surface
of discourse. If we accept Foucault's imagery and see power as productive, we can see how the interpretation of human conduct and the critique of ideology are part of the same process. It is the critique dimension that tends to be neglected in the development and assessment of
empirical theories.

The existence of ideological commitments in theories is often neglected because, as Taylor pointed out, many of the ideological, or as
he put it, "value frameworks" lurking behind empirical propositions are
widely shared or relatively unproblematic. He notes, for example, "that
Catholics in Detroit tend to vote Democratic can consort with almost
anyone's conceptual scheme, and thus with almost anyone's set of political values."[4] As soon as more elaborate explanatory problems
or more complex concepts are involved, such as trying to account for
the existence of various kinds of "political conflict," however, the ideological support system of a theory or explanation becomes more controversial, whether or not it is referenced by the theorist.

At this point one may well question whether if empirical theories are
ideologically predicated, they are not therefore so cognitively suspect
that there is no objective basis for validating them. The position here is
not that the process of testing a theory of some empirical domain involves
disguising ideological interests in a seemingly procedure display; I am
claiming, rather, that any knowledge of something that is acquired with
the aid of scientific procedures is predicated on *both* ideological choices
and scientific norms and that these choices and procedural norms must
be deployed in a complementary way to produce an understanding. The
ideological choices are involved in constituting the entities and relationships that we theorize about and are also involved at various stages in
setting criteria for measurement and validation. Once meaning criteria

are established, once we have a "what" to treat scientifically, the inference processes involved in justifying knowledge claims require impartiality. For example, suppose we are building a theory of political participation, and by "political participation" we mean what Nie and Verba mean. "By political participation we refer to those legal activities by private citizens which are more or less directly aimed at influencing the selection of governmental personnel and/or the actions they take."[5] An ideological element is involved in this meaning of political participation, but an unbiased validation procedure for inquiry is conducted *within* this meaning context. Operating within the bounds of this conception of political participation, we might build a theory that eventuates in a proposition to the effect that the more control a private citizen has over who gets to work, the more likely it is that he/she can influence the selection of governmental personnel and/or the actions they take. A specific hypothesis might therefore be that the presidents of large corporations are more likely to be effective political participants that the owners of mom-and-pop grocery stores. One would hope that in the testing of such a hypothesis, the respect for scientific procedures would be maintained. This would mean, among other things, that one's values and attitudes would not interfere with the test (although they might affect the interpretation as to what could be regarded as a test). For example, a pro or con attitude toward large corporations or toward mom-and-pop grocery stores should be held in abeyance so that the appropriate impartiality could be maintained. If we then said "we know" that persons like the president of General Foods are more effective political participants than the owners of mom-and-pop grocery stores, we would be making a claim about the impartiality of our procedures, not revealing an attitude toward the persons involved in our hypotheses. But there are clearly many value preferences involved in "knowing something about political participation," not the least of which is Nie and Verba's apparent preference that citizen participation in politics remain indirect (channeled through political officials) and conservative (within the existing framework of laws, whatever the power allocation those laws may represent). That kind of partiality does not interfere with scientific theory building; it supplies the value-based, ideological predicates. When we make the discourse of science part of our framework for knowing something about political participation, we accept certain prescriptions about the role of particular attitudes that could influence scientific procedures. We therefore devise procedures that cannot be impugned by someone's showing that he or she was affected by those attitudes. This does not mean, however, that *all* attitudes or values play no role in the inquiry. In any scientifically oriented political analysis, a scientific discourse is only one of the discourses which govern the understanding that is to emerge from the investigation. Before the "political phenomena" can be subjected to the inferencing patterns belonging to scientific discourse, they must be meaningfully constituted, that is, developed within the framework of a discourse whose norms generally represent an interpretation of what persons are and what a society is. An empirical theory therefore contains an implicit argument about how human interactions ought to be organized, and if that argument were pursued it would produce justifications that begin with what we understand as ideological commitments and that rest ultimately on preferences for an elaborated form of life or mode of human existence. For example, some understandings of war protesters were developed within psychiatric discourses suggesting that their behavior could be explained with pyschopathological theories. This promotes the argument that persons who protest against American involvement in international conflict are best understood as psychological deviants. To begin to build an understanding of antigovernmental protest with a psychotherapeutic discourse instead of a political discourse within which protest would be understood as "political participation" is to promote an ideological position, one in which protests are deprived of legitimacy. To construct such protests as political phenomena is of course no less ideological, for it has the effect of politically legitimating such activity. What provides support for either of these competing frames of reference are arguments about how political activity ought to be construed within the American society.

The purpose here is not only to point out that empirical theory is value laden or that there is an ideological component in theory building but also to emphasize that the norms promoted in producing understandings are themselves a subject matter worthy of investigation. In this connection it is important to recall the burden of the position on language developed thus far. If the speech–phenomena relationship is viewed as dependent so that what we speak or theorize about emerges as a result of the norms which create meaningful categories and relationships, the focus of political analysis must be broadened to comprehend the political relations inherent in the creation of phenomena as well as the relationships among the phenomena. It is now necessary to go beyond the merely methodological argument that this position on language implies and indicate how a methodology is linked to a content. Recognizing the content that a discourse carries, we can analyze that discourse from the viewpoint of the data or substance it carries rather than simply as a tool for approaching a wholly separate domain of data. Because the political domain resides in our methods (languages of inquiry) as well as what we use them on, it is appropriate now to shift the focus of analysis and involve myself in an attempt to characterize that domain.

If we are interested in political phenomena, we must decide about the boundaries we should use to quarantine political phenomena from other phenomena. Such a decision puts us in a position, for example, to understand a given "protest" in either a psychological or political way— the problem posed above. In most societies there is usually one political discourse that predominates. This is to say simply that there is a political discourse differentiated from others by norms that are either enforced or generally accepted, norms that identify attributes of persons, actions, and relationships among persons thought to be legitimately part of a political process. If we are concerned with identifying who is exercising political power in a given arena, it is necessary to make decisions about what attributes of society and what attributes of persons (both characteristics and behaviors) are to be regarded as part of the political arena and, further, to decide which of the attributes are relatively more important than others. It matters quite a lot, for example, whether one regards a person's direct participation in decisions as necessary for that person to have his or her interests represented or whether it is sufficient that someone with the same or similar interests participates. In addition, many persons whose attributes are not politicized might, if these were, produce what they themselves regard as important results. At present there are no explicit rules about discrimination on the basis of a person's height, but it is well known that advancement in both public and private bureaucracies is height related (perhaps because tallness carries certain charisma or perhaps it is a spurious relationship based on ethnic correlations with height). If for the sake of illustration we regard height as a politically relevant attribute, we become sensitive to the power differential of people who vary on this attribute and, to the extent that we are involved in inquiries about distribution of power, are inclined to heed this attribute in our concepts and measurements.

This point can be further illustrated with an example of an attribute that has been recently politicized, a recognition amounting to an important change in the American political culture. Through the first half of this century, a person's material well being (food, shelter, employment) but not psychological state of being (self-esteem, sense of belonging, work satisfaction) was regarded as a legitimate ingredient in the political process. Accordingly, the public debate and governmental recognition of policy alternatives focused primarily on the distribution of material satisfactions. It was unlikely that anyone would enter a debate on a public issue to point out that a particular policy choice would affect the psychological status of a particular group of people. However, since the racial-integration decision (*Brown* v. *The Board of Education of Topeka*), which overturned the "separate-but-equal" doctrine supporting school segregation and related political participation by ethnic minorities, it has been a commonplace for persons or groups to make political demands on the basis of the psychological impairment that various kinds of discriminatory practices produce. We now witness frequent resorts to the psychological impact of public policy as persons who have traditionally lacked power (ethnic minorities, women, etc.) act to reorient the place they occupy in people's consciousness and thereby create a situation in which they can enjoy an altered, more felicitous self-consciousness. This represents a radical redefinition of the political arena whereby a wholly new attribute of persons—their feelings of worth and effectiveness—have come to be regarded as meaningful parts of the political process.

Obviously, what politics concerns is problematic and controversial. To understand how to approach the elusive and controversial task of identifying the political, it would be useful, therefore, to understand what is involved in approaching what have come to be called "essentially contested concepts."

Politics as a Contested Concept

Recognition of the controversies that surround the appropriate meanings of some social and political concepts—even to the concept of politics itself—has led to the resurrection of a relevant approach to such concepts invented by W. B. Gallie more than two decades ago. Gallie noted that some concepts associated with human activities, either organized or semiorganized, seems to provoke disagreement as to their appropriate use. The pervasiveness of the disagreement with respect to these concepts, he said, is such that, "when we examine the different uses of these terms and the characteristic arguments in which they figure, we soon see that there is no one use of any of them which can be set up as its generally accepted and therefore correct or standard use."[6] When there are genuine, ongoing disputes associated with a given concept, which are seemingly endless or not resolvable by referral to some agreed-upon criterion, the concept is what Gallie calls "essentially contested." Among the examples Gallie cites are concepts such as "democracy" and "social justice," which give evidence of being contested in that they tend to be used both aggressively and defensively.

A similar but less acknowledged analysis of such concepts was offered by Stuart Hampshire. Speaking of what he called "essentially disputed concepts," Hampshire observed that "there are some concepts that are permanently and essentially subject to question and revision, in the sense that the criteria of their application are always in dispute and are recognized to be at all times questionable." Hampshire goes on to note that certain concepts would have to remain subject to dispute because they are connected with "variable human emotions" which are, in turn, connected with "changing social forms." Under such circumstances, he states, we cannot except "undisputed and standardized criteria of application."[7]

It is important to recognize that Hampshire, like Gallie, is not simply claiming that some concepts *seem* to be subject to dispute, that is, that people in fact disagree about their appropriate application. The sense of both Gallie and Hampshire's use of essentially contested and disputed concepts is that they are contested in a strong sense—something intrinsic to certain kinds of concepts invites contention. This kind of claim is surely connoted by the use of the adverbial modifier "essentially." Recognizing the potential value of the Gallie-Hampshire notion, several political scientists have attempted to clarify what could appropriately be meant by essentially contested concepts, assuming that such concepts are contested in the strong sense. In one of the more systematic appraisals of the value of such concepts, William Connolly has identified their contestability as a function of their involving contending interpretations, which contain appraisive dimensions, of their complexity—they are related to clusters of other concepts, which contribute to their possible meanings—and the openness as to their criteria of application. After scrutinizing various concepts that appear to fulfill his criteria—Democracy and politics for example—Connolly concludes that contested concepts have a close connection between their normative point or orientation and the criteria of their application, for example, Democracy is oriented toward participatory governance, and criteria for applying it to various cases involve interpreting what is participating.[8]

The idea of essentially contested concepts appears to be useful, therefore, in guiding our understanding of certain controversial concepts in the social sciences. However, the use of the idea has provoked, in one significant instance, considerable contention. Steven Lukes argued that power is an essentially contested concept. In his analysis, Lukes developed a "three-dimensional view" of power, which recognizes that besides the decisions (dimension one) and nondecisions (dimension two) which impact on what people want, there are interests that persons have which may vary with what they recognize as their preferences.[9] Power, in Lukes's view, can therefore be exercised in some cases in a way that avoids observable conflict but is contrary to some persons' interests, even if that conflict avoidance is what all the affected parties claimed to want. What Lukes adds to traditional power conceptions is the notion that some conflict is latent in that one can distinguish between subjective and "real" interests, the former being interests that persons translates into wants and/or demands that they might want to place in the public arena and the latter being interests which persons have but have not translated into wants or demands because they lack an effective understanding of what the interests are or of how to legitimate them by proferring them in a publicly oriented discourse. In comparing his conception of power with the earlier versions emanating from the well-known community power analyses, Lukes notes that every power conception rests on a view of human interests. It is in this sense, he asserts, that power is an essentially contested concept.

This assertion seems sensible within the context of the above understanding of essentially contested concepts. To claim that power is being exercised in a given case, one must hold some view of the relevant individual and collective interests that can be at stake, and such normative commitments are both subject to dispute and are, in fact, often disputed. Lukes's analysis is illuminating inasmuch as it locates much of the now venerable community-power controversy—the dispute among American sociologists and political scientists about how to determine if a given community has an elitist or pluralistic power structure—properly in the realm of ideological commitment rather than where it was for many, in the methodological realm.[10] What produced the controversy was Lukes's claim that his three-dimensional view of power is superior to other, one- and two-dimensional views. This claim, taken together with the claim that power is an essentially contested concept, implying that its meaning is subject to irreducible value conflict, would appear to place Lukes in the position of making contradictory assertions. But to point this out, as indeed one reviewer of his analysis did, is to promote an ungenerous view of Lukes's argument for the superiority of his conception of power.[11] One can make the more generous assumption that Lukes's view of power is better within the common understanding of many, even though power is a contested concept. It is likely that many who hold one- and two-dimensional views of power do so because they are insensitive to the impact on what they would regard as important interests of various institutional decision-making procedures and/or because they are vague in distinguishing interests from conscious attitudes. Once they are given a more complex model and are armed with some analytic devices they hitherto lacked, they might agree that Lukes offers a superior view.

It is possible, therefore, that one could accept Lukes's three-dimensional *view* of power, predicated on a more comprehensive model of where decisions are in effect made and on a distinction between attitudes and interests, and still disagree with him (and others) as to what constitutes legitimate interests. Of course, some difficulties are involved in separating the meaning of power—which is contestable—from the analytic framework within which one looks for it. Lukes's three-dimensional *view* of power draws upon some aspects of a *meaning* of power with implicit normative commitments. To argue that noncognized interests ought to be part of a conception of power is to promote some aspect of persons as relevant to the public domain. It therefore takes extraordinary generosity to absolve Lukes altogether from the contradiction involved in claiming both that power is essentially contested and that his "view" of power is better than some others. Lukes himself, in fact, has rightly pointed out the illegitimacy of radically distinguishing contests about what inheres in a concept and those that involve the values upon which the concept depends. As he replied to a critique of his position, the point of his argument is that "disputes about the proper interpretation and application of certain concepts *are* disputes between contending moral and political perspectives—that different interpretations (which I call 'views' and Rawls calls 'conceptions') of such concepts arise out of and operate within different perspectives."[12]

Does the "essentially contested concepts" notion survive the Lukes, et al, exchange? Recently, John Gray has attempted to fashion a viable view that is informed by past debate. He suggests that we regard essentially contested concepts as those that refer to a common core of meaning but whose history of use involves disputes about criteria of application. He suggests, further, that such disputes extend to contextually related concepts such that a cluster of coherent, interrelated disputes is involved. The level of dispute extends ultimately, he argues, so that "divergent patterns of thought . . . partly constitutive of rival ways of life are involved." They are thus disputes that cannot be settled with resort to either formal or empirical means but have, rather, a metaphysical character.[13] Wishing to avoid a radical relativism, Gray bids us to regard philosophical disputes about the value of rival ways of life as subject to resolution in principle. When we recognize that the level of dispute is philosophical, an invitation to an inquiry known as doing a political philosophy aimed at discovering the good life is involved.

Gray's view, like Connolly's, alerts us to the kinds of commitments involved in disputes about the meaning of social and political concepts, but a disabling element in the current understanding of essentially contested concepts remains. Although political scientists attempting to employ the idea of such concepts have suggested that claiming a concept is essentially contested is claiming more than that its meaning is in fact disputed, they have tended to use a restrictive view of contestability, one which reintroduces the ambiguity between what it means for a concept to be contested and what it means for it to be contestable. For example, Gray introduces his approach by stating, "essentially contested concepts find their characteristic uses within conceptual frameworks which have endorsement functions in respect of definite forms of social life."[14] But as was pointed out in chapter 3, any concepts that reside within normatively oriented discourses can be presented in nonnormative or descriptive discourses and vice versa. The fact that a particular concept happens to be contested probably means, as Gray suggests, that the other related concepts involving preferences for alternative forms of life are also controversial. But a concept that tends not to be contested could become so. Connolly moves in the direction of showing how this is the case when he speculates about how the criteria for what is regarded as genocide could be revised as new experiences as interpreted as relevant.[15] Interpretations are, of course, always subject to controversy, so it is always possible to contest the idea of genocide. *Any* concept that refers in any way to persons or to collective relations among persons is potentially contestable. Disagreements about what constitutes laziness rarely are pushed far enough to provoke defenses of "forms of life," probably because issues of responsibility that are relatively small in scope are being contested in such a case. But the justifications of a meaning position on the proper application of the concept of laziness could produce a moral/philosophical-level dispute on the proper mode of living for persons in general. What is recognized as controversial comprises the conscious ideological commitments that people carry around. The fact that the meaning rules of a given concept are not in dispute does not make them less contestable in principle.

This suggests it would be less misleading simply to recognize that concepts which refer to any social dimension of persons, either explicitly or implicitly, are contestable and that a thoroughgoing dispute about the meaning of such concepts will, of necessity, produce ideological- and moral-level commitments. Given the structure of a society and its pattern of political relations at a given time, we can usually identify some concepts whose meanings are more likely to produce moral- and ideological-level disputes, but to accept that particular set of concepts as being somehow more essentially disputable than others is to be unnecessarily conservative; it is to accept the prevailing understanding of the appropriate and legitimate range of controversy. I shall therefore drop "essentially" from the idea of contested concepts and develop a justification for regarded politics as a concept worthy of being contested.

The kind of disagreements about how one should use the term "political" are similar to the power controversy that Lukes sought to clarify by using the idea of essentially contested concepts. Just as the identification of who holds power in a community requires propr commitments to a view of human interests, which supports a particular meaning of power, the identification of the political domain requires an elaborated normative commitment. The kind of variability that the concept of the political enjoys, owing to the kinds of proper commitments about the nature of human interests that abound, has been discussed by Alan

Montefiore, who like Connolly, sees politics as an essentially contested concept:

> Politics, in the sense which seems most helpfully relevant, is the area of public policy; and public policies are those which may affect any (though not necessarily every) nonassignable member of the relevant community. The notion of a community as an essentially variable, relative and contestable one, which means that the notions of "public" and "politics" are in their turn essentially variable, relative and contestable. But this is an advantage rather than a disadvantage, since it serves to bring out something of the interrelation of the different areas and levels of politics; of how and why it is that what may seem to be political at one level or from one perspective may seem not to be so from another; and may even to suggest a natural explanation of the phenomenon that quarrels over what is public or private, what is political or nonpolitical, what is or what ought to be the structure of society itself, may sometimes turn out to be among the most important political quarrels of all.[16]

It is apparent that if one is committed to a conception of politics like Montefiore's, one recognizes that it is misleading to talk about politics in descriptively oriented statements without addressing a variety of contextual issues, for the subject matter of politics is unclear apart from an elaborated notion of what kinds of relationships ought to be regarded as political. Clearly, then, the significance of every "political" inquiry is subject to judgments on the view of the political context they represent. We are thus left to deal with the fact that the issue of "the political" complicates political inquiry. As Montefiore puts it, "The evident complication is that one cannot identify the material as that to which the concepts relate in direct and total independence of the meaning assigned to the concepts through whose application the identification is made. One has, therefore, to proceed indirectly, adjusting one's terms of discourse as one goes along."[17]

The Domain of Politics

In the opening chapter I suggested that the concept of politics can be regarded as appropriately attached to those processes which involve sanctioned individual and collective control over valued experience. This notion was more or less serviceable in the context in which it was offered, but now that we are scrutinizing the concept of politics per se, it needs elaboration. The definition as it stands cannot be usefully applied to concrete circumstances or statements in what purport to be political controversies without additional stipulations about how each of the terms in the definition is to be used. The political commitments that must be expressed in order to refer to political relations, then, will come in the process of giving the definition meaning, that is, in establishing the rules or norms that will link word and object and provide a context for that linkage. Paying attention to such commitments, moreover, should allow us to move from understanding the political domain to understanding political action—what it means to be political. The kinds of political commitments involved in giving the definition a meaning and potential for application can be illustrated by focusing on the major concept in it, "control." By discussing various ways to construe the concept of control we can at least begin to close the circle as we continue to speak around the domain of politics and about political activity.

When discussions take place over the relative merits of different kinds of political systems and the emphasis is on such contrasts as that between capitalist and socialist or communist systems, the concepts of "control" and "freedom" figure prominently. Pro-capitalists often regard noncapitalist countries, where government "controls" the press, as lacking "freedom" of expression. The discussion often tends, in addition, to involve notions of "controlled" versus "free" economies. Those who line up in favor of capitalist systems, for example, are wont to argue that it is desirable to be free to produce or to purchase what one wants with the money one has "earned." Not surprisingly, adherents of systems with collectivized economies use the notions of control and freedom differently. Without getting into an elaborate consideration of criteria for assessing the merits of different political systems, it is worth noting how misleading such discussions are when they do not hold up to critical scrutiny the norms that give meaning to the concepts of control and freedom involved.

At an abstract level, the concept of freedom that functions in modern capitalist societies has been stated succinctly by Macpherson.

> Man is the proprietor of his own person. He is what he owns. The human essence is freedom properly limited only by such rules as are needed to secure the same freedom for others. On these assumptions, the best society (indeed the only possible good society) is one in which all social relations between individuals are transformed into market relations to which men are related to each other as possessors of their own capacities (and of what they have acquired by the exercise of their capacities).[18]

To understand how such a concept of freedom functions, however, we need to know more precisely how it is used. What, for example, might be regarded as a dispossession of person's control over their capacities? We can pursue a relevant example.

In the United States at the moment, when a person decides to purchase an automobile, he or she is not visited by a government official
who slaps handcuffs on the potential consumer or resorts to some other
kind of force and says, "All right, you and I are going down to see the
Pontiac dealer." Such a technique of control over an automobile purchase would be regarded as more than merely controversial. It would,
given the American political ideology, constitute an outrageous interfer-
ence with a person's "freedom of choice." There are certainly many
less direct restraints on a person's choice of an automobile in America.
These kinds of constraints of "freedom of choice" are embedded in the
structure of economic relations and therefore end up masquerading under different labels—for example capital derived from investors who expect quarterly profit statements, thereby discouraging long-term planning that would result in a better product. These kinds of constraints on
"freedom" are, of course, often recognized as such. There are genuine
ideological controversies about the impact of various economic institutions in the United States, and some people debate the impact of various
investment-capital mechanisms. But while freedom as it is viewed
within the context of American ideological orientations is widely regarded as an issue in processes which, by direct force or structurally related incentives, affect the choices of producers and consumers of goods
and services, the freedom question rarely if ever arises in connection
with processes of "thought control."
The fact that automobile manufacturers buy up massive amounts of
advertising space in the media and put together messages designed on
the basis of sophisticated theories of how to affect persons' thinking is
not ordinarily noted in discussions about "freedom." Doubtless, for
every academic social scientist who sees his or her vocation as one of
increasing peoples' awareness, there are two more selling their ideas on
how to constrain or manipulate that awareness to the producer of a
product who is trying to attract customers (some of these are also "academics"). What does this tell us, if anything, about political relationships in the United States? It tells us about political relationships that
are implicit in the way the concepts of freedom and control are ordinarily used. To elaborate on this answer, from the viewpoint of the individual in society, it tells us that when it comes to avoiding psychological
pressures or controls on a person's ability to make free choices, the responsibility rests with the individual who is the potential controllee *(ca-
veat cognitor)*. Looking at this from the viewpoint of those who sell various products and services, the rule is, if you can afford the media space
you can try to manipulate whoever's consciousness is reached as long
as you do not engage in a particular narrow range of fabrication. Of
course there exist various regulations about what kind of material one

can use to influence people's thinking in particular arenas, for example, school boards regulate what children read in the schools, but the important point is that the concept of "freedom" as it is used in the context of mainstream American ideological thinking is not a virtually content-free notion, implying the total absence of any controls. Various uses of the concept involve implicit norms about what kinds of controls are legitimate and what kinds are illegitimate.

There are in the United States some kinds of constraints on mind control. For example, if you purchase a product after having been hypnotized by an agent of the seller, you can claim "undue influence" and seek redress, but if you buy a product in order to be like the person advertised using it, as promised in the seller's advertising, and find that the hoped-for change is not credible to those you wished to impress, you have no recourse. As suggested above, the rule is that if you are duped by a message in the public media, it is your responsibility. Such rules are used to construct the meanings of politically relevant concepts that, taken as a whole, constitute the political domain. To raise questions about such rules, moreover, is to invite political controversies of a more radical nature than those which neglect this level, for example, controversies over the trade-offs involved in balancing freedom and equality. If we pursue the freedom-versus-control example and recognize this deeper level of controversy that it raises, we can better understand a major concept that integrates various activities called political analysis, the concept of "political culture." The concept was systematically developed and elaborated in a popular text on "comparative government" written in the 1950s. At that time, concepts like culture that played an important role in disciplines such as sociology and anthropology were being adopted by political scientists hoping to build frameworks for understanding the attitudinal contexts in which governmental institutions develop and function. For example, Samuel Beer and his associates used the concept political culture, which was more or less an extension of the concept of culture used by sociologist Talcott Parsons, to apply to persons' cognitive orientations toward the political processes in their societies.[19] Beer argued that by focusing on the cognitive orientations, consisting of values, beliefs, and emotional attitudes, which comprise a political culture, one can understand the political behavior of a society.

Beer and his associates went on to develop a more detailed typoology, distinguishing, for example, between procedural and goal values. Procedural values are "conceptions of authority," or notions about legitimate versus illegitimate ways of making political decisions, whereas goal values are conceptions about the purposes that ought to be achieved in and by the political process. Their typology, like typologies developed by others, includes a more general-purpose cognitive component, "beliefs," to cover the images that persons have of "what is" as opposed to what ought to be, and another component, "emotional attitudes," to cover the nonrational attachments that persons have to various political symbols.

Whatever the comparative advantages of the Beer, et al, model of political culture—it is probably as good a framework as any for understanding explicit attitudes and ideologies among the citizens of a given polity—such models are severely limited by their positive focus, that is, by their emphasis on cognitions which are part of a person's conscious awareness. The Beer model, in short, emphasizes only the surface of political culture. Beneath this is a network of implicit or tacit ideological orientations that would be untapped by the typical survey of political attitudes.[20] Consider person's cognitive orientations toward the concepts of freedom and control as discussed in the above example about how choices are controlled in making a purchase. As was suggested, most Americans have the attitudes that (1) the ability to spend one's money free from external constraints is desirable (perhaps a "goal value" in Beer's framework), and (2) the best way to maintain that freedom is with a market economy (probably a "procedural value" in that framework). The constraints or influences that develop from the "open market" in the form of thought control through the producer's use of the media is not a subject of American political attitudes in their ordinary sense. Ideological debates about freedom and control rarely, if ever, evoke statements about how the freedom to spend one's money is constrained by a person's self-image and how self-images are created by modes of social organization and exploited by advertisers who can trade on these self-images to market products.

How, then, can we speak of this other political culture, which is represented not in the beliefs, attitudes, and values that orient persons toward what they regard as the political process but which resides in the implicit premises and rules constituting in effect, the objects, events, and ideas that come to people's attention as the subjects of their political cognitions? One recent attempt to add some sophistication to Beer's conception of political culture is instructive here. Equating the concept that a political culture with that of ideology, William Bluhm has suggested that a political culture comprehends "two kinds of political behavior, which can usefully be called 'forensic' and 'latent' ideology." Forensic ideologies are the part of the political culture addressed by the Beer model. They are what Bluhm calls "the elaborate, self-conscious word systems, formulated at a rather abstract level, which constitute the language of political discussion in times of severe stress or strain."[21] Latent ideologies are an implicit part of political culture or, in Bluhm's terms, implicit sets of political words.

Bluhm argues that latent ideologies tend to be expressed in more settled times, in contrast with forensic ideologies, which emerge in debates
during politically stressed periods. But this stipulation confuses an otherwise useful distinction. Whatever the level of public attention on what
are generally regarded as "political events," that is, however politically
active and aware the public may be at a given time, the levels of ideology conception can be regarded as applicable. Latent ideologies, as I am
conceiving of them, exist at a meta level. They are the set of rules that
constitutes the meanings of the objects and events that people develop
explicit or conscious ideologies about. Thus forensic or conscious ideologies represent public awareness of political processes, but that awareness is predicated on latent ideologies which can be regarded as part of
persons' ideological deep structure. This deep structure is not necessarily evoked, whether there is political turbulence or quiescence. Turbulence or controversy generally produces the verbalization or projection
onto the political domain of forensic ideologies. To evoke and perhaps
disturb a latent or tacit ideology that is constitutive of the phenomena
people relate to ideologically, one must suggest, not simply that various
interests are neglected or that justice is not being done, but that the interpretive framework constituting the various "interests" thought to be
at stake is improper, that is, that we are conceiving of things (or conceiving things) inappropriately.

This focus on latent ideologies allow us to illuminate the various
meanings that can attach to such references as "the politics of the family," "the politics of medicine," "the politics of work," and to appreciate therefore what it means to act politically. For example, there are
at least three different kinds of meanings that can be involved in "the
politics of the family." First, in referring to such a politics, one might
simply be suggesting that, to understand politically the relations *within*
the family, we regard the family as a closed political system. Then, depending on our ideas of politics, we can analogize such that each family
member becomes a citizen. We can then elaborate by exploring leadership roles and decision-making processes involving rule making within
the family. Treating the politics of medicine in this way would similarly
involve regarding the medical profession as a political system and then
focusing on relationships among association members from a political
standpoint. And a like treatment of the politics of work would apply
some model of political relations to a group of workers as though the
aggregate of work associates constituted a political community. "Political analysis" of various groups in a society is often predicated on this
kind of analogizing. There is a second kind of meaning to the politics of
the family, medicine, and work, however. When theorists and analysts
make such references, they are often applying some kind of political cat-

egories and understandings to relationships between some group or association and the society as a whole. "The politics of the family" could thus refer to the political role that families, as units, play in the society. Similarly, the politics of medicine and work would, within this second meaning context, refer to some political aspects of relationships between organized medicine and the rest of society—such as lobbying by the medical association in behalf of or against health legislation—and between a work association like a union and the rest of society—for example, union endorsement of a political party platform.

Finally, a third kind of meaning can attach to references to the politics of the family, medicine, and work. This kind of meaning is quite close to what Foucault has suggested in his discussion of "tertiary relations" (see chapter 5), for it refers to the relationships among persons that are presupposed in the meanings of such things as families, medicine, and work. Within this third frame of reference, then, such phrases as the politics of the family, medicine and work refer to the political significance of the rules or standards that constitute something as a family, medicine, or work. For example, what makes a particular sequence of activity work rather than play or leisure is the rules which designate who can do what, where, and under what circumstances and have it be regarded as a remunerable contribution. Such rules obviously allocate various kinds of control differentially; they are sanctioned to the extent that they belong to a predominant speaking practice, and they certainly affect valued experience—hence their political significance. In this framework, then, the locus of the "politics of the family" is the set relationships within the society that produces rules which constitute what a family is. Thus there may be certain prohibitions in an urban community about what can be called a family in order to regulate such aspects of land use as who can live where. Such prohibitions, which help constitute a family, can be understood in the context of all the complex relationships of humans to each other and to land—"private property" and "investment" being but two concepts that represent such relationships. Families are thus constituted within the entire set of rules that allocate authority responsibility and control within the society. Similarly, the politics of medicine in this framework relates to the authority, responsibility, and control implications of the rules which constitute what is part of the practice of medicine and what is not. To the extent, for example, that aspects of parent–child relationships are medicalized, those who are medically certified can control that relationship. That particular kind of control is often represented in the concept of child abuse, when "child abuse" emerges as a phenomenon within medical discourse, that is, when parents who batter their children are regarded as people with an "illness." If "child abuse" is a medical phenomenon, it represents relationships between parents and children, physicians and children, physicians and parents, and all of these to the rest of society. These are not apparent as relationships, however, unless we examine the speech–phenomena linkage while regarding child abuse, not as a thing that is simply referred to in speech, but as a code representing a complex array of relationships. This third aspect of politics—the political relationships sequestered in speech practices or discourses—is a relatively neglected subject of political inquiry, largely because it requires viewing language as constitutive rather than, the predominant view, as descriptive of phenomena.

Therefore to act politically within this third aspect of the meaning of politics is to disturb an existing frame of reference. It is to seek to affect the rules that constitute one's actions and to seek to affect the community through one's actions. In chapter 5 I pointed out how Foucault's investigations elucidate this third aspect of politics. His contribution to producing a political understanding at this level is even more manifest in his most recent study of sexuality. In this analysis, which focuses on the sexual objects that emerge in various discourses in various historical periods—hysterical women, neurasthenic girls, sadistic husbands, onanistic boys—Foucault develops what he calls an "analytics of power." He shows how the identities that are distributed by discourses on sex, especially the medical and sociological, are part of a process of normalization wherein persons are subjected to the existing collective structures, occupational above all. We are misled, he argues, if we try to understand the link between power and sexuality by focusing on the particular legal proscriptions that *regulate* sexual behavior. What we need, he says, is to "conceive of sex without the law, the power without the king."[22] The power that subjugates persons to various institutionalized practices is immanent in the available sexual identities that are *constituted* in the medical, psychological, biological, and sociological discourses which help to create a docile labor force. Power is thus exercise not through the direct will of a sovereign nor through legal proscriptions but through the creation of objects and persons. Power is immanent, therefore, in rules that constitute these persons and things. Having argued that the constitutive rules of phenomena, which are sequestered in language in general and speech practices in particular, contain a politics worth investigating, it would be useful to exercise this viewpoint with an example.

The Politics of Constitutive Rules

The latent ideological level of political culture—the level consisting of rules that constitute both the entities and episodes a society recognizes and the understandings in which the entities and episodes are embedded—is difficult to discuss precisely because it consists of commitments that are not usually explicitly verbalized. Consider the phenomenon of stuttering. What stuttering or any "speech disorder" *is* becomes constituted as a phenomenon as a result of implicit norms about what kinds of speech performances are normal or acceptable, and these norms of acceptability are understandable in the context of a broader set of rules that links persons to each other and to their environment. For example, collective activities requiring relatively rapid verbal communication are more "disabling" than those that do not. By disabling I mean creating a context in which persons' speech characteristics are more likely to be regarded as inadequate. To understand the politics of stuttering, then, is first and foremost to understand the authority and responsibility rules that create boundaries which in effect distinguish enabled versus disabled speakers. If we therefore become interested in the "politics of stuttering," in a particular society, we must begin by raising the boundary questions related to what stuttering is. Thereafter it makes sense to ask explanatory questions—those related to how stuttering as a phenomenon is embedded in one or another frame of references within which explanations of why it happens and/or how it might be alleviated might be raised. The answer to the boundary and explanatory questions would tell us both how the phenomenon of stuttering is constituted and how it is controlled by virtue of where the responsibility for dealing with it lies. In industrialized societies it is relatively noncontroversial, except in some therapeutic circles, that the control should center on the stutterer's mouth. By this I mean that a latent political ideology directs society's gaze in a particular way (into the stutterer's mouth), producing a particular distribution of responsibility and control. Helped by a "speech therapist," the stutterer will learn to control movement of the part of the anatomy that produces gratuitous or meaningless sounds. The usually controversial part of this frame of reference relates to who is responsible for paying the stutterer's therapist. Some might argue that it is the stutterer's parents (in the case of a child) or the stutterer (in the case of an adult), and some might argue that the therapy ought to be paid for out of public funds. Also various intermediate positions might urge public funding of speech therapy for those whose ability to pay falls below a particular threshold.

But why should one regard the mouth as the zone for professionals to work on, with varying degrees of assistance from the stutterer, what is usually called the "speech defect." The appropriate answer to this "why" question will produce the latent political ideology directing the kind of attention the problem receives, given the way it is construed. As with any aspect of human conduct, a complex array of causal factors could be implicated. The direction and focus of the investigation, and ultimately the therapeutic gaze, is selective, and what is selected does not exhaust the entire network of possible implication.

Where but in the stutterer's mouth could we effect a change that would probably or at least conceivably result in a more normal speech pattern? There are various choices, but for the sake of illustration we can focus on the concept of stress and its individual and structural implications. It is easy to establish that stuttering is one among many "abnormal behaviors" that are often stress related. This being the case, an often effective response to stuttering would be an assault on the chain of causation that leads to the stutterer's stress. In a stuttering child one might well ignore the mouth and focus on the parent–child relationship(s); the parents might be putting pressure on the child, which, if removed, might end in the "stuttering problem." Or, going farther out in the causal sequence, the parents might be under pressure, given such situations as a stressful work setting or a stressful marital relationship. Thus the removal of work-related stress for one of the parents might ultimately remove pressure from the child and end the stuttering. We could continue the analysis, traveling farther and farther from the stutterer's mouth, perhaps considering work in our society in general and its various detrimental effects, and then moving on to the structure of our economy as a whole. We cannot decide where to direct and ultimatey to end the journey outside of a guiding ideological framework for the excursion. The way we tend to speak about phenomena like stuttering is conditioned by the discourses within which such phenomena are embedded. Speech pathology, for example, is not a phenomenon lying around waiting to be discovered. It emerges from a discourse oriented around various modes of responsibility and control. The fact that speech conditions are regarded as problems is a function of a latent ideology, which is structurally represented by the vocations of persons like speech therapists. We look into the mouths of stutterers, in short, because we regard it as relatively more legitimate to load the responsibility for stuttering on the stutterer than elsewhere. Once we realize that this model of responsibility is controversial, we can consider placing some of the responsibility elsewhere. However, we would tend to implicate stress and act to control it only if we had a model within which the effect of stress-producing aspects of social organization could be regarded as legitimate targets for adjustment. At present, such a model lacks currency. Or we might say, stress is at present not politicized. It is not a concept embedded in a political discourse, not an outcome of human organization that tends to be regarded as something that public authorities should regulate.

When we cast about for something to implicate we therefore consider "cause" in the standard sense, but cause is not a sufficient condition for assigning responsibility. Showing, for example, that an administrative unit's allocation of funds led to the removal of a person's job, that this resulted in the person's moving his family to find work, and that this, in turn, seemed to precipitate his child's stuttering does not necessarily imply that the administrative decision-makers are accountable and must either compensate the family or reconsider their decision. As was pointed out in chapter 4 on the theory of action, the creation of stuttering is attributable to the administrative decision only if there are rules linking the "behavior" of the administrators to the resultant stuttering such that "creating stuttering in the child" is to be regarded as part of the action of the administrators.

Such rules, called constitutive rules since the concept was introduced in chapter 2, provide a significant portion of the political relations of a society. To analyze such relations, we must develop a framework for analyzing what might best be termed the politics of constitutive rules. The analysis of such a politics must be other than solely causal, for as was indicated in the discussion of how cause and responsibility interrelate, the rules of meaning that constitute behaviors as actions and events direct the choice from among a variety of possible causes that could be implicated in a given analysis. This choice is a political choice, because to allocate responsibility is to imply a correlative model of control, and to the extent that we recognize the control as legitimate by the way we speak, it is a sanctioned control.

There is a more precise way to indicate how the analysis of the politics of constitutive rules can be deployed, in contrast to ordinary causal analysis. As has been indicated throughout the analysis since the inquiry into theories of meaning in chapter 2, to inquire into meaning is to ask how terms and expressions are used. This represents a concern with semantic meaning, as opposed, for example, to experiential meaning. Semantic rules are those governing the process by which we translate what we experience into what we say, whereas experiential meaning, by contrast, is governed by the rules that translate what we do into a psychological discourse within which we can represent what we are experiencing as we do something.

It has been pointed out that persons have relatively more control over experiential meaning than they do over semantic meaning, for whatever one may intend to do—whatever meaning one may wish his or her behavior to have in a given circumstance—what is in fact done depends on rules with a social meaning that one person cannot change by an act of will. Now, to take this analysis further, we can elaborate the framework for speaking about meaning, for the rules that give human conduct significance are not isolated commitments unrelated to each other. They exist within various discourses, many of which are interdependent. Recognizing this, we would explicate the previous example of the politics of stuttering by saying that the discourse in which stuttering tends to be located, given our political culture, links it with more general notions such as "speech pathology," and with other notions at the same level of abstraction that refer to the biological equipment—tongues, vocal cords, and so on—with which we make meaningful sounds. Stuttering does not as often emerge within the discourse we use to speak about stress, and even when it does, that discourse rarely includes social–structural phenomena and never political phenomena.

This discussion has shown in effect that to speak of speech defects is to accept a model of responsibility and a conception of the legitimate kinds of adjustments that can be attempted to alter performances. One can, of course, take a more radical, structural approach than my example suggests and seek to manipulate the structure within which disabilities like speech defects are identified. To take such an approach is to engage in radical political activity. A structural change can have the effect of changing demands for performances such that various performance capacities that may be regarded as defective in the old structural context are not so regarded in the new.

Discursive Practices as Political Practices

In order to provide a systematic approach to the relationship between discursive choices—alternative ways of understanding represented in different speech practices or discourses—we can scrutinize what amounts to Foucault's substitution of an interpretive understanding for the more traditional causal explanation.

Foucault has spoken of this kind of analysis—the location of phenomena within the fields of discursive and nondiscursive relations—as the "play of dependencies," stating, "I would like to substitute this whole play of dependencies for the uniform, simple notion of assigning causality; and by eliminating the prerogative of the endlessly accompanying cause, bring out the bundle of polymorphous correlations." These dependencies are of three types. The first is "intradiscursive"—dependencies (between the operations, the concepts of a same formation).[23] These dependencies are represented by the linkage between any two or more elements of a discourse. Self-esteem, for example, is to be found in a developmental psychology discourse. Within such a discourse one can find self-esteem linked with various experiences a person has in the transition from childhood to adulthood, experiences whose meaning is of course shaped by the discourses within which they appear. If one therefore becomes interested in explaining self-esteem in a theoretical investigation and limits oneself to the developmental psychology discourse, the results will involve the linkage between self-esteem and such other things as the quality of one's relationships with one's parents, as was, for example, the emphasis in Rosenberg's study of the adolescent self-image.[24] Causal analysis, such as Rosenberg's investigation of self-esteem, tends therefore to be part of an understanding that is confined within one discourse. One can, of course, develop a causally oriented investigation that is interdiscursive, as when one examines psychosomatic phenomena, that is, relations between phenomena linking psychological and biological understandings.

But a broader kind of interdiscursive relationship than the causal kind is involved in psychosomatic effects. When Foucault speaks of "interdiscursive dependencies," he refers to the way an understanding within one discourse affects the kind of understanding one can have in another.[25] This is his second kind of dependency. Foucault illustrated this kind of dependency in his analysis in *The Order of Things* in which he argued that a meta-level discourse, such as the theory of representation applied to language, affected the development and direction of various substantive discourses, for example, those of natural history, economics, and grammar. Similarly, I have argued throughout much of this analysis that the metalanguage of social science is intimately linked with various substantive discourses in the social sciences, as in the above example of how the radical separation between theoretical terms and data in a meta-level discourse is connected with substantive decision-making theories that take no cognizance of the way decision makers conceptually manage what ultimately becomes "the decision-making situation."

Finally, the third kind of dependency is "extradiscursive" ("between discursive transformations and others which have been produced elsewhere than in discourse"). I pointed out above that changes in the power situation in the United States (nondiscursive changes), as in effective demands by ethnic minorities for redress of various inequalities, account for how the notion of self-esteem previously unconnected with public-policy concepts has become part of political discourses. This example provides a context for discussing what one can do by substituting Foucault's analysis of discursive practices, presented here in an elaborated form through the discussion of dependencies endogenous and exogenous to discourse, for simple causal analysis. There are undoubtedly interesting causal questions of the simple variety that link self-esteem with "political phenomena." For example, one could analyze how the existence of formally elected political leaders of a given ethnicity affects the self-esteem of persons of the same ethnicity by providing symbolic status. But by placing self-esteem in the field of discourse-related dependencies—intradiscursive, interdiscursive, and extradiscursive—we clearly have a more comprehensive and politically sensitive way of analyzing its relationship with political phenomena. Cause is certainly involved in such an analysis. For example, we might be able to demonstrate that the increasing politicization of self-esteem, the trend for it to become a more familiar part of political discourse, began with ("was caused by") the place that self-esteem started to occupy in educational discourse (linked with "achievement"). Then, given the spillover or linkage between educational theory and the occupational structure—in Foucault's terms an interdiscursive relationship between educational and economic discourses—there developed a recognition that self-esteem is related to work performance. Given the value placed on work performance ("productivity"), particularly by relatively powerful members of society, it is a short step to the idea of self-esteem attaining political legitimacy. Whether or not this account is accurate, the sequence indicates the complementary roles that causal analysis and the analysis of discursive practices can play.

What the analysis of discursive practices provides that the simple notion of cause does not is a framework for understanding political practices in a broad sense. Much of what political controversy consists of becomes explicable when we analyze the interplay of discursive practices. Recalling that politics was identified as the sanctioned control of valued experience, we may easily make the case that the pattern of discursive practices in a society represents an important part of that control. It has already been shown how a discourse like psychiatry confers control over mental deviance on particular practitioners and their clients (as opposed to patients), a different kind of control from that obtained if mental deviance were "structuralized" (developed and explained as a product of social organization and thus embedded in a structural discourse) rather than medicalized. The more comprehensive overview provided by the discussion of discursive dependencies should indicate how the linkages between and within various discourses affects the extent to which various aspects of human relations are politicized. Sometimes the nature of discursive practices confers a control on all those with effective access to the public domain. When an element in a discourse is linked into the political discourse of a society it is, depending on the kind of linkages involved, more or less politicized. To the extent that it is politicized it is regarded as a matter of conflicting values and interests, so that raising questions about where control over it ought to be lodged becomes relevant. For example, to the extent that women's self-concepts are understood exclusively as psychological—having meaning only within a psychological discourse—attempts to improve them will be either individual (women themselves will have to take responsibility) or therapeutic (psychiatrists, psychologists, and/or other counselors can become involved). If, however, women's self-concepts become part of a political understanding—for example, if women's having positive self-concepts comes to be regarded as a resource that is a public responsibility to produce and maintain—the control over such self-concepts changes by implication and public officials and citizens can become implicated in dealing with the problem. Under such circumstances political processes are evoked as conflicts develop over what kinds of public costs are to be borne for producing women's self-esteem—for example, laws requiring businesses to grant maternity leaves which produces an expense of person-work-hours lost in exchange for the advantages. Whether or not women's self-concepts are politicized explicitly by becoming, as indeed they have, part of political discourse, the location of such phenomena in any kind of discourse reveals a preference for some mode of responsibility and control and hence a political standpoint.

Understanding discursive practices, therefore, can help us to appreciate the extent to which seemingly nonpolitical phenomena have a political significance. As Foucault has noted, the task of his kind of analysis is "to indicate and show up, even where they are hidden, all the relationships of political power which actually control the social body and oppress or repress it."[26] How the analysis of discursive practices provides insights into hidden dimensions of control was suggested in chapter 5 in the discussion of what Foucault calls tertiary or discursive relations, and immediately above in the contrast of structuralizing versus medicalizing mental deviance. A discourse can be understood in terms of both the control it vests in various persons or practitioners and in terms of its exclusivity, that is, in terms of who is excluded from control. For example, the medicalization of mental deviance vests control in the hands of psychiatrists and, given that medicine is a closed fraternity, excludes all nondoctors. Or, similarly, when "food" is embedded in a discourse that contains relationships between producers and consumers, that is, in an economic discourse (as was pointed out above), the control over what we can eat is vested in those who control food-related economic processes, large agribusinesses for example. Lacking an authoritative discourse that links food to health and health to political processes (i.e., the constitutive rules of health—determining what health *is*—are not politicized), we are not in a position to politicize food and thereby possibly to open up to broad participation the control over an important substance related to the general well-being.

There are undoubtedly various ways to represent the discussion of where the political domain is located in discourse and how it might be analyzed. One way is represented in figure 2, which is an attempt to clarify aspects of the discussion. It should be noted, however, that this particular representation is incomplete, representing only some of the relationships among discursive and nondiscursive relations which exist in a larger set of possible relations.

Because the major focus of the interest in discourse relates to politics, political discourse occupies the central position in the discursive universe abstracted for purposes of illustration. The other discourses represented, psychological, economic, biological, and medical, are selected because they have figured prominently in examples discussed thus far. In addition, the relationships shown by the arrows and areas of overlap are there, not to indicate all of the possible kinds of discursive patterns, but to highlight a particular process that can develop in the field of discursive relations, the process of politicization.

To demonstrate how the diagram complements the earlier discussion, we can rehearse an example presented in chapter 5. As was noted there, Foucault has pointed out that a development in the nondiscursive domain, the development of probability theory, resulted in the alteration of medical discourse. This alteration came about because probability theory facilitates the kind of inductive inferences from a large data base (through its relationship to statistical inference) necessary for the operation of an empirical science. Therefore, as a result of their "conceptual mastery of probability" along with other developments, medical practitioners began to organize themselves into a science rather than a craft. This resulted, as Foucault has shown, in the development of the hospital as a controlled domain for inferences and, of course, an alteration of medical discourse, based on the new roles that doctors, patients, and others play when diseases are part of broad classifications and patients begin to provide, therefore, knowledge to expand medical science (rather than just fees for service). Once medical discourse has been affected, its change can have a variety of possible impacts on political discourse specifically, and on the controls arising from new interdiscursive relations in general. For example, with the development of publicly funded hospitals, a public health administration develops to regulate medical practice and an attendant intersection of medical and political discourse. The elements in such a discursive intersection deal with, among other things, the kind of experimentation and therefore risks allowed in treating patients not only to help them but also to advance medical science.

The dotted lines extending into the political discourse from each of the other discourses in the diagram represent the part of each of them that is politicized, or is recognized as politically relevant in some institutionalized way, as in the example of the new medical-discourse/political discourse relationship illustrated in figure 2. Similarly, as has also been illustrated, the concept of self-esteem, which has historically been

Figure 2. Politics and Discourse

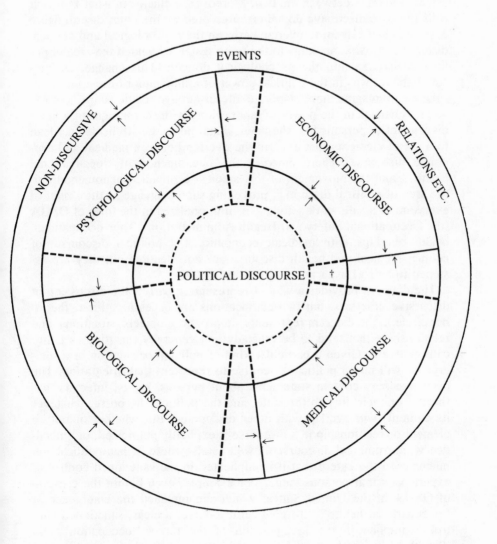

* "self-esteem
† "occupational health"
→ "extra and inter discursive dependencies"

an element in only psychological discourse, is now part of political discourse as well, in that it is regarded as a resource everyone must have in order to acquire other things (such as jobs) to which they have rights. Thus as an element in both political and psychological discourse, self-esteem overlaps between the two. Moreover, a change in what Foucault calls the extradiscursive domain (represented by the outer disc in figure 2) pushed self-esteem to overlap between the psychological and political discourse or, what amounts to the same result, expanded the area of political discourse into the psychological domain. This change, as indicated above, was in the political power of ethnic minorities.

One can imagine more elaborate interdiscursive relationships. For example, changes in the power of labor, along with recruitment of a more diverse set of persons into the medical and public health fields may lead to a set of elements that exist in the overlap between medical and economic discourse. There emerges the phenomenon of "occupational health," and the movement of this medical-economic phenomenon into the area of political discourse, provoking such language as the "right of everyone to a safe work setting," institutionalized in the form of OSHA (the Occupational Safety and Health Administration). Thus occupational health overlaps with medical, economic, and political discourse (of course, medical and health discourse are not identical but they are assumed to be so for purposes of this example).

The diagram provides a way of representing part of the discussion of discursive practices, but two clarifications are necessary. First, the inner circle in the diagram represents simply those objects, situations, and relationships that tend to be officially and generally regarded as politically relevant. Given a particular kind of political orientation in a society, we will find a political discourse to represent that orientation. The discourse may contain statements about persons' rights, interests, authority, or their duty to the state, and the political discourse, whatever its content, will overlap with other discourses. But whether or not an element or relationship in a discourse is explicitly politicized, or embedded within political discourse as well as elsewhere, it has political significance to the extent that it is implicated in the sanctioned control of experiences that persons value. For example, even before the creation of OSHA in the United States, which accompanied the emergence of "occupational health" into political discourse, a clear, sanctioned control is implied in the juxtaposition of the terms "occupation" and "health" even without its being explicitly politicized. To combine occupation and health as ideas is to create a discursive relationship between work conditions and the idea of health. Given that this discursive relation is legitimized (that it carries even an informal sanction insofar as it is evidenced in statements of interested parties) it confers on health-related and interested persons some control over work settings.

Second, the diagram makes it appear that the relative territories occupied by the various discourses are fixed. But indeed part of the political process in a society involves controversy over the scope and content of the political domain and thus over the nature of political discourse. This is what was meant above by the notion that politics is a reflexive concept, that there is a politics of politics. Therefore, to represent the struggle by various persons and groups of persons to politicize different elements of human relations, we would need a protean diagram which, in each of its different forms, would represent the differing political perspectives in a society.

At a minimum, then, the discussion of the political implications of alternative discursive practices demonstrates the kinds of choices available in constructing a political world. Foucault, as I noted in chapter 5, has diminished his own role as investigator/author, claiming to be simply showing how *the* discourses on which he has focused represent power, authority, and responsibility relations. But despite his claims to playing no role, he makes a consistent choice in characterizing the practices he studies and discloses. He brings a political frame of reference or discourse to his analyses of other discourses. Is Foucault making an arbitrary choice? In presenting an essentially political frame of meaning, is his interpretation of practices in discourses no better or worse than some other might be? Frames of meaning are not entirely self-contained. They rely for their persuasive and disclosing powers on some shared common understandings. For example, a particular psychological frame of meaning becomes superior to another when it provides for a "better" understanding of social interaction, but regarding it as better depends on a common understanding of what social interaction is about. Thus, although Foucault is exercising a choice, he is also disclosing something. We can say, as a result of Foucault's analyses of discursive practices, that we "know" more about the politics of medicine, the politics of penology, and so forth. That is, we can say this because, to some extent, we bring a common understanding of authority and control (some of the components of a political understanding) and of professions, disciplines, and bureaucracies to Foucault's invitation to mediate the frames of reference promoted by one of these groupings with the political frame of reference Foucault provides. In making this kind of invitation, Foucault is promoting a possible world, one more highly politicized than the one he analyzes, but this is always what the interpretation of human conduct involves: the use of one frame of meaning or reference to understand another. To create an understanding is therefore to engage in a polemical act. It is not somehow less objective to interpret human conduct within a frame of reference than it is to explain it with a scientific theory. As I have noted above, the validity of a scientific hypothesis *within* one frame of reference also involves implicit commitments about what the world should be.[27]

With this in mind, it is reasonable to say that *my* invitation to understand what fuller model of political inquiry may be possible is predicated on the commitment that developing a political self-understanding at the same time one understands political things is emancipatory. If we maintain an epistemological commitment to a dialectically interdependent relationship between speech and phenomena, we can recover both the politicizing and depoliticizing that resides in our speech practices. Part of this epistemological commitment is a particular way of framing questions. When, instead of asking, "Why are we repressed?" Foucault asks, "Why is it that we make the repression hypothesis the major component of our understanding of the history of sexuality?" he is framing a question more in accord with this epistemological perspective.[28] By doing so, he is able to point out how we desexualize some things while sexualizing one particular aspect of human relations. We neglect, he points out, relationships between sexual categories and political power, for example, the use of sexuality for maintaining social stratification, which is embodied in proscriptions of interethnic and interclass marriage. Similarly, by posing as our major political question, "Why do some people participate in politics while others do not?"—meaning, Why do some people vote or try by other means to influence elections and the behavior of elected officials while others do not?—we depoliticize everything else. We need to ask why we restrict our political discourse to such an understanding of political life. By expanding our political discourse, we can politicize other aspects of human relations just as Foucault has sexualized other aspects of human relationships. By looking for political significance in our discourses that are not ordinarily construed as political, we allow ourselves to see how the exercise of control over speech practices is a significant aspect of political relations. For example, to limit the idea of a prisoner to the way prisoners are identified in the penal language of governmental/bureaucratic processes is to defer to existing power configurations in a society. If we create a critical political awareness by suggesting that schools, work organizations, and even cities are, by dint of their principles or organization, engaging in carceral functions such that one can examine their inhabitants on the basis of the extent to which they are imprisoned, we are politicizing the functions of education, work, and city planning.[29] What do we know as a result? The process of critically challenging prevailing discursive practices within a political frame of reference both discloses aspects of political relations unavailable as such in other understandings and suggests a possibility of other modes of existence unimagined within the prevailing modes of speaking/thinking.

Language and Politics

Influenced by Foucault's archeological method, I have in my analysis emphasized the ways that human conduct is controlled and understood within the discourses that give it meaning. Insofar as we do not invent language or meanings in our typical speech, we end up buying into a model of political relations in almost everything we say without making a prior, deliberative evaluation of the purchasing decision. This being so, we might ask where there is room for an effective political consciousness that one can claim as one's own. Where, in this model of language and politics is there a place for an active awareness of how one can engage in constitutive acts, reorientations of meaning that affect the interpretation of our experience by restructuring the rules prescribing where control over that experience is to reside? There are two kinds of answers to this question. The first presumes a methodological focus in which the major concern is political understanding. The relevant answer, within this focus, relates back to the old adage, Knowledge is freedom. Translated into the present context it can be restated as, "To understand politics, one needs a valid and useful metapolitics." Understanding what language does, we can discover and even control aspects of political life that would otherwise remain unacknowledged.

We need, in short, a perspective on the speech–phenomena relationship that allows us to monitor the politicizing implicit in alternative discursive practices. Once we are thus alerted, our methodological focus shifts to include not only "political" objects and events that we seek to explain but also the political practices hidden in the discursive practices responsible for producing those objects and events.

The other kind of answer presumes that our focus is on political action rather than understanding (although it should be apparent that any understanding carries action-constituting norms). Within the political-action focus we are concerned to avoid linguistic traps that confine our options as members of a political community. Hannah Pitkin's discussion of language membership, as contrasted with political membership, provides a context for exploring avenues that detour the dead ends involved in the ordinary linguistic routes we travel.[30] She refers to how our "language membership" constitutes a set of internalized norms that individuals cannot effectively manipulate because their significance derives from collective rather than individual experience. "Language seems to provide a model of membership," she writes, "showing how norms can be learned, acquired without choice and without a real alternative, and yet end up being obligatory." But, she argues, language membership and political membership ought not to be equated. Despite the fact that our membership in a political culture gives us a political self that significantly controls our political actions, "what we will want to do, how we will perceive political events, what political means will be possible for us and so on,"[31] there remains aspects of politics outside of this model of a political self.

In developing these aspects, Pitkin is showing how the analogy between persons' political affiliations and language affiliations breaks down in certain situations. She is taking language as the paradigm case of the nonconscious acceptance of norms and contrasting those dimensions of political life that involve explicit constitutive actions on the part of political participants. She notes, for example, that individuals rarely stage linguistic revolutions but do consciously and deliberately innovate political change. She argues, further, that language is not, as a rule, politicized, that there are not interest and power conflicts surrounding language change except in special cases, whereas politics consists primarily in such classes of interests and power. And, finally, she argues that political processes involve explicit enforcements or sanctions, whereas linguistic norms are internalized and thus operate without external sanctions. Given this distinction, she notes, it would be dangerous to model politics on language because it might lead to a nonrecognition of the actual enforcement that political authorities employ.[32]

Pitkin's contrast between political and linguistic membership is useful in that political action is explicit and controversial whereas linguistic action (speech practices) tends to be implicit and noncontroversial. It is important to recognize that "language membership" is a more passive kind of citizenship than "political membership" and that modeling the latter on the former might result in justifying a conservative, passive-to-the-exercise-of-authority conception of politics. The two memberships should not be radically distinguished, however, because it is also useful to emphasize the overlap between language membership and political membership. Even though an analogy between the two breaks down in important respects, political processes are produced and therefore derive their meanings in the context of linguistic memberships. If, as I have suggested throughout my analysis thus far, adherence to the speech practices that comprise linguistic membership *is* adherence to political practices, an active posture toward one's political membership is possible only through a more active posture toward one's linguistic membership, and that activity must take the form of energetic, imaginative interpretation of the political practices embedded in various discourses. Even though, as Pitkin argues, the politicization of language is the exception rather than the rule, our speech practices, even at time when they are not explicitly politicized, carry political commitments. If we neglect the political relations that are discursive, that are in what we speak and how we speak, we have seriously diminished the arena of political action. Innovative political action, which has a constitutive effect on political life, *consists in* linguistic action, in changing the rules that link what we say to our experience. Without elaborating on a now familiar case, women's politics is an area in which much of the important political action involves linguistic action. A more powerful political membership for women is evolving as, "woman" begins to mean something other than it has traditionally. This altered meaning results from locating women in different discursive practices and/or altering the discursive practices in which they now reside. Politics and language are intimately commingled. Because our linguistic habits tend to be shaped by a relatively passive language membership, we are apt to neglect the political import of our characteristic modes of speaking. If we ignore the rules that create *what* we speak about and *how* we speak about it, this passivity spills over into our political membership, promoting an insensitivity to much of our political life. To enlarge the realm of politics—to politicize more aspects of human relations—one must analyze language as a domain of political relations and thereby use it rather than be used by it.

Notes

Chapter 1

1. Gregory Bateson, "The Cybernetics of 'Self': A Theory of Alcoholism," in *Steps to an Ecology of Mind* (Frogmore, St. Albans, Herts.: Paladin, 1973).

2. Max Weber, *The Methodology of the Social Sciences* (New York: Free Press, 1949), p. 52.

3. Talcott Parsons, "Introduction," to Max Weber, *The Theory of Social and Economic Organization,* ed. Talcott Parsons (New York: Free Press, 1947).

5. Alfred Schutz, *The Phenomenology of the Social World,* trans. George Walsh and Frederick Lehnert (Evanston, Ill.: Northwestern University Press, 1967).

6. S. Sidney Ulmer, ed., *Introductory Readings in Political Behavior* (Chicago: Rand McNally, 1961), p. 2. Although this statement is now roughly two decades old, it remains close to current representations of the understanding of those pursuing scientific theory-building strategies in political science. See, for example, the summary of the orthodox view of theory building provided by J. Donald Moon, "The Logic of Political Inquiry: A synthesis of Opposed Perspectives," in Fred I. Greenstein and Nelson W. Polsby, eds., *Handbook of Political Science,* vol. 1 (Reading, Mass.: Addison-Wesley, 1975).

7. See Mary Hesse, "In Defense of Objectivity" *Proceedings of the British Academy* 58 (1973):8.

8. Jurgen Habermas, *Knowledge and Human Interests* (Boston: Beacon Press, 1971), p. 303.

9. A. J. Ayer, *Language, Truth and Logic* (New York: Dover, 1936), p. 9.

10. Husserl's philosophy of mind is presented in *Ideas: General Introduction to Pure Phenomenology,* trans. W. R. Boyce Gibson (New York: Humanities Press, 1931), and *Logical Investigations,* trans. J. N. Findlay (New York: Humanities Press, 1970), 2 vols.

11. Alfred Schutz, "Common Sense and Scientific Interpretations of Human Action" (hereafter, "Common Sense"), in *Philosophy of the Social Sciences,* ed. Maurice Natanson (New York: Random House, 1963), p. 333.

12. Leo Strauss, "The Crisis of Our Time," in *The Predicament of Modern Politics,* ed. Harold Spaeth (Detroit: University of Detroit Press, 1964), p. 91.

13. Martin Heidegger, *Being and Time* London: Oxford University Press, 1967), esp. pp. 89–90 and 248–49.

14. Habermas, *Knowledge and Human Interests,* pp. 309 and 312.

15. John Austin, *How to Do Things with Words* (Cambridge, Mass.: Harvard University Press, 1962), p. 148. (Hereafter, *How to Do Things.*)

16. Otto Neurath, "Sociology and Physicalism," in *Logical Positivism,* ed. A. J. Ayer (Glencoe, Ill.: Free Press, 1959), p. 284.

17. Ibid., p. 293.

18. Strauss, "Crisis of Our Time," p. 50.

19. Schutz, "Common Sense, " p. 333.

20. Dilthey's position is presented systematically in Habermas, *Knowledge and Human Interests,* chapter 7.

21. See Wittgenstein, *Philosophical Investigations* (New York: Macmillan, 1953), and Hans-Georg Gadamer, *Truth and Method* (New York: Seabury, 1975).

22. Paul Ricoeur, "Structure and Hermeneutics," in his *The Conflict of Interpretations: Essays in Hermeneutics* (Evanson, Ill.: Northwestern University Press, 1974).

23. Jurgen Habermas, "Wahrheitstheorien," in *Wirklichkeit und Reflexion: Festschrift fur Walter Schulz* (Pfullingen: Neske, 1973), pp. 211–65.

24. Peter Winch, *The Idea of a Social Science* (New York: Humanities Press, 1965).

25. Quentin Skinner, " 'Social Meaning' and the Explanation of Social Action," in Peter Laslett, W. G. Runciman, and Quentin Skinner, eds., *Philosophy, Politics and Society,* 4th ser. (Oxford: Basil Blackwell, 1972).

26. Charles Taylor, *The Explanation of Behavior* (London: Routledge & Kegan Paul, 1964), pp. 27–33.

27. A. I. Melden, "Action," in *Essays in Philosophical Psychology,* ed. D. F. Gustafson (New York: Doubleday, 1964), pp. 58–76.

28. May Brodbeck, "Meaning and Action," in *Readings in the Philosophy of the Social Sciences,* ed. May Brodbeck (New York: Macmillan, 1968), pp. 58–78.

29. Carl Hempel's recent positions can be obtained in his *Aspects of Scientific Explanation* (New York: Free Press, 1965). (Hereafter, *Aspects.*)

30. See, for example, Eugene J. Meehan, *Explanation in Social Science* (Homewood, Ill.: Dorsey, 1968), and Barney G. Glaser and Anselm L. Strauss, *The Discovery of Grounded Theory* (Chicago: Aldine, 1967).

31. Michael Scriven, "Explanation and Prediction in Evolutionary Theory," *Science* 28 August 1959, pp. 477–82.

32. Michael Scriven, "The Covering Law Position: A Critique and an Alternative Analysis," in *The Nature and Scope of Social Science: A Critical Anthology* (New York: Appleton-Century-Crofts, 1969), pp. 94–116.

33. Ibid.

34. Rudolph Carnap, *The Logical Syntax of Language* (New York: Harcourt, Brace & World, 1937), p. 25. (Hereafter, *Logical Syntax.*)

35. Ibid.

36. Julius Kovesi, *Moral Notions* (London: Routledge & Kegan Paul, 1967).

37. See Rudolph Carnap's "Testability and Meaning" in A. J. Ayer, ed., *Logical Positivism*.

38. Philippe Ariès, *Centuries of Childhood* (New York: A. Knopf, 1962).

39. This approach to the concept of violence is, like Galtung's, controversial (Johan Galtung, "Violence, Peace and Peace Research," *Journal of Peace Research* 6 [1969]: 167–91). Some prefer a more restricted conception, e.g., Giuliano Pontara, "The Concept of Violence." *Journal of Peace Research* 15 (1977): 19–32. However one develops the boundaries of the concept, there is an inseparable ethical component to it. This is pointed out in J. Gronow and J. Hilppö, "Violence, Ethics and Politics," *Journal of Peace Research* 7 (1970): 311–20.

Chapter 2

1. Recent treatments of the philosophy of the social sciences that have been influenced by the later Wittgenstein and other modern linguistic philosophers include: Alan Ryan, *The Philosophy of the Social Sciences* (London: Macmillan, 1970); Hanna Fenichel Pitkin, *Wittgenstein and Justice* (Berkeley: University of California Press, 1972); Richard J. Bernstein, *The Restructuring of Social and Political Theory* (New York: Harcourt Brace Jovanovich, 1976); and Anthony Giddens, *New Rules of Sociological Method (New York: Basic Books, 1976).*

2. Husserl's position on language is best developed in his *Logical Investigations,* trans. J. N. Findlay (New York: Humanities Press, 1970), 2 vols.

3. Martin Heidegger, *The Piety of Thinking* (Bloomington, Ind.: Indiana University Press, 1976), pp. 26ff.

4. Jacques Derrida, *Speech and Phenomena* (Evanston, Ill.: Northwestern University Press, 1973).

5. Newton Garver, "Preface," to ibid.

6. For an extensive discussion on the uses or meaning of the concept "meaning," see C. K. Ogden and I. A. Richards, *The Meaning of Meaning* (New York: Harcourt, Brace & World, 1923).

7. See John Austin's essay, "The Meaning of a Word," in *Philosophical Papers,* ed. J. O. Urmson and G. J. Warnock (London: Oxford University Press, 1961).

8. Charles Morris, "Foundations of the Theory of Signs," in *International Encyclopedia of Unified Science,* ed. O. Neurath, R. Carnap, and C. W. Morris (Chicago: University of Chicago Press, 1955).

9. Described in Henri Poincaré, *Science and Hypothesis* (New York: New Science Press, 1905).

10. Willard Van O. Quine, *From a Logical Point of View* (Cambridge, Mass.: Harvard University Press, 1953), p. 43.

11. See Frege's writings in *Philosophical Writings of Gottlob Frege,* ed. Peter Geach and Max Black (Oxford: Basil Blackwell, 1970).

12. Ludwig Wittgenstein, *Tractatus Logico-Philosophicus,* trans. D. F. Pears and B. F. McGuinness (New York: Humanities Press, 1961). (Hereafter, *Tractatus.*) Bertrand Russell's denotational theory of meaning is presented in his *An Inquiry into Meaning and Truth* (London: Allen & Unwin, 1940).

13. Wittgenstein, *Philosophical Investigations.*

14. Wittgenstein's *Tractatus,* p. 27 (preface).

15. Ibid., p. 67 (4.024).

16. Hempel, *Aspects* p. 101.

17. Ibid., p. 12.

18. Moritz Schlick, "The Turning Point in Philosophy," in Ayer, ed., *Logical Positivism,* p. 57.

19. See, for example, Achinstein and Barker eds., *The Legacy of Logical Positivism* (Baltimore: Johns Hopkins University Press, 1969).

20. See Hempel, *Aspects,* p. 105, and Sir Isaiah Berlin, "Verification," in *The Theory of Meaning,* ed. G. H. R. Parkinson (Oxford: Oxford University Press, 1968), p. 21.

21. A. J. Ayer, *Language, Truth and Logic,* p. 25.

22. Ibid.

23. Berlin, "Verification," p. 22.

24. Sir Karl Popper, *The Logic of Scientific Discovery* (New York: Science Editions, 1961).

25. Hempel, *Aspects,* p. 105.

26. Otto Neurath, "Sociology and Physicalism," in Ayer, ed., *Logical Positivism,* pp. 287–88.

27. Rudolph Carnap, "Psychology in Physical Language," in Ayer, ed., *Logical Positivism,* p. 172.

28. Rudolph Carnap, "Testability and Meaning," in *Readings in The Philosophy of Science,* ed. Herbert Feigl and May Brodbeck (New York: Appleton-Century-Crofts, 1953), pp. 47–92.

29. Ibid., p. 69.

30. Ibid.

31. See Rudolph Carnap, *The Logic Foundations of the Unity of Science,* vol. 1, no. 1, of the *International Encyclopedia of Unified Science* (Chicago: University of Chicago Press, 1938); and Karl Hempel, "The Empiricist Criterion of Meaning," in Ayer, ed., *Logical Positivism,* pp. 121–22.

32. Friedrich Waismann, "Verifiability," in Parkinson, ed., *Theory of Meaning.*

33. Ibid., pp. 39–40.

34. Hempel, *Aspects,* p. 117.

35. John Searle, "How to Derive an 'Ought' from an 'Is,' " in *The Is/Ought Controversy,* ed. W. D. Hudson (New York: Macmillan, 1969) (hereafter, *Is/Ought*), pp. 120–34.

36. G. E. M. Anscombe, "On Brute Facts," *Analysis* 18 (1958): 69–72.

37. Gilbert Ryle, *The Concept of Mind* (London: Hutchinson, 1949).

38. Two critiques of contemporary approaches to international conflict make this point well. See Edward Friedman, "Chinese Foreign Policy and American Social Science," *Bulletin of Concerned Asian Scholars* 6 (April–August 1974: 7–12; and Andrew Mark, "Numbers Are Not Enough," *Comparative Politics* 7 (July 1975): 597–619.

39. Robert Dahl, *Modern Political Analysis* (Englewood Cliffs, N.J.: Prentice-Hall, 1963), p. 12.

40. Ibid., p. 13.

41. Carnap, *Logical Syntax,* p. 279.

42. Ludwig Wittgenstein, *Lectures and Conversations on Aesthetics, Psychology & Religious Belief,* ed. Cyril Barrett (Oxford: Basil Blackwell, 1970), p. 1.

43. Wittgenstein, *Philosophical Investigations,* p. 5e.

44. Ibid., p. 12.

45. Ibid., p. 17.

46. Ibid., p. 664.

47. This is from Charles I. Stevenson, *Ethics and Language* (New Haven: Yale University Press, 1944), p. 73.

48. Wittgenstein, *Philosophical Investigations,* pp. 179, 180.

49. See chapter 1, n. 14, above.

50. Wittgenstein, *Philosophical Investigations,* p. 7.

51. Austin, *How to Do Things,* pp. 15–16.

52. Ibid., p. 52.

53. Ibid., pp. 91, 134.

54. Austin pointed out that his analysis could be generalized to cases other than the first person which predominate in his examples, ibid., p. 73.

55. Ibid., p. 142.

56. Ibid., pp. 144–45.

57. George Kerner, *The Revolution in Ethical Theory* (Oxford: Oxford University Press, 1966), p. 156.

58. This distinction between perceptual versus linguistic orientations in phenomenological philosophies discussed by Don Ihde, "Language and Two Phenomelogies," in *Martin Heidegger in Europe and America,* ed. Edward G. Ballard and Charles E. Scott (The Hague: Martinus Nijhoff, 1973), pp. 150–53, (Hereafter, *Martin Heidegger.*)

59. Taken from Derrida's explication of Husserl, *Speech and Phenomena.*

60. Ibid., pp. 21, 22.

61. Ibid., p. 73.

62. H. P. Grice, "Utterers Meaning, Sentence-Meaning, and Word Meaning," *Foundations of Language* 4 (1968): 225–42.

63. Derrida, *Speech and Phenomena,* p. 100.

64. Ibid., p. 90.

65. Heidegger, *Piety of Thinking,* pp. 26, 29.

66. Quotations in John Sallis, "Language and Reversal," in Ballard and Scott, eds., *Martin Heidegger,* p. 132.

67. Ibid., p. 134.

68. Heidegger, *Piety of Thinking,* p. 28.

69. Ibid., p. 25.

70. William P. Alston, "Meaning and Use," in Parkinson, ed., *Theory of Meaning,* p. 141.

71. Gilbert Ryle, "Ordinary Language," in *Ordinary Language,* ed. V. C. Chappell (Englewood Cliffs, N. J.: Prentice-Hall, 1964), p. 27.

72. John Austin, "Other Minds," in Urmson and Warnock, eds., *Philosophical Papers,* pp. 76–116.

73. Stanley Cavell. "Must We Mean What We Say?" in Chappell, ed., *Ordinary Language,* p. 78.

74. Jean Baudrillard, *The Mirror of Production* (St. Louis: Telos, 1975).

Chapter 3

1. Hume, *A Treatise of Human Nature,* (Oxford: Oxford University Press, 1888), p. 460.
2. Margaret MacDonald, "The Language of Political Theory," in *Logic and Language,* ed. A. Flew (New York: Anchor, 1965), p. 175.
3. R. M. Hare, *The Language of Morals* (Oxford: Oxford University Press, 1952), p. 243.
4. C. I. Lewis, *Values and Imperatives,* ed. J. Lange (Stanford, California: Stanford University Press, 1969), p. 71.
5. Kovesi, *Moral Notions,* pp. 9–10, 12.
6. Michael J. Shapiro, *Ethical and Political Theory* (Morristown, N.J.: General Learning Press, 1976), p. 12.
7. Paul Henle, "Method in Ethics," in *Readings in Ethical Theory,* ed. Wilfred Sellars and John Hospers (New York: Appleton-Century-Crofts, 1952), pp. 188–99.
8. Georges Gusdorf, "Values as Principles of Action," in *Contemporary European Ethics,* ed. Joseph J. Kockelmans (New York: Doubleday, 1972), p. 223.
9. Ibid., p. 227.
10. G. E. Moore, *Principia Ethica* (Cambridge: Cambridge University Press, 1903), p. 8.
11. P. F. Strawson, "Ethical Intuitionism," *Philosophy* 24 (1949): 28.
12. G. J. Warnock, *Contemporary Moral Philosophy* (London: Macmillan, 1967), p. 63.
13. Stevenson, *Ethics and Language,* p. 11.
14. Ibid., p. 62.
15. Ibid., p. 199. See also my discussion of naive subjectivism in Shapiro, *Ethical and Political Theory,* p. 16, for a similar point.
16. Charles I. Stevenson, "Ethical Fallability," in *Ethics and Society,* ed. R. J. De George (New York: Anchor, 1966), p. 215.
17. Ibid., pp. 200–01.
18. Paul Edwards, *The Logic of Moral Discourse* (New York: Free Press, 1955), p. 147.
19. Ibid., pp. 182–83.
20. Michael Scriven, "Science, Fact, and Value," in *Philosophy of Science Today,* ed. S. Morgenbesser (New York: Basic Books, 1967), p. 175.
21. Ibid., pp. 176, 180.
22. W. D. Hudson, *Modern Moral Philosophy* (New York: Anchor, 1970).
23. John Searle, "How to Derive an 'Ought' from an 'Is.' "
24. R. M. Hare, "The Promising Game," in W. D. Hudson, ed., *Is/Ought,* pp. 144–56.
25. See the discussion on prescriptivism in Hudson, *Modern Moral Philosophy,* pp. 239–48, quotation, p. 249.
26. Michel Foucault, *The Birth of the Clinic* (New York: Pantheon, 1973).

Chapter 4

1. Otto Neurath, "Sociology and Physicalism," in Ayer, ed., *Logical Positivism,* p. 293.

2. Ibid.

3. Jacques Monod, *Chance and Necessity* (New York: Knopf, 1971).

4. An example is Dilthey. See Habermas, *Knowledge and Human Interests,* chapter 7.

5. Max Weber, *The Theory of Social and Economic Organization* (New York: Free Press, 1964), pp. 94–95.

6. May Brodbeck, "Meaning and Action," in Brodbeck, ed., *Readings in the Philosophy of the Social Sciences,* pp. 58–78.

7. Ibid., p. 74.

8. Brodbeck, "Meaning and Action," and Donald Davidson, "Actions, Reasons and Causes," *Journal of Philosophy* 23 (November 1963): 685–700.

9. A. J. Ayer, "Man as Subject for Science," in *Philosophy, Politics and Society,* ed. Peter Laslett and W. G. Runciman, 3rd ser. (Oxford: Basil Blackwell, 1967), pp. 6–24.

10. Brodbeck, "Meaning and Action," p. 71.

11. David S. Shwayder, "Topics on the Background of Action," *Inquiry* 12 (1970), 34, 45.

12. Sigmund Freud, "The Moses of Michelangelo," in *Collected Papers,* vol. 4 (London: Hogarth, 1925), 279.

13. Alfred Schutz, "Common Sense and Scientific Interpretations of Human Action," in Natanson, ed., *Philosophy of the Social Sciences,* pp. 342–43.

14. A similar observation is made by Giddens, *New Rules of Sociological Method,* p. 31.

15. Alfred Schutz, "Equality and the Meaning Structure of the Social World," in *Collected Papers,* vol. 2, ed. Arvid Brodersen (The Hague: Martinus Nijhoff, 1964), 226–73.

16. Harold Garfinkel, *Studies in Ethnomethodology* (Englewood Cliffs, N.J.: Prentice-Hall, 1967).

17. Ibid.

18. Schutz, *The Phenomenology of the Social World,* p. 61.

19. Paul Ricoeur, "The Model of the Text: Meaningful Action Considered as Text," *Social Research* 38 (autumn 1971): 529–62.

20. Ibid., pp. 534, 541.

21. Charles Taylor, "Interpretation and the Sciences of Man," *The Review of Metaphysics* 25 (September 1971): 27.

22. Quoted in Rosalind Coward and John Ellis, *Language and Materialism* (London: Routledge & Kegan Paul, 1977), p. 7.

23. Grice, "Utterers Meaning, Sentence-Meaning, and Word Meaning," pp. 225–42.

24. Melden, "Action," in Gustafson, ed., *Essays in Philosophical Psychology,* p. 59.

25. John Austin, "A Plea for Excuses," in *Philosophical Papers* (London: Oxford University Press,) p. 189.

26. H. L. A. Hart, "The Ascription of Responsibility and Rights," in A. Flew, ed., *Logic and Language,* p. 151.

27. Ibid., p. 154.

28. Ibid., p. 167.

29. Ibid.

30. Joel Feinberg, "Action and Responsibility," in *Philosophy in America,* ed. Max Black, (Ithaca, N.Y.: Cornell University Press, 1965), pp. 136, 139.

31. John Rawls, "Two Concepts of Rules," *Philosophical Review* 64 (1955): 3–32; and John Searle, "What Is a Speech Act?" in Max Black, ed., *Philosophy in America,* pp. 221–39.

32. P. T. Geach, "Ascriptivism," *Philosophical Review* 69 (1960): 221–25.

33. Austin, "A Plea for Excuses," p. 194.

34. Geach, "Ascriptivism."

35. Davidson, "Actions, Reasons, and Causes," p. 45.

36. A. I. Melden, *Free Action,* (London: Routledge & Kegan Paul, 1961).

37. Austin, "A Plea for Excuses," p. 201.

38. Anthony Kenny, "Intention and Purpose in Law," in *Essays in Legal Philosophy,* ed. Robert Summers (Oxford: Basil Blackwell, 1970), pp. 146–63.

39. Skinner, " 'Social Meaning' and the Explanation of Social Action," in Laslett, Runciman, and Skinner, eds., 4th ser., *Philosophy, Politics and Society,* p. 148.

40. See Jack Bilmes, "Rules and Rhetoric: Negotiating the Social order in a Thai Village," *Journal of Anthropological Research* 32 (1976): 44–57.

41. This aspect of understanding decision making is represented in Harold Garfinkel and Saul Mendlovitz, "Some Rules of Correct Decision Making that Jurors Respect," in Garfinkel, *Studies in Ethnomethodology,* pp. 104–15. Among the best general presentations of the "reality construction" approach to social analysis is Peter Berger and Thomas Luckmann, *The Social Construction of Reality* (New York: Doubleday, 1966).

Chapter 5

1. John Austin, "A Plea for Excuses."

2. Ibid., pp. 180, 189, 204.

3. Roland Barthes, *Elements of Semiology* (London: Jonathan Cape, 1967), p. 28.

4. Jacques Lacan, *The Language of the Self* (Baltimore: Johns Hopkins University Press, 1968).

5. Michel Foucault, *Language, Counter-Memory, Practice,* ed. D. F. Bouchard (Ithaca, N.Y.: Cornell University Press, 1977), p. 199.

6. Jonathan Culler, *Structuralist Poetics* (London: Routledge & Kegan Paul, 1975).

7. Michel Foucault, *The Archeology of Knowledge* (New York: Pantheon, 1972), p. 194. (Hereafter, *Archeology.*)

8. Ibid., p. 31.

9. Gadamer, *Truth and Method,* pp. 238ff.

10. Ricoeur, "Structure and Hermeneutics," in his *Conflict of Interpretation,* p. 51.

11. Hans-Georg Gadamer *Philosophical Hemeneutics* trans. and ed. David E. Linge (Berkeley: University of California Press, 1976), p. 26.

12. Ricoeur, "Structure and Hermeneutics," p. 30.

13. Ibid., p. 33.

14. Foucault, *Language, Counter-Memory, Practice,* pp. 130–31.

15. Foucault, *Archeology,* p. 138.

16. Ibid., p. 75.

17. Ibid., p. 38.

18. Ibid., p. 121–22.

19. Ibid., p. 120.

20. P. F. Strawson, "Truth," in *Logico-Linguistic Papers* (London: Methuen, 1971), p. 196.

21. Habermas, *Knowledge and Human Interests,* p. 309.

22. Michel Foucault, *Discipline and Punish* (New York: Pantheon, 1977), p. 27.

23. Ibid., p. 26

24. Foucault, *Archeology,* p. 120.

25. Michel Foucault, *Madness and Civilization* (New York: Pantheon, 1965).

26. Ibid., pp. 45, 46.

27. Ibid., p. 64.

28. See chapter 3, n. 26

29. Foucault, *Birth of the Clinic,* p. xix.

30. Ibid., pp. 6, 10.

31. Ibid., pp. 16, 17.

32. Ibid., p. 25.

33. Some see the position in *The Archeology of Knowledge* as a departure from what has been argued in *The Order of Things,* e.g., Dominque Lecourt, *Marxism and Epistemology: Bachelard, Canguilhem and Foucault* (London: NLB, 1975).

34. Michel Foucault, *The Order of Things* (New York: Pantheon, 1971), p. xix.

35. Foucault, *Archeology,* p. 51.

36. Thomas Kuhn, *The Structure of Scientific Revolutions,* 2nd ed. (Chicago: The University of Chicago Press, 1970).

37. Ibid., p. viii.

38. Ibid., p. 94.

39. Bernstein, *The Restructuring of Social and Political Theory,* p. 93.

40. Foucault, *Archeology,* pp. 4, 6.

41. Ibid., pp. 31–32.

42. Ibid., p. 33.

43. Ibid., p. 34.

44. Ibid., pp. 38, 45

45. Ibid., p. 50.

46. Ibid., p. 51.

47. Ibid., p. 79.

48. This comparison is suggested in Lecourt *Marxism and Epistemology.*

49. Michel Foucault, "History, Discourse, and Discontinuity," *Salmagundi* no. 20 (summer–fall 1972): 243.

50. Foucault, *Archeology,* p. 45.

51. Ibid.

52. Ibid.

53. Thomas Szasz, *The Myth of Mental Illness* (New York: Dell, 1961), and *Ideology and Insanity* (Garden City, N.Y.: Anchor, 1970); R. D. Laing, *The Divided Self* (Baltimore: Penguin, 1965), and *The Politics of Experience,* (New York: Pantheon, 1967).

54. Peter Sedgwick, "Mental Illness *Is* Illness," *Salmagundi* no. 20 (summer–fall 1972): 196.

55. Peter Sedgwick, "Goffman's Anti-Psychiatry," *Salmagundi* no. 26 (spring 1974): 26.

56. See Lester King, "What Is Disease?" *Philosophy of Science* 21 (July 1954): 193–203.

57. Aubrey Lewis, "Health as a Social Concept," *British Journal of Sociology* 4 (June 1953): 109–24.

58. Sedgwick, "Goffman's Anti-Psychiatry," p. 26.

59. Sedgwick, "Mental Illness *Is* Illness," p. 215.

60. Ibid.

61. Georges Canguilhem, *Le Normal et le Pathologique* (Paris: Presses Universitaires de France, 1966), pp. 12–13.

62. Foucault, *Discipline and Punish,* p. 26.

63. Ibid., p. 55.

64. Ibid., p. 54

65. Ibid., p. 304

66. Murray Edelman, "The Political Language of the Helping Professions," *Politics and Society* 4 (1964): 295–310.

67. Vilhelm Aubert and Sheldon Messinger, "The Criminal and the Sick," *Inquiry* 1 (1958): 137–60.

68. Clarice Stoll, "Images of Man and Social Control," *Social Forces* 47 (December 1968): 119–27.

69. Edelman, "Political Language of the Helping Professions."

70. Robin Lakoff, *Language and Woman's Place* (New York: Harper & Row, 1975).

71. Michel Foucault, *The History of Sexuality,* vol. 1 (New York: Pantheon, 1978).

72. Foucault, *Discipline and Punish,* p. 307.

73. Foucault, "The Discourse on Language," in *Archeology,* p. 215.

74. Foucault, *Language, Counter-Memory and Practice,* pp. 131–36.

Chapter 6

1. Quentin Skinner, "Meaning and Understanding in the History of Ideas," *History and Theory* 8 (1969): 47.

2. Quentin Skinner, "Some Problems in the Analysis of Political Thought and Action," *Political Theory* 2 (August 1974): 277–303.

3. J. G. A. Pocock, "Verbalizing a Political Act," *Political Theory* 1 (February 1973): 33.

4. Ibid., p. 29.

5. Ibid., p. 33.

6. J. G. A. Pocock, "Ritual, Language, Power: An Essay on the Apparent Political Meanings of Ancient Chinese Philosophy," in his *Politics, Language*

and Time (New York: Atheneum, 1971), pp. 42–79, and *The Machiavellian Moment* (Princeton, N.J.: Princeton University Press, 1975).

7. For Gadamer's position, see his *Truth and Method,* and *Philosophical Hermeneutics.* A similar critique of Skinner, Pocock, and others can be found in John G. Gunnell, *Political Theory: Tradition and Interpretation* (Cambridge, Mass.: Winthrop, 1979).

8. Ricoeur, "The Model of the Text," pp. 529–62.

9. Hans Reichenbach, *The Philosophy of Space and Time* (New York: Dover, 1958), p. 14.

10. Patrick Suppes, "What is a Scientific Theory?" in Morgenbesser, ed., *Philosophy of Science Today,* p. 56.

11. Ibid., p. 62.

12. Norwood Russell Hanson, "Observation and Interpretation," in Morgenbesser, ed., *Philosophy of Science Today,* pp. 89–90.

13. Sheldon Wolin, "Political Theory as a Vocation," *American Political Science Review* 63 (December 1969).

14. Florian Znaniecki, *Cultural Sciences* (Urbana: University of Illinois Press, 1952).

15. Suppes, "What Is a Scientific Theory?"

16. Michael J. Shapiro, "Social Control Ideologies and the Politics of American Education," *International Review of Education* 20 (1974): 21.

17. Scriven, "The Covering Law Position," p. 96.

18. Shapiro, "Social Control Ideologies," p. 24.

19. This is described in several places. See, for example, Thomas Kuhn, *The Copernican Revolution* (Cambridge, Mass.: Harvard University Press, 1957).

20. Scriven, "The Covering Law Position," p. 99.

21. The Chinese orientation toward health is described in Joshua Horne, *Away With All Pests* (New York: Monthly Review Press, 1969).

22. Colin Tatz, "The Politics of Aboriginal Health," Supplement to *Politics* 7 (November 1972): 14.

23. Ibid., p. 15.

24. Georges Canguilhem, "The Role of Analogies and Models in Biological Discovery," in *Scientific Change,* ed. A. C. Crombie (London: Heinemann, 1963), p. 514.

25. Ibid., p. 512.

26. Abraham Kaplan, *The Conduct of Inquiry* (San Francisco: Chandler, 1964), p. 265.

27. Canguilhem, "The Role of Analogies and Models in Biological Discovery."

28. The theory of directed graphs is developed in F. Harary, R. Z. Norman, and D. Cartwright, *Structural Models* (New York: Wiley, 1965).

29. Richard B. Braithwaite, "Models in the Empirical Sciences," in *Logic, Methodology and Philosophy of Science,* ed. E. Nagel, P. Suppes, and A. Tarski (Stanford: Stanford University Press, 1962), pp. 224–31.

30. Harary, et al., *Structural Models.*

31. Michael J. Shapiro and G. Matthew Bonham, "Cognitive Process and Foreign Policy Decision-Making," *International Studies Quarterly,* 17 (June 1973): 147–74, and G. Matthew Bonham, Michael J. Shapiro, and George J.

Nozicka, "A Cognitive Process Model of Foreign Policy Decision-Making." *Simulation & Games,* 7 (June 1976): 123–52.

32. James G. March, "Model Bias in Social Action," *Review of Educational Research* 42 (fall 1972): 413–29.

33. Talcott Parsons, "Definitions of Health and Illness in The Light of American Values and Social Structure," in *Social Structure and Personality* (New York: Free Press, 1964).

Chapter 7

1. The "false consciousness" doctrine is critically reviewed in Martin Seliger, *The Marxist Conception of Ideology* (Cambridge: Cambridge University Press, 1977).

2. The positive view of ideology is presented clearly in William Bluhm, *Ideologies and Attitudes: Modern Political Culture* (Englewood Cliffs, N.J.: Prentice-Hall, 1974).

3. Clifford Geertz, "Ideology as a Cultural System," in David Apter, ed., *Ideology and Discontent,* (New York: Free Press, 1964), p. 71.

4. Charles Taylor, "Neutrality in Political Science," in Laslett and Runciman, eds., *Philosophy, Politics and Society,* 3rd ser., p. 57.

5. Norman H. Nie and Sidney Verba, "Political Participation," in *Handbook of Political Science,* vol. 4, ed. Nelson W. Polsby and Fred I. Greenstein (Reading, Mass.: Addison-Wesley, 1975).

6. W. B. Gallie, "Essentially Contested Concepts," *Proceedings of the Aristolelian Society* 56 (1955–56): 167–98.

7. Stuart Hampshire, *Thought and Action* (New York: Viking, 1959), p. 230.

8. William Connolly, *The Terms of Political Discourse* (Lexington, Mass.: D. C. Health, 1974), chapter 1.

9. Stephen Lukes, *Power: A Radical View* (London: Macmillan, 1974).

10. The literature on the community-power controversy is too voluminous to cite. The one-dimension-power people to whom Lukes refers are the elitists and pluralists, the former being represented by C. Wright Mills and Floyd Hunter, among others, and the latter represented by Robert Dahl, Nelson Polsby, Raymond Wolfinger, and others. The two-dimensional conception is found in the work of Peter Bachrach and Morris Baratz.

11. Brian Barry, "The Obscurities of Power," *Government and Opposition,* 10 (1975): 250–54.

12. K. I. Macdonald, "Is 'Power' Essentially Contested," *British Journal of Political Science* 6 (1976): 380–82; Stephen Lukes, "Reply to K. I. Macdonald," *British Journal of Political Science* 7 (1977): 418–19.

13. John Gray, "On the Contestability of Social and Political Concepts," *Political Theory,* 5 (August 1977): 331–48, 334.

14. Ibid., p. 332.

15. Connolly, *Terms of Political Discourse,* pp. 38–39.

16. Alan Montefiore, "The Concept of the Politics," in *Neutrality and Impactiality,* ed. Alan Montefiore (Cambridge: Cambridge University Press, 1975), p. 42.

17. Ibid., p. 275.

18. C. B. Macpherson, "Market Concepts in Political Theory," *The Canadian Journal of Economics and Political Science* 27 (November 1961): 496.

19. Samuel Beer, et al., *Patterns of Government,* 2nd ed. (New York: Random House, 1962).

20. The tacit dimensions of knowledge and understanding are extensively discussed by Michael Polanyi in *Personal Knowledge* (New York: Harper & Row, 1964).

21. William Bluhm, *Ideologies and Attitudes* (Englewood Cliffs, N.J.: Prentice-Hall, 1974).

22. Michel Foucault, *The History of Sexuality,* p. 91.

23. Michel Foucault, "History, Discourse and Discontinuity," p. 232.

24. Morris Rosenberg, *Society and the Adolescent Self-Image,* (Princeton, N.J.: Princeton University Press, 1965).

25. Foucault, "History, Discourse and Discontinuity," p. 232.

26. Michel Foucault in an interchange with Noam Chomsky, moderated by Fons Elders in *Reflexive Water,* ed. Fons Elders (London: Souvenir Press, 1974), p. 171.

27. Giddens argues, wrongly I think, that authenticating a frame of meaning is different from validating propositions about the world (Giddens, *New Rules of Sociological Method,* p. 145). My argument is that validating a proposition presupposes a particular authentification.

28. Michel Foucault, *The History of Sexuality,* p. 8.

29. "Carceral function" is used by Foucault in *Discipline and Punish.*

30. Hannah Pitkin, *Wittgenstein and Justice* (Berkeley: University of California Press, 1972), chapter 9. For a useful discussion of the idea of linguistic cages, see Robert Goodin, "Laying Linguistic Traps," *Political Theory* 5 (November 1977): 491–504.

31. Pitkin, *Wittgenstein and Justice,* pp. 199, 201.

32. Ibid., pp. 202–03.

Index

Actions, human: behavior distinguished from, 122; concept of, 16, 112, 117–18; explanation of, 119–26, 127; in progress (compared with acts/accomplishments), 105–07; results or consequences of, 103, 120–22. *See also* Conduct; Conduct, interpretation of; Responsibility
Adorno, Theodor W., 140
Alcoholics Anonymous, 4
Alston, William, 59–60
Analytic-synthetic distinction: Quine's attack on, 31, 40, 84
Anglo-American tradition, *see* English linguistic philosophy
Anscombe, G. E. M., 42, 49, 88, 90
Archeology of Knowledge (Foucault), 131, 145, 146, 149, 152
Ariès, Philippe, 21
Aristotle, 175
Ascriptivism, 117
Austin, John, 25, 26–27, 41, 62, 86; and context, 47, 51–52, 57, 58; *How to Do Things with Words,* 12, 50, 54; and "inadvertence," 116; influence of, 60, 76, 165–66; and intention concept, 107–08, 109, 120, 127–28; language-analytic position of, 44, 58, 59, 80, 129; and "speech-act" or "performative sentence," 50–55, 69–70, 78, 87–88, 90, 137, 166; and "use" concept, 60–61, 66, 108
Australia: infant mortality in, 186–87
Ayer, A. J., 9, 34, 36, 39, 65, 98

Bachelard, Gaston, 146
Barthes, Roland, 129–30, 133
Bateson, Gregory, 4–5
Beckett, Samuel, 152; *The Unnamable,* 146
Beer, Samuel, 214–15
Behavior: "displacement" and compulsive, 128; distinguished from action, 122; distinguished from conduct, 101

Benjamin W., 140
Berlin, Sir Isaiah, 36
Bernstein, Richard, 147
Bhagavad-Gita, the, 35
Birth of the Clinic, The (Foucault), 143–45, 149
Bluhm, William, 215–16
Braithwaite, Richard B., 191, 193
Brentano, Franz, 9, 44
British Empiricists, 9. *See also* Positivism
Brodbeck, May, 97, 98
Brown v. *The Board of Education of Topeka,* 205
"Brute facts," 42, 49, 88, 111

Cambridge philosophy of language, *see* English linguistic philosophy
Canguilhem, Georges, 146, 149, 158–59, 189–91
Carnap, Rudolph, 19–20, 34, 35, 37–40, 43, 47, 65, 169
Cartesian dualism, 4–5
Cartwright, D., 191, 193
Cavell, Stanley, 61, 62
China: public health in, 185–86
Concept: contestability of, 210; development of, *see* Meaning; of politics, *see* Politics
Conduct: distinguished from behavior, 101; Garfinkel's model of, 104–05; language and, 127–31. *See also* Actions, human
Conduct, interpretation of: different senses of, 97–98; and intention, 107–08, 109–10; rule-governed, 99; Schutz on, 10, 13, 17, 100–105. *See also* Actions, human; Intentionality concept; Subjectivism/subjectivity
"Confirmability," 38–39
Connolly, William, 207, 209, 210, 211
Constitutive rules: contrasted with regulative rules, 113–17; politics of, 218–22
Context, *see* Language

"Coordinative definition," 171
Copernican system, 183
Correspondence, rules of, 70–71
Critical theory, 11, 14
Cullers, Jonathan, 131

Dahl, Robert, 62; *Modern Political Analysis,* 46
Davidson, Donald. 118
Decision making (political/scientific), 125–26, 176, 180–83, 186–87, 194, 205, 214, 223. *See also* Responsibility
Deductivism, 8, 17–18
"Defeasibility," 111, 113
Derrida, Jacques, 27
Descriptivism, 87, 88–90, 93, 218
Dewey, John, 76
Dilthey, Wilhelm, 14
Directed graphs (digraphs), *see* Graph theory
Discourse: descriptive vs. evaluation, 66, 68; and discursive practices, Foucault's analysis of, 130–56, 159–64, 179, 196, 202, 222–26, 228–31; medical, 135–36. 146, 151, 217, 226, 228; moral, functional approach to, 86–94; normative, and political understanding, 65–94; and normative-empirical distinction, 65–72, 83, 86, 91–94
Disease, 185–86. *See also* Health
Dualism, Cartesian (mind-body), 4–5

Easton, David, 6
Edelman, Murray, 162
Edwards, Paul, 82–84, 86
Einstein, Albert, 31
"Emotionalism," 93
Emotivism, *see* Subjectivism/subjectivity
Empiricism: British, 9; consequences of, 41; criteria of meaning of, 34–35, 37, 39, 40–46, 137; and "empirical theory," 165, 168–69, 177, 201; "essential incompleteness" of descriptions, 39, 40, 41; and evaluation of empirical explanation, 18, 181–84; and normative-empirical distinction, 65–72, 83, 86, 91–94; philosophy of modern, 7; and "pseudo-empirical" statements, 67; rejection of/flaws in, 14, 15, 18, 27, 32, 40, 43, 46, 62, 75, 107, 141, 147, 163, 169–70. *See also* Positivism
English linguistic philosophy, 59, 76, 107, 127, 129, 136–38, 144, 151, 166–67
"Epistemes," 146–47, 148
Epistemology: Foucault and, 136–41, 230
Equality: as political concept, 123; Schutz's discussion of, 103

Erklären(causal-explanatory)approach,97
Ethnomethodology, 104
Euclidean geometry, 19, 29–31, 188

"Falsifiability," 36
Feinberg, Joel, 113, 114, 115
"Foreconceptions," 59
Foucault, Michel, 25, 26, 92, 124, 127, 217, 218; discursive practices analyzed by, 130–56, 159–64, 179, 196, 202, 222–26, 228–31; writings of, 131, 141, 143–46, 149, 152, 223
Fourier, Jean Baptiste, 189
Frankfurt school of philosophy, 11, 14–15
Freedom, concept of, 212–15
Frege, Gottlob, 32–33, 56
French linguistic tradition, 129–30, 137
Freud, Sigmund, 99, 133, 163

Gadamer, Hans-Georg, 14, 25, 132, 167
Gallie, W. B., 206, 207
Garfinkel, Harold, 104, 105
Garver, Newton, 27
Gauss, Karl Friedrich, 30–31
Geach, P. T., 114–15, 116–17
Geertz, Clifford, 200–201
Goffman, Erving, 156
"Good," concept of, 77–78, 157
Government: Dahl's definition of, 46
Grammar, *see* Language
Graph theory, 194; and directed graphs (digraphs), 191–93
Gray, John, 209–10
Greek philosophical tradition, 8, 11, 58
Grice, H. P., 57
Gusdorf, Georges, 75–76

Habermas, Jurgen, 8–9, 12, 15, 138–39, 140–41
Hampshire, Stuart, 206–07
Hanson, Norwood Russell, 172
Harary, F., 191, 193
Hare, R. M., 68, 87, 88–89
Hart, H. L. A., 110–14, 116–17, 120, 151, 184
Health: as concept, 155–57, 159–60, 161, 225; "occupational," 228; politicization of, 185–87
Heidegger, Martin, 25, 41, 55, 56, 75, 134; and "being-in-the-world," 14, 57–58, 106; and concept of intention, 16; and view of language, 27, 58–59, 129, 146, 166
Hempel, Carl, 6, 17, 18, 36, 181; and empiricism, 34–35, 37, 39, 40
Henle, Paul, 74

Hermeneutical approach, *see* Meaning

Horkheimer, Max, 140

How to Do Things with Words (Austin), 12, 50, 54

Hudson, W. D., 89

Hume, David, 68, 69, 73, 87; quoted, 66–67

Husserl, Edmund, 6, 14, 27; and concept of intention, 16, 44, 102; phenomenological philosophy of, 9–10, 55–57, 58

"Hyperactive child" as object/concept, 180–81

"Hyperfactualism," 6

Ideology(ies): American orientations of, 213–15; "forensic" and "latent," 215–16, 218–19, 220; -science relationship, 200–204; social control, 180–87. *See also* Value(s)

Illocutionary force (level of meaning), *see* Meaning

"Infelicities" concept, 51, 52

"Institutional fact," 42, 88, 90

Intentionality concept, 96–97, 107–10, 120, 128; different interpretations of, 16, 102, 105; and "object-awareness," 9, 44; and responsibility, 112, 117, 121–22. *See also* Motives; Responsibility

Intuitionism, 76–79, 90

"Is-ought" relationship, 67–70, 72, 76, 87, 88, 90

Julius II (pope), 99–100

Kantian unconscious, 133

Kaplan, Abraham, 189

Kenny, Anthony, 120–21

Kovesi, Julius, 20, 69

Kuhn, Thomas, 147–49, 166; *The Structure of Scientific Revolutions*, 146

Lacan, Jacques, 130

Laing, Ronald D., 154

Lakoff, Robin, 162

Language: content of, 23; and context, 24, 47, 52, 57, 58; as data for analysis vs. tool, 14, 58, 168; and "depth" vs. "surface" grammar, 48–49, 68, 73; empiricist approach to, 46, 137; enunciative modality (passive voice) used in, 135–36; and human conduct, 127–31; and "language games," 47–50, 53; and language membership, 231–32; and male dominance, 162; and meaning, 26–64; and metalanguage (of positivists), 21; "ordinary," 26, 47, 59; persons as users of, 59, 129–30; -politics relationship, 22, 231–33;

positivist position on, *see* Positivism; and rhetoric, 27, 53, 87, 166; and semantic (vs. pragmatic) rules, 29, 60–61, 81, 89, 108–09, 117, 169, 170, 221; -speakers relationship, 59, 129–30; and speech pathology, 219–22; and speech-phenomena relationship, 19–22, 43, 58, 62, 69, 86–87, 94, 151, 169, 204, 218, 231; and syntax, 28–29, 81, 148, 169, 170; "use" theories of, 59, 60–62, 66, 108; "verbal clusters" in, 133. *See also* Discourse; English linguistic philosophy; French linguistic tradition; Meaning

Legitimacy concept, 62–63

Lévi-Strauss, Claude, 133

Lewis, C. I., 68, 69, 76, 90

Lobachevskian system of geometry, 30

Locutionary force (level of meaning), *see* Meaning

Lukes, Steven, 207–09, 210

MacDonald, Margaret, 67

Mach, Ernst, 18

Macpherson, C. B., 212

Madness and Civilization (Foucault), 141, 149

March, James, 195

Margenau, Henry, 171

Marx, Karl (and Marxism), 63, 139–40, 152, 160, 163, 199; quoted, 179, 201

Meaning: and concept development, 175–78, 187, 197; "emotive," 65; experiential, 98, 101, 200–201, 221; hermeneutical approach to, 132, 133, 134; inadequate/misleading theory of, 5; language and, 26–64; levels of (locutionary, perlocutionary, illocutionary), 53–55, 60, 80, 87, 166; levels of (moral judgments), 91; "picture theory" of, 33, 49, 189; polyguity of (for moral judgments), 83; "referential theory" of, 33; "verifiability theory" of, 9, 29, 34–39, 40, 41; word-object relationships in, 28, 137, 144, 178. *See also* Language

Medicine, *see* Discourse; Health; Psychiatry

Melden, A. I., 16, 109, 118

Merleau-Ponty, Maurice, 55

Meta as term, 2; and metaethical questions, 72, 73, 81

Michelangelo, 99

Model(s): analogical, 189, 190–91, 194, 195–96; cognitive functions, 187–93; homological, 189; and "model bias," 195; normative functions, 194–98; as term, 187–88; theoretical, 188–89

Modern Political Analysis (Dahl), 46

Monod, Jacques, 96
Montefiore, Alan, 210–11
Moore, G. E., 77, 78, 157
Moral judgments: descriptivist-prescriptivist agreement on, 89; fundamental and nonfundamental, 83–84, 86; levels of meaning of, 91; polyguity of, 83
Moses, Michelangelo's figure of, 99
Motives: "in-order-to" vs. "because of," 101–02. *See also* Intentionality concept

Naturalism, 73–76, 78, 90, 97; and antinaturalists, 97, 98
Natural science, *see* Science
Neurath, Otto, 12, 37–38, 95
Newton, Sir Isaac, 31
Nie, Norman H., 203
Nietzsche, Friedrich, 141
Norman, R. Z., 191, 193
Normative discourse, *see* Discourse

"Object-awareness," 9, 44
Objectivist approach, 13; and "objective meaning," 102
"Observation predicates," 43
Occupational Safety and Health Administration (OSHA), 228
"Open question" argument, 77
"Open-texture" concept, 39, 40, 69
Order of Things, The (Foucault), 145–46, 152, 223
Oxford philosophy of language, *see* English linguistic philosophy

Paradigms, concept of, 147, 148, 166
Parsons, Talcott, 214
"Performative" sentence ("speech-act"), 50–55, 69–70, 78, 87–88, 90, 137, 166
Perlocutionary force (level of meaning), *see* Meaning
Persuasion concept, 147, 148
Phenomenological philosophy, 16, 56, 57, 58, 76, 100–105, 107, 190; Husserl as originator of, 9–10, 55
Philosophical Investigations (Wittgenstein), 33, 49, 50
"Picture theory" of meaning, *see* Meaning
Pitkin, Hannah, 231–32
Plato, 7
"Play of dependencies," 222–23
Pocock, J. G. A., 166–67
Poincaré, Henri, 30, 31
Political practices, in relation to discursive practices, 129
Political relations in speech practices, 140; in relation to Foucault's level of analysis, 153–55

Politics: of constitutive rules, 218–22; contested concept of, 206–11; "of the family," "of medicine," "of work," 216–18; implicit and explicit levels of theory of, 93–94; language and, 22, 231–33; and "political culture" concept, 214; and political domain, 199, 204–06, 210, 211–18; and "political experience" as entity, 19; and political (vs. language) membership, 231–32; and political relations, 199–233; of politics, 229
Popper, Karl, 36
Positivism: development of position, 27–39; German tradition of (Weber and), 5–6; logical, 8; and neo-positivism of Foucault, 136, 144, 162; and positivist position on meaning, 9–13, 17–24, 33, 40, 43, 45, 65–66, 103, 124, 136; rejection of, 24, 162, 163; traditional, and language, 20–24. *See also* Empiricism; Vienna Circle
Power: "analytics of," 218; knowledge and, 139, 142, 147–49, 160; "three-dimensional view" of, 207–08
Prescriptivism, 87, 88–89
"Protocol sentences," 37–38
Psychiatry, 153–54, 204, 224, 225; and "antipsychiatrists," 156–57, 158
Psychology: descriptive vs. experimental, 44; phenomenologically oriented, 55
Ptolemaic system of astronomy, 40, 183
Public domain, concept of, 92–93

Quine, Willard Van O., 31–32, 40, 84–86

Rawls, John, 113
"Recalcitrant experience," 31–32, 85
"Reduction sentences," 39
Reichenbach, Hans, 171, 172
Reimannian metric, 31
Responsibility: -action relationship, 99, 110–19, 121–22, 184; model of, for speech disorder, 219–22; -rights discussion, 110, 120. *See also* Decision making (political/scientific); Intentionality concept
Ricoeur, Paul, 14, 25, 105–06, 132, 133, 167
Romeo and Juliet (Shakespeare), 100
Rosenberg, Morris, 223
Russell, Bertrand, 33, 47
Ryle, Gilbert, 44, 61

Saussure, Nicolas de, 129, 133
Schlick, Moritz, 34, 35, 39

Schutz, Alfred, 6, 55, 57; on interpretation of conduct, 10, 13, 16–17, 100–105

Science: defined, 96; -ideology relationship, 200–204; and "scientific political analysis," 7; and scientific theory, 170–72, 201; and unified-science approach (symmetry of natural and social science), 12, 95–100, 119

Scriven, Michael, 18, 84–86, 181–82, 183

Searle, John, 41, 42, 87–90, 113

Sedgwick, Peter, 157–58

Self-understanding, 132; and self-concepts of women, 224–25; and self-esteem, 223–24, 226–28

Semantic rules, *see* Language

"Sensory periphery," 86

Sexuality: Foucault's analysis of, 162, 218, 230

Shwayder, David S., 99

Skinner, Quentin, 15, 123, 165–66, 167

Social science: "model" as term in, 187; traditional approaches of, 125, 126; and unified-science approach, 12–13, 95–100, 119. *See also* Model(s); Science

Sociopolitical relations, 94, 127; and social control ideologies, 180–87. *See also* Ideology(ies)

Speech, *see* Language

"Speech-act," *see* "Performative" sentence

State, U.S. Department of, 45

Stevenson, Charles I., 79–82, 84

Stoll, Clarice, 161

Strauss, Leo, 11, 13

Strawson, P. F., 78, 138

Structuralism, 132–35

Structure of Scientific Revolutions, The (Kuhn), 146

Subjectivism/subjectivity, 20, 56, 57, 100–107; and emotivism, 79, 80, 82, 84, 86, 89, 90; "naive," 80; and normative discourse, 79–86

Suicide as phenomenon, 150–51

Suppes, Patrick, 171–72, 174

Syntax, *see* Language

Szasz, Thomas S., 154, 156

Taylor, Charles, 16, 106, 202

Tractatus (Wittgenstein), 33–34, 47, 49

Unified-science approach, *see* Science

Unnamable, The (Beckett), 146

"Use" theories of language, *see* Language

Validation process, *see* "Verifiability," "verificationist theory"

Value(s): concept of "formation of," 150; Foucault on, 138, 140, 150; "frameworks," 202; Gusdorf's definition/theory on, 75–76; labor theory of, 140; Scriven on system of, 85–86. *See also* Ideology(ies)

Verba, Sidney, 203

"Verifiability," "verificationist theory," 9, 29, 34–39, 40, 41

Verstehen (interpretive-understanding) approach, 13–14, 97

Vienna Circle, 5–6, 7, 9, 12, 19–20, 37, 95, 136, 169; "verificationist theory" of, 29, 34

Waismann, Friedrich, 39, 40, 41, 69

Warnock, G. J., 79

Weber, Max, 5–6, 46, 97

Winch, Peter, 15, 126

Wittgenstein, Ludwig, 12, 25, 26–27, 41, 54, 86; and context, 51–52, 58; and "form of life," 14, 106, 210; influence of, 60, 165; language-analytic position of, 44, 57, 58, 59, 68; and "language games," "depth grammar," 47–50, 53, 68; "picture theory" of, 33, 49, 189; and "use" concept, 60, 66, 108; writings of, 33–34, 47, 49, 50

Wolin, Sheldon, 172

Women: linguistic practices and, 162; political membership for, 233; and public policy, 206; self concepts of, 224–25; and "work" concept, 177

Word-object relationships, *see* Meaning

"Work" as concept, 172–78

Znaniecki, Florian, 173